KNOW ME
TO TEACH ME

Louise Michelle Bombèr is qualified as both a specialist teacher, a therapist and a DDP certified practitioner. She is the Clinical Lead and the Director of TouchBase Centre CiC in Brighton. The aims of TouchBase are to support those who have experienced adverse childhood experiences to function well at home, in their schools and out in the community. Louise and her team offer a range of support services for children and young adults (5 to 25) who have experienced significant relational traumas and losses to move towards learned security and recovery. They also support family, friends and professionals around these children.

Louise set up the National Attachment Lead Network to connect up education staff who seek to be Attachment Aware and Trauma Responsive in their practice (attachmentleadnetwork.net). She also created TIE - trauma informed education - a developmental pathway for Attachment Leads who want to continue developing their practice using Theraplay® and DDP (traumainformededucation.org.uk).

As well as writing many articles and courses, Louise is the author of the bestselling and highly respected book *Inside I'm Hurting*, translated into French and Italian. She also wrote *What About Me?*, contributed to *Teenagers & Attachment* (Ed. Andrea Perry) and co-authored *Settling to Learn: Why Relationships Matter in School* with Dr Dan Hughes. Louise also contributed to a specialist family law book *Capacity to Change* outlining what needs to be considered for traumatised children and their lives in school. More recently Louise has written the *Attachment Aware Schools Series: Bridging the gap for troubled pupils* to support schools to create effective small teams around pupils - Team Pupil.

Louise is passionate about ensuring all play their part in the recovery journey through present, attentive, attuned and responsive relationships. Together in community, she believes dignity can be restored and hope found … Contact info@touchbase.org.uk

KNOW ME
TO TEACH ME

Differentiated discipline for those recovering
from adverse childhood experiences

**The latest neuroscience
applied and made practical!**

Louise Michelle Bombèr

worthpublishing.com

ATTACHMENT AWARE SCHOOLS COLLECTION®

The Attachment Aware School series

    Book 1   The Key Adult in School

    Book 2   The Senior Manager in School

    Book 3   The Key Teacher in School

    Book 4   The Team Pupil in School

    Book 5   The Parent and Carer in School

Attachment for Teachers

Attachment in the Classroom

Better Play

Conversations That Matter

Inside I'm Hurting

Know Me to Teach Me

Little-Mouse Finds a Safe Place

Making Friends

Overcoming Barriers to Learning

School as a Secure Base

Settling to Learn

Teaching the Unteachable

Teenagers and Attachment

Temper Temper!

What About Me?

What Can I Do With The Kid Who...?

You think I'm Evil

First published 2020 by Worth Publishing Ltd
worthpublishing.com

© Worth Publishing Ltd 2020

British Library Cataloguing in Publication Data
A catalogue record for this book is available from the British Library

ISBN 9781903269404

Cover and text design by Anna Murphy
Illustrations pp. 140-41 and p. 259 by Molly Murphy

Dedicated to one of my adult clients who was so misunderstood at home,
school and later in her work place and out in the wider community.
You know who you are. I don't feel sorry for you. I grieve with you for all that should
have been. May this book move us all one step further towards true
understanding so that we can support those with a legacy of both trauma
and attachment disruption, to live life fully, without fear.

We all share a common enemy, and that common enemy is childhood adversity ...
Burke-Harris 2018, p. 195

Acknowledgements

My dear husband Jon who believes in all I do, releasing me at home to read, reflect and write at all kinds of times! To my much loved four-legged friends - cockapoo Maisie and my cat Winston who have supported my own regulation and relationship needs, whilst writing this book.

To all those in the TouchBase engine room who are my fellow travellers, together with me, on this journey of facilitating inclusion. To the dedicated team of practitioners at TouchBase Centre CiC who genuinely care and want to be the best they can be for the children, young people and parents/carers with whom they work. A special thank you to Isabella-Mae Harris who supported me with some of the admin needed for this book, and to Helen Wright with some of the research.

To the growing Attachment Lead Network across the UK, who I know are living brave, in order to ensure that the policies and practices in their schools are trauma responsive, many of whom have contributed to this book and more, and are named throughout.

To all the pupils and staff who contributed their voices to my research, from the following schools and more! Bannerman Road Community Academy, Bristol: Beckmead College, Croydon: Cardinal Newman School, Brighton: Carr Green Primary School, West Yorkshire: Coombe Road School, Brighton: Firs Farm Primary, Enfield: Hove Junior School, Brighton: ICollege, Newbury: Joy Lane Primary School, Kent: Patcham Junior School, Brighton: Patcham High School, Brighton: Pocklington Juniors, York: Ratstrick High School & Sixth Form, Calderdale: Reculver CE Primary School, Kent: Rudyard Kipling School, Brighton: St Andrew's School, Brighton: The Wensum Trust, Norfolk: West Heath School, Kent: Wyke Regis Primary Foundation, Dorset: and students who have recently left school.

To my first two clinical supervisors who provided me with all the foundations I needed, for all I do now - Dr Paul Holmes and Penny Auton. To my DDP supervisors Dr Kim Golding and Dr Mikenda Plant for their continued insight and wisdom. To Dr Vivien Norris who oversees Theraplay®UK, Fiona Peacock and Jo Williams for their experience and expertise into how Theraplay® Informed Practice is being integrated into schools, across the UK.

To Dr Stephen Porges for our special meeting and your amazing generosity in ensuring your Polyvagal theory is made practical across every sector. I hope I have done you proud! To Dr Bruce Perry, for sharing more of your Neurosequential Model© (NMT) of therapeutics with me and for all your research into this area, which I know will be a lifeline for so many currently 'stuck'. To Dr Dan Hughes for believing in me and my work in schools, and for your model of DDP that has become a part of all I am and do!

To Hilary Kennedy who runs AVIG UK. And a big thank you to Kate Miller from Connected Moments for sharing the VIG pyramid she created. To James McTaggart for generously sharing his helpful behaviour model. A big shout out to my friend and colleague in this field of work, Karen Treisman. Thanks for all you do to support advocacy in this whole area too (we could talk for hours!).

For sharing their experiences and insights - Emma Houldsworth, Director of Plot 22, Simon Cobb, Director of Stoneham Bakehouse and Tim Holtham, Director of Brighton & Hove Table Tennis Club.

To my longstanding editor Andrea Perry, who is now also a close friend. To Martin Wood from Worth Publishing; behind the scenes, a big supporter of all of this pioneering work. To Anna Murphy for all the creative design and illustrations included in this book. To Alice Harper for the boy on the cover, and Molly Murphy for her incredible dog pictures. You clearly know dogs well!

And to all the children, young people, young adults, adoptive parents and carers I have stood alongside over the years ... you have taught me what I now understand, and integrate into my practice ...

For such a time as this ...   Esther 4 v14. Bible - New International Version

Foreword

Know Me to Teach Me is a classic. I do not say this lightly as I have read literally hundreds of books and this is one of the most practical and useful I have ever read. I believe it will stand the test of time. More than this, the appeal of the book will be relevant to anyone curious about why children and adults behave the way they do. It is written simply and communicates the insights of theory and practice with the strategies to effect meaningful change and transform behaviour. It shows distressed behaviour is not to be feared, but understood.

I wish Louise had written this a decade ago because it would have enabled me, as an educator and a father, to deal with the many stones in my shoe I've been carrying around for years. How do we educate children in a way that respects their biology? In a way that respects the dignity of the individual biologically, physiologically and psychologically. *Know Me to Teach Me* achieves what many books have failed to do before, it provides insight into differentiated discipline whilst maintaining the integrity of a scientific model which achieves results. An informed way of thinking, that starts from where the child is and celebrates the uniqueness of every child and young person. Not only is this book useful for practitioners, it's so important for families too: as a parent I am already applying what I have learned from it.

I was fortunate to meet Louise at a National Conference by UK Adoption. Louise was the keynote and I was the chair. I remember vividly sitting listening to her speak and I took several pages of notes and immediately returned to my school and applied and shared what I had learned. This is the beauty of this book. It is simple, accessible, functional and can be built upon.

For two decades I have been working with children affected by Adverse Childhood Experience and trauma and recognised a child's behaviour is the start of a conversation. I know after reading this book it will begin many conversations across your work setting and in the home. Not only does Louise provide much needed insight, she provides templates, checklists, scripts and summaries. Included in the book is a Relationship Policy aligned with the invaluable content of the book, one many schools would benefit from to guide their future direction of travel.

She references and unpacks Polyvagal theory and the Neurosequential model in a way that is practical and easily understood, and this is why this book is so important. It empowers people to learn the biological basis of behaviour. It's grounded in relationships and relational practice.

In short: this book is a gift, a treasury of insight. Whether you are a parent or a professional it matters not, what matters is you should read this book. Treasure it and I wish you the very best as you translate the insights into gains in your relational practices at home and in school.

Nicky Murray
Headteacher of Claypotts Castle Primary School
Dundee, Scotland
April 2020

A note at the time of the Covid-19 crisis 2020

In *Know Me to Teach Me*, Louise clearly and diligently helps us to understand the impact of developmental trauma based on the latest science and psychological theory. It is time for the education sector to take notice and it is also heartening to hear of the experiences of those education teams that are leading the way with this.

This book is being published during a world-wide crisis as Covid-19 sweeps through many countries. Schools are shut. Anecdotally I am hearing of many children who are settling well into being at home. Some are missing the structure and friendships at school, but many are not. The impact of early adversity can make life more difficult and school can offer challenges despite the dedication and commitment of the educators. As behavioural and emotional challenges have reduced for them, even at a time of increased anxiety and fear for all of us, educators need to take notice. These children may find returning to school quite traumatic. Old fears of abandonment and separation anxiety are likely to be high as they learn to be apart from their parents again. They need their educators to understand this and to give them the space they need to manage the adjustment of being at school again.

Conversely, there are also children managing lockdown whilst having to live in unsafe homes with increasingly stressed parents. Incidents of domestic abuse appear to be increasing and as parents are preoccupied with their own worries and fear, there is no-one to think about what the children need. These are the children who may have found school to be a refuge; somewhere that their basic needs for shelter, food and physical safety could be found. These children will return to school wobbling emotionally. They will need educators who can manage their feelings of frustration at seeing earlier progress going backwards and can trust that learning will begin again if they remain patient and meet the immediate needs of the child.

Educators need the confidence to give all vulnerable children the time and space they need, despite the pressure to help them to catch up in their education. Without sufficient emotional support it is unlikely that these children will ever make the educational gains they are capable of. This book is arriving at the right time to help build this confidence. When schools open again, this book will be on hand to provide many creative and innovative ideas. Generations of teachers will provide enhanced educational experiences if they take notice of Louise's knowledge and wisdom. And generations of children going forward will benefit.

Kim S. Golding
Clinical Psychologist, Author and DDP trainer
April 2020

Contents

The difference this makes │ EVIDENCE FROM PRACTICE

Since we have been using a neurodevelopmental approach within our Virtual School, we have seen significant shifts in the ability of our pupils to settle in school. Some of our more complex children are even making it back into mainstream classrooms, as the impact of this way of working has helped them to become more regulated and able to focus back on learning.

The approaches we use, such as Sensory Attachment Intervention, Theraplay® and Dyadic Developmental Practice, are enabling our pupils to build trusting relationships with their key adults and develop a sense of safety both in school and at home. Whilst we can't take away what has happened in the past, these approaches assist us in our work to address the impact of developmental trauma on a child's ability to learn and achieve.

Jane Pickthall, Head of The Virtual School in North Tyneside and Trustee of
The National Association of Virtual School Heads

NOTES ABOUT THE BOOK

1 To protect the confidentiality of individual children, carers or professionals, names and autobiographical details have been altered in every case quoted apart from where permission has been given in writing. Any case examples written are composite and drawn from a number of similar examples known to the Author from her experiences over many years of working with children and adolescents.

2 To simplify the text, the terms 'child' and 'pupil' have been used on occasion to represent both children and young people. The strategies described are relevant to both primary and secondary phases, unless stated otherwise.

3 To simplify the text, the term 'parent' is used on occasion to represent those now providing the primary care for children with attachment difficulties. This term will therefore include birth parents, adoptive parents, foster carers, family and friends.

Chapter 1

Introduction

Tracing back to the beginning

Educational processes are working very hard to dismiss the body's responses to environmental features. If we observe children in a classroom, we note a variety of behavioural features that illustrate that some children are safe and can sit comfortably in the same environment that triggers, in other children, the hypervigilant behaviours characterising a lack of safety.   Porges 2011, somaticperspectives.com

Small, weak, defenceless and vulnerable we come into this world, wired to connect. Through our whole lives, from our first breath to our last, we're on a biologically driven journey; our survival instincts working to enable us to feel safe in our bodies, our environments and in our relationship with others. What are known as Adverse Childhood Experiences (ACEs) (Felitti & Anda 1998) disrupt this original pathway towards safety and connection. The track instead diverts off into the deserted wilderness of toxic stress, fear and terror, a legacy for insecure attachment. A legacy for homes, schools and the wider community at large.

As Burke-Harris (2018) states, 'Adversity happens everywhere, among all races and geographic areas' (p. 158). Disruption within relationship with other people, especially those who were supposed to encourage and comfort you whilst you were growing up, means stress, toxic stress. Toxic stress impacts human biology. Toxic stress results in a disruption to the stress response. Tragically, dysregulation and distrust are two of the most significant villains which come into play, as developmental vulnerabilities, as a result. In this book, we'll look at how these two villains may imprint how we view ourselves, others, the contexts we find ourselves in and how they may negatively shape our futures. *May* shape our future, because it's not an inevitable trajectory - if help is provided. And that's what this book will be all about - how to provide the right kind of support, at the right time, in the right way, to get the lives of traumatised children and young people back on track.

Childhood adversity can manifest in distressed behaviours that can puzzle, disturb and shock us. Whilst some adults offer empathic, relational responses, others use punitive/rule-based or behaviourist/consequence-based management, in the name of zero tolerance. The latter engenders fear and compliance. I firmly believe, as I've said in my earlier books, that 'Every relationship has the power to confirm or challenge all that's gone on before' (Bombèr 2007). So these children and young people can either end up being supported, or being compromised further.

Childhood adversity is now known to lead to all kinds of health difficulties because of the toxic stress involved, difficulties including inflammation, which lies behind many serious physical diseases, as well as serious mental health problems. So it's essential that we really think about what we're doing at home, school and out in our wider community contexts. Are we engendering social cohesion, or segregation? Health or disease? Inclusion and belonging, or exclusion and rejection? Empathy, relationship and hope or punishment, estrangement and hopelessness?

We're probably not even aware that our action (or lack of it) could be colluding with the move towards the negative trajectory, or to a fuelling of the continuing public health crisis. There is so much we remain largely unaware of. That is, until now ... thankfully, simple actions that everyone can take, informed by an awareness of the impact of Adverse Childhood Experiences (ACEs), which can make all the difference in the world. It's now time to integrate everything we know from the worlds of attachment, trauma and neuroscience into how we interpret what's going on, and most importantly, *what we do about it*. In our homes and communities, but perhaps nowhere more so than in schools, where all our children and young people spend so much of their young lives.

Some readers may have seen *Resilience* (Dartmouth Films, 2017, *see* **References**), a documentary about research into the challenging impact of ACEs on our trajectory through life, and what we can do about it - what's referred to as *'the science of hope'*. Towards the end, there's a comment, 'If you get this (information and understanding) out to the general population they will invent very wise actions'. Well - here goes! That's what this book is all about. The wise actions we can all take to make a genuine positive difference in the lives of children and young people who've experienced the most challenging of starts in life. And yes, that includes how we can bring healthy discipline into our schools in a trauma-responsive, attachment aware way. This isn't an either-or situation. I want to stress that *discipline is not the enemy*. Used in the right way, we can ensure that our children learn what is emotionally and socially healthy and appropriate so that they, and those around them, can function at their best and go on to lead rewarding lives.

But first, let's set the scene some more.

The protection good enough care provides

Children and young people who have experienced 'good enough' care back at home have generally lived with three essential foundations for thriving: safety, security and stability. They have usually been provided with the right conditions (of, for example, comfort and joy) to facilitate the developmental capacity and internal resources necessary to navigate their way through family, school and work life really well. Our practice as educators isn't as up to date as it could be, but these pupils generally emerge from our education systems equipped and unscathed (or at least with only a few minor cuts and scratches). When we're working with 'secure' children, we can get away with not knowing that much. They will usually make it, regardless of (or even despite) us.

However, traumatised children and young people who have experienced many instances from the current list of ACEs (p. 22) or indeed any other relational traumas and losses, can suffer deeply as a result of our collective ignorance. Amongst our excluded pupils, think how many have been in care: think what a huge percentage of individuals in the criminal justice system were children in care (CIC) at some point as well. If we naively continue with 'business as usual', these young people will continue to find life at school very hard, emerging from our education system scarred for the rest of their lives, as all too many have done before them. We need to use a wide range of evidence-based, mind-body interventions in all aspects of school life, and support these particular children and young people with the care they really need.

The more I learn and understand, the more I realise that many of our cultural ways, policies, practices and systems in the UK are at odds with what's needed for healthy nervous systems to function best. When conditions are optimum for their nervous systems, our pupils in schools are able to fully settle into learning, and make the most of their potential academically, socially, and as citizens-to-be … When the conditions are not right, those children and young people who have previously been exposed to traumatic events are at risk of being retraumatised, not understood, punished, labelled, and excluded. Learning about human biology and the nervous system can really, really help us, especially when things go wrong, when, traditionally, 'discipline' is called for. We need to take a long, hard look at what makes us human, what makes us tick, how we function best and the implications for best practice in schools. As Nouwen (1982) states, 'Compassion means full immersion in the condition of being human'. Ignoring or disrespecting some fundamental truths can lead to dire circumstances, not just for them, but for all of us, the collective whole.

The case against 'managed moves'

Sadly in my work within education I've come across some young people who have had the most difficult starts in life being given 'managed moves'. I believe a managed move is just different terminology for exclusion from everything familiar and known to them. These pupils' therapeutic needs all increased significantly and in all cases, despite our team being initially involved in preventative recovery work, our advice was not sought. Thankfully these sorts of cases are in a minority in the areas where I work, since inclusion there is the priority: but nevertheless, each one of these young people will have this additional relational trauma and loss to recover from. They were already fragile, and I do strongly believe that with the recommended advice contained within AATR (Attachment Aware, Trauma Responsive) trainings and publications, such outcomes can be averted. When there are difficulties in school, a flexible approach is essential and *differentiated discipline* (p. 63) is necessary. Not a plan to move them on!

And the children and young people agree. In writing about exclusions, the Children's Commissioner (2019) commented, 'the 2017/18 Ofsted annual report ... stated that they had seen a continuing trend of rising exclusions among children and young people with SEND': and the report notes that ... 'Children also called for teachers to be more flexible in giving them chances to change their behaviour. Children wished that they had been given more opportunity by schools as some felt that they had been written off too quickly. There was a sense that if schools were more accommodating of SEND children, then those children would likely be more accommodating in return'.

> They could have gave me another chance and listened to what I had to say and then learned that I couldn't take the stress of that day.
> Secondary school age boy (p. 17)

Building on my earlier writing, in this book I'm going to map out how we can make yet more informed choices about what we do and when we do it. We're going to make a journey together, based on what we now know from the worlds of science and therapy, to integrate what this means for our homes, schools and wider communities within an increasingly compassionate response.

Frankly, some of our pupils up and down the country who have high ACE scores need a medal for having survived thus far! Their young bodies and minds have responded with a *normal* reaction to *abnormal* circumstances. But their survival has come at a truly significant cost to both their minds and their bodies, as a result of everything they've lived through. At school every week I meet those who are paying the cost, many years later. Like Stacey, who still has nightmares at the age of 16 about what happened early in her life, despite having been adopted into a loving home at the age of two. And when I say nightmares, I mean so terrifying that they actually generate a panic attack, just telling her adoptive mum and me about them. Like Arthur (13), who is really anxious in crowded environments like shopping centres, or assembly, or in between classes. He goes really pale and becomes immobilised. And like Sanjeep (15), who becomes re-triggered instantly if anyone touches him when he isn't expecting it, for example when someone brushes past him in the corridor. He can move into a terror response and start lashing out.

What these children and young people have lived through has seriously impeded their everyday functioning and affected the way they interpret everything that goes on inside and around them. In turn this means that what we are saying and doing around them in school will not be interpreted in the way we may have intended. This is so significant. Much of what we say and do can so easily be 'lost in translation', without us even realising. Unless we notice and understand what's happening, we can inadvertantly perpetuate the cycle of misunderstanding between us by sticking with and insisting on our own interpretation, so we both completely miss each other, in our shared communication. In Chapter 2 we'll look at the children who are currently being misunderstood, isolated and excluded because of this core vulnerability, and we'll consider alternative ways of being and doing so that we can facilitate *relational proximity*, not *relational withdrawal* (p. 65). In other words, we need to come alongside their misinterpretation with empathy and understanding, instead of exclusion and rejection; provide them with a bridge back to healthy relationship with us and with themselves; and thus enable them to settle back into learning and thriving as a valued member of our school communities.

Surely that's what we want for every pupil in our school? At the end of the day, it's down to us, the adults to use our knowledge wisely. Because thankfully, despite the negative biological, neurological, psychological, behavioural and emotional consequences of having lived through multiple ACEs, there really is a science of hope, as *Resilience* suggests (*above*). Our biographies do not need to turn out to be our biologies. There is ample opportunity to get back towards our original, intended pathway, all through the life span.

But the longer we wait, the longer it will take to get back on track. Our brains need more repetitions of new behaviour the older they get, in order for healthy new neural pathways to wire together. And what's most needed for such deep change for children and young people who have experienced developmental trauma is - us! The adults. The very tool that many of us in education have underestimated - ourselves! *Recovery from early ACEs doesn't happen in isolation, but in community.*

Together we will explore how to respect and honour our biology as human beings. How to get onto this healthy pathway. We will learn why the troubled children and young people in our schools can't make it on their own, and how we all function best in the context of relationship. Our pupils are going to need you and me to support them on their journey towards recovery, being grounded and acquiring *'learned security'*, and thus able to enjoy and benefit from life in school.

Relationships provide social air

Recovery happens within a community of people, especially when primary relationships were at the root of the original disruption, distress, trauma and loss. We have an ethical responsibility as adults to reduce the dosage of adversity on children and young people and to strengthen our own relational capacity, whatever our role or responsibility, to provide the healthy *relational buffering* (p. 112) these children and young people so desperately need. I'll go into all these elements in later chapters. We will need to find ways to travel with them, despite their distrust in us. We'll explore how to facilitate experiences of relationship together, to gently challenge their perceptions about grown-ups and to raise their awareness, so that they can firstly experience and then secondly learn, how to be both grounded and present, in order to function well. We'll explore how attending to our own state of regulation and wellbeing can be the lifeline needed for regulation in children and young people.

The saying we all know about 'putting our own oxygen masks on first, before helping anyone else', still holds much sway. In effect, we'll be engaging in similarly necessary and lifegiving actions to help our pupils get back on track, of how things should have been for them, the first time around. This book will invite you to become the 'social air' needed for recovery, so that these children and young people can breathe in, breathe out, and live, freely live; not merely survive on a destructive downward spiral, as too many currently are. This approach will inevitably calm and quieten the distressed behaviours we currently observe in our classrooms, too often attracting rigid disciplinary measures and even exclusion. Exclusion from the very place that could actually offer these pupils a lifeline to second chance learning - school.

We'll be applying some of the basic principles of the now widely respected Polyvagal Theory (p. 102) to our understanding of what's happening for these children and young people in our current education context and climate. Doing so will give us opportunity to update our ways of being, our practices and our policies, in line with this ground-breaking neuroscience, thanks to the work of Dr Stephen Porges. Obviously this work has implications not only for schools, but also how our homes and communities are organised and function. We'll learn together how healthy, robust relationships, sleep, exercise, nutrition, mindfulness and mental health support within homes, schools and out in the wider community can contribute so much benefit.

Potential benefits

✔ Decrease stress hormones ✔ Decrease inflammation ✔
✔ Increase neuroplasticity ✔ Delay cellular ageing ✔ Enhance regulation ✔
✔ Quieten faulty alarm systems ✔ Increase connection ✔
✔ Increase socially appropriate behaviours ✔ Reduce exclusions ✔

Cans of worms?

I hear a lot from educationalists, parents and carers about their nervousness about 'opening a can of worms'. Understandable though that apprehension is, fortunately, we have no reason to be afraid. We'll be getting involved in essential rebuilding and restorative work, by providing enabling conditions for these children and young people to really be able to thrive. And if they talk - great! If they open up to you - great! Then you'll have the opportunity to be a fellow human being, a mature adult, alongside them, being empathic. If you feel back-up is needed because of the sorts of things they are beginning to disclose, then of course consider finding a good therapist, familiar with the terrain of relational trauma and loss, to join your team. Please note I said 'join'! The experts in this area are not going to be *instead* of you, but *as well as* you! Of course we need to be wise about where our boundary lines lie, in terms of knowledge, skill and expertise, but please don't ever discount yourself as a fellow traveller, whatever your role or responsibilities! We are all needed … our relationships matter.

I strongly believe that children and young people will only talk in a way that's really helpful for them when they feel safe enough. I realise this is contrary to some practice in the UK at the moment, whereby, for example, a child is told they are going to do lifestory work with an adult, often led by the adult's timing, rather than the child's. We need to pace our interventions, and learn the best ways of building the kind of genuine relationships with them that will enable them to feel safe in themselves - not just to be told they are safe by adults. Without becoming therapists, we can learn from many different approaches such as DDP (Developmental Dyadic Practice) (**Useful Organisations**), a respectful and powerful way of supporting children and young people into recovery, applicable in so many varied contexts including school (Chapter 7 **Relate**). A safe way of being, using sensitive, attuned timing.

Before we can create a map for a pupil's recovery we'll need to navigate the chaos of trauma, by strengthening our own capacity for attunement. If we can understand what's going on in front of us, what has happened to a child and how that's connected to the child's current presentation, we'll find our empathic responses will increase. The pupil in turn will feel less threatened by us and more likely to engage in their *social engagement* system (p. 26) which is good news for behaviour in our schools and inclusion targets. *Attunement* (the capacity to notice what might be going on in any given moment in school, in the mind and body of a pupil p. 127) is going to play a significant part in our work. We'll learn from research how rich communication can be from birth (Trevarthan 2014, Chapter 5), if we can work out what's being 'said'. We'll recognise that attunement is an art, and that we can become stronger and more practised as we become more aware, learning from colleagues within the VIG world (Video Interactive Guidance) (**Useful Organisations**).

We'll look at how following the 'neurosequential order' (Perry, 2014, 2017, 2020) will help (p. 145), and the types of 'biology respecting' interventions we all need to use as we come alongside individuals, families, schools, colleges, universities and communities, courtesy of Dr Bruce Perry's invaluable contributions to this field of work (Chapter 5). Then the stage will be set for facilitating the right kind of support for traumatised children and young people to move into recovery. They'll become better able to function well in relationship, engaging and participating effectively within our schools and in our world, making valuable contributions. We'll look in depth at the **4 R's - Regulate**, **Relate**, **Reason**, and **Repair**. I'll provide creative ways of being to enable us to be as inclusive as we possibly can be. Within all this will be the premise that discipline is linked to teaching, not punishment: the child or young person needs to be in the right state to learn, in order to be taught. So we'll be addressing the need for sensitive timing, and how to choose the right moment to help them develop their internal controls.

Throughout this book I'll challenge us to re-think what school is and how it operates, hopefully helping you to create an exciting vision of what it could become. It really doesn't depend on huge financial costs (although some more money would be appreciated right now! As schools are struggling more than they ever have). It does however depend on shifting our thinking, to develop different mindsets. We need brave leaders to enable us to prioritise interpreting the traumatised child's perspective in the midst of a world with so many competing and contradictory demands.

You'll find many different types of interventions that can strengthen what's known as the child or young person's 'vagal tone', a key element in becoming robust enough to manage stress (p. 116). It really is possible to strengthen natural resilience! Despite their 'window of stress tolerance' (p. 121) being initially very limited, we'll discover that there's a huge amount we can do to extend it to a far more reasonable size, to help them function much better. We can't hope to eliminate stress: life is inherently stressful for all of us, and anyway some stress is useful. There are the everyday, low level stressors and the extraordinary stressors which hit us, out of nowhere, in the different seasons of our lives. But whilst helping our pupils practise and learn how to get stronger with stress management, we, the adults will intentionally become their stress regulators. We will work towards minimising or dampening down, wherever possible, the frequency and intensity of the stressors we have control over. This will give the children and young people the breather they need, to have the opportunity to grow.

And this is what's so important. By having that 'breather', we'll be enabling our traumatised pupils to grow their capacity for settling to learn, for enjoying belonging, for developing new neural connections for healthy minds and bodies. *It's not just a process of removing stress, and then sitting back. It's about how and what we actively do with our traumatised pupils as the calmer times start to get longer.*

If you have any connection or role with children, young people and adults who have been impacted by relational trauma or loss, then this book can really enhance your understanding of them. Whoever you are in relation to a child you care about, it can help you - it really does 'take a village to raise a child'. You'll recognise the implications for how parents teach their children and for how schools are set up and run, including our use of discipline both at home, school and within other contexts, out in the wider community at large. And perhaps I should say, brace yourself! Since I think you're bound to find this will challenge many practices currently valued in family homes, allowed in schools and accepted within our culture, across the UK.

But take heart: there is a different way, and once enriched by our new knowledge, we can all be 'relational activists', making constructive change together. Now is the time to update how we get alongside traumatised children and young people who deserve our very best. Please note that this material is in no way intended as a manualised approach. It's intended as a map of being, for those of us seeking to journey together with those who are hurting, in the context of unique relationships with one another. As Ogden (2015) states, 'It is what transpires within the relationship that is at the core of transformation' (p. 22).

For such a time as this. In honour of all the foster carers and adoptive parents out there: all those educators and clinicians striving to do their best: for all the children and young people: the inclusive revolution has begun …

The benefits of AATR training

The difference this makes | EVIDENCE FROM PRACTICE

Honestly that training was the best in my career and it's so true that once you know it, you can't unknow it. It's really made us think about things differently.

Alison West, Assistant Head Teacher & Attachment Lead, Enfield

All schools should invest in training based on attachment and early trauma. They should allow all staff to have an understanding of the needs of the children in order to offer them the correct support. Too often these children are labelled as 'naughty' or 'lazy', and school becomes another negative experience, another daily battle for them and another place where they cannot trust the adults around them. Every school should strive to be that 'safe place' for every child. A place they can talk openly, be heard and understood. A place where the adults know how to support their adverse needs and help them to overcome them.

Charlotte Wood, Pastoral Lead, Bury

I have now done attachment training and ACE training in all the schools in our Trust. Feedback has been amazing and all schools want more. I am developing a Trust model policy.

Tracy Jones, Vice Principal, Trust SEND Lead & Attachment Lead, Bristol

More thoughts about the benefits of AATR training

* Useful techniques to help children calm down
* Valuable information
* The information was very insightful
* The training was extremely interactive
* It was very engaging
* Make delivery to schools mandatory
* It was so helpful knowing the relationship between biology and trauma, how trauma may affect behaviour and the relevance of the vagal nerve
* Now I understand the biology behind trauma
* Although the understanding is 'out there', not enough is done to enable it to happen in schools
* Breathe! It is an ongoing process but we CAN help!
* We must always remember the order of the **4 R's**, focussing on the importance of regulation. Don't fight the physiology. Work with it
* The training is helping me to become a better practitioner and inspiring me to be the person that can make a difference
* This course has been an amazingly useful training experience for my work with children, adults and myself
* Really well delivered - the science behind the understanding of behaviour

Chapter 2

The Excluded and Isolated

We allow our ignorance to prevail upon us and make us think we can survive alone, alone in patches, alone in groups, alone in races, even alone in genders.
Maya Angelou (11/3/90 during an address in Louisiana)

A crisis

We have children and young people in our homes, schools and out in community right now who are behaving in unexpected, unusual ways. If we recognise behaviour as communication, we see the behaviour as indicative of the trauma and attachment inadequacies and failures they have experienced. But so often their distressed behaviours are not 'interpreted' in this way. All too often we react and make quick assumptions and judgements about the 'badly behaving pupil' based on our own history, understandings and our value systems. There are also other misinterpretations and misunderstandings at play, in our homes, schools and out in the wider community at large. Many of these children and young people are viewed as mad or bad. Most challenging behaviours are seen as intentional.

It's still unusual, at the moment, to interpret everything we experience from others, especially children and young people, through a reflective, compassionate lens, or to reflect on why someone is doing whatever they are doing. We simply see or experience what we think of as 'bad' behaviour, and have a reaction. It's often one of negative, emotion-laden judgement, and then we have the instant wish that the bad behaviour would stop, so that we can relax and our sense of things being OK and under control can be restored. If we see this kind of behaviour happening in the street or in our classrooms, it's so easy to view it through a simplistic, evaluative lens, and see the parent or teacher involved being somehow not 'good enough' at keeping control. It's as if we don't realise that we all have a part to play in what's happening with our fellow human beings, and that there is often a much bigger, more complex narrative going on, that we are only reading part of.

I believe we are in crisis at this time, with exclusions reaching incredible levels - and around *42 children 'expelled'* [permanently excluded] *each week* (Independent, July 2019). Picture it: like the 'football pitch a minute' going up in smoke in the Brazilian rainforest (BBC, July 2019) - that's around one-and-a-half classrooms full of pupils each week: and the prison population soaring as well. If we could get the necessary understanding out to schools and the wider education context first, what a difference this could make to all the other contexts these children and young people find themselves in. We could all do with pressing the pause button as a matter of urgency. Not for a much needed holiday, even though far too many staff are struggling and burnt out trying to teach in old traumatised systems, but for everyone to be trained up in attachment aware and trauma responsive practice. How about a week off usual school commitments for us all to receive this training and to have the opportunity to update both policy and practice?*

I know you might well be laughing and thinking what a luxury that would be. But I believe it would be time so well spent. In fact, it would be precisely the investment we need. Sadly, the AATR (Attachment Aware and Trauma Responsive) movement is not spreading fast enough to prevent raised eyebrows, disapproving looks, thoughtless words and thousands of unnecessary exclusions (informal and formal) each week. It's true that many schools have now heard about attachment theory, and increasing numbers

---

* I'm aware at the time of writing during the Covid 19 crisis, that many education staff are making great use of their time studying and updating their skills despite all their other responsibilities: preparing themselves to better support their pupils once the lockdown has ended. I really applaud their dedication.

are now covering this in initial teacher training, albeit often in a limited way: but how does this theory impact practice, in terms of teaching and learning in our schools, wider communities and homes? Especially for those with disrupted attachment, who have been flooded with toxic stress in their early lives, rather than being bathed in safety, regulation and joy.

The knowledge we have now must impact and change *practice*. It really must. There are a couple of hopeful signs. In October 2019 the (AAPG) on Knife Crime made seven clear recommendations that will support this: the fifth reads as follows:

> Everyone working in the education sector must be trained to understand vulnerability and trauma. Best practice should be identified and spread.

And the 2018 DfE Guidance for Designated Teachers explicitly states that one of their roles is to:

> ... understand the impact trauma, attachment disorder [17] and other mental health issues could have on looked-after and previously looked-after children and their ability to engage with learning. It is also important that the Designated Teacher ... and other school staff [recognise that] issues will continue to affect previously looked-after children and that the school will need to continue to respond appropriately to their needs.
>
> [17] 'Being attachment aware' ie ensuring that the school understands attachment theory and the impact of attachment disorders on a child's emotional development and learning and adopts a whole school approach to identifying and supporting pupils with attachment difficulties.
>
> p. 26, and footnote 17 [my parenthesis]

I would draw attention to the fact that this should not just remain the responsibility of the DT but of the whole school community! It states *'and other school staff'*. Too often DTs are expected to hold this responsibility on their own, and yet for them to be enabled to do their job properly, they need an AATR context to do it in!

But education practitioners were not warned that 'attachment awareness' would imply new and alternative practices in the classroom. Unfortunately, in many schools, attachment theory has become an interesting short-term bolt-on, to support existing crumbling infrastructure, rather than underpinning bold, courageous steps of re-thinking how we do school. Those who have been brave enough to start doing this are often in a minority; some have given up as they realised they couldn't stand up to the giants of current education authorities, such as Ofsted, in isolation, especially when the focus has seemed to be solely on curriculum, rather than on wellbeing.

However a second encouraging development came in September 2019, when Ofsted revised their inspection framework. It will now be assessing what a school does to support behaviour and attitudes, as well as personal development. The government too has committed to improving mental health provision for children and young people, with education as its priority, by introducing a designated senior lead for mental health into schools, amongst other measures. However cynical we may have become, and whilst we don't want any child to be pathologised and labelled, we need to share our attachment aware and trauma informed practice, and make the most of these initiatives. We still have a way to go: I will make further recommendations throughout this book, and I hope you will be inspired to think of more.

We need clarity and purpose; a vision for how school can function when everything we now know about the impact of ACEs is properly integrated into school practice. We must put mental health and wellbeing at the top of our priority list for education, as a matter of urgency.

I continue to receive many emails from panicked adoptive parents and foster carers who actually do grasp the gravity of this situation. These are *not*, as they are sometimes dismissingly labelled, 'over-protective parents', but parents who live and breathe the out-workings of relational trauma, day in and day out, knowing full well the destruction it brings to hearts and minds; and in some cases they are already seeing the impact upon young bodies too. They realise that we are actually in the midst of a crisis within education, but that many who hold the keys to power, authority and influence are sleepwalking in this toxic arena called trauma. They are acutely aware that the long-lasting, devastating impact on individuals, families, schools and communities when toxic cycles are not interrupted, is barely taken into account. The biggest stressor for adults fostering and adopting is how we currently run our education system, with policies and practices which don't take into account the need for trauma responsive practice. Just ask any adoption or fostering teams in the UK right now and you will find this to be true. Many family placements break down because of the pressures looked-after and adopted children and young people experience within the education context. A heart-breaking loss and continuation of cycle of rejection, toxic stress and trauma - personally costly for them and their families, at all levels, and costly also to the rest of society.

Many committed parents and carers move around the UK in the search of professionals who will understand and support the children they brought into their family to re-parent, using therapeutic parenting, and to support on into recovery. They don't want their children re-traumatised by an ignorant system. Some even end up in law courts having to protest their children's additional needs to education authorities. I'm very saddened when it comes to this. Let's look at some figures.

PERMANENT AND FIXED TERM EXCLUSIONS IN ENGLAND 2017-18 (gov.uk accessed JULY 2019)

- Since 2012/13 the rate of permanent exclusions has been rising significantly
- In 2017/18, 7900 pupils were permanently excluded from all state funded primary, secondary and special schools, representing a 70% increase from 2012/13
- The number of fixed term exclusions has increased by 54% since 2012/13
- Persistent disruptive behaviour is the most common reason for both permanent and fixed period exclusions overall, with the increases being driven mainly by secondary schools.
- Pupils eligible for free school meals have seen a large increase in fixed term exclusions

The 2019 report from IPPR *Making The Difference* stated that along with the growing number of official exclusions in the UK, there are also significant issues with how *unofficial exclusions* are being used by schools. It also highlighted that excluded children and young people are often the most vulnerable of all children.

- Twice as likely to be in the care of the state
- Four times as likely to have grown up in poverty
- Seven times as likely to have a special educational need
- Ten times as likely to suffer recognisable mental health problems

Exclusions from Mainstream Schools 7/5/19 on
childrenscommissioner.gov.uk

These are truly shocking statistics. And as I think we all know, the figures outlined above will be lower than the actual figures as they don't take into account those in isolation/seclusion units within schools, those who have been off-rolled, otherwise known as 'back-door exclusions', or those who have experienced 'managed moves': *'... We're not sure our school is the right school for your son or daughter'* ...

So there is a tribe within education who have been traumatised, which is currently being moved about from school to school, in the name of zero tolerance, potentially re-traumatising them, new rejections further deteriorating their fragile state: so much going on that needs to be challenged. Instead, this tribe should be receiving *additional trauma responsive support*. There should be *increased funding* for schools to provide the necessary preventative support these children and young people need, and *good governance* as to the policies and practices being used, amongst our most vulnerable. This would be an ethical response from a properly mature and caring society.

What we need to know

Traumatised children and young people are surviving, not living. However safe we think they are in school, their nervous systems are actually doing what we should all do in the face of overwhelming threat - trying to survive. They are not 'disturbed', in the old-fashioned and judgemental labelling of those mentally unwell. What they have experienced was indeed highly disturbing (and maybe still is), and their bodies and minds needed to shift accordingly to accommodate and to adapt to toxic stress. They have adapted well to seriously maladaptive experiences. These children and young people have learned they need to manage their lives through hypervigilance, rather than with spontaneity, because of what they've had to live through. They need to be on the watch, watching their own backs, in case of further threat. Under the circumstances, in fact this actually was and remains sensible and wise.

Adverse Childhood Experiences and toxic stress

In 1998 the first significant and long-term research study was published on the correlation between ACEs and adult physical and mental health outcomes by Dr Vincent Felitti & Dr Robert Anda. The findings were truly remarkable. There were a number of possible experiences listed and participants had to count up how many they had lived through, the total becoming known as the ACE score. The highest ACE score one can have is 10. Felitti & Anda correlated this score with health risk behaviours and outcomes. They discovered that ACEs were extremely common: so it wasn't a matter of identifying another vulnerable group, but of realising that they impact many of us. They also discovered that those with an ACE score of four or more were especially at risk of physical and mental health difficulties (Burke-Harris 2018).

Adverse Childhood Experiences (Felittie & Anda 1998)

◎ Physical abuse   ◎ Sexual abuse

◎ Emotional abuse   ◎ Physical neglect

◎ Emotional neglect   ◎ Exposure to domestic violence

◎ Household substance abuse   ◎ Household mental illness

◎ Parental separation or divorce   ◎ Household member incarcerated/imprisoned

From this list, depressingly, we can see that a lot of toxic stress (including pre-birth stress) occurs in the home context with those who were meant to be the 'safe hands' in the Circle of Security (*see* **Useful Organisations**) around a child whilst growing up. What's critical to note here is that this particular type of stress is both overwhelming and terrifying: with nowhere to go for safety or respite, where the child is exposed to ongoing, elevated levels of adversity, which are often, by their nature, unpredictable. When our stress response system is constantly turned on with little or no time for repair and recovery, our minds and bodies are hijacked, especially when they are developing. Dr Bruce Perry (p. 143) states that it is important to find out when relational traumas and losses happened: the stage of development and whether there were any adults to provide support at that time to buffer the toxic stress, or not.

We're not designed to manage this kind of stress, and especially not unaided, so it brings with it all kinds of complications including significant compromises to physical health, wellbeing and the capacity to function at home and at school. This is trauma … complex trauma. Complex trauma is different to other types of trauma. Complex trauma impacts psychological development, executive functioning, affect regulation (management of emotions and physical states) and physical health (Bombèr, 2011).

Multiple, chronic and prolonged, developmentally adverse traumatic events, most often of an interpersonal nature ... and with early life onset.   Van der Kolk 1996

Traumatised nervous systems can't discriminate between contexts. These pupils also regularly miscue us, hiding their true, softer, more vulnerable needs. Again, another wise action, for self-protection. This is because of their experiences of past grown-ups, projected onto their expectations of all grown-ups. No mature adult has helped them learn yet that some people are different. You will often discover, on tracing back to a pupil's starting point, that they have experienced multiple *intimacy betrayals* along the way; these impact how they now view adults. This, together with their 'blocked trust' (Bomber & Hughes 2013 p. 298), regularly remains unsupported and unchallenged. And in fact it's tragically easy to see how their distrust will be further strengthened as they are moved about, within depersonalised, large systems called 'school', where usually 'one size fits all'.

As Ogden states, 'Nonverbal expressions visibly reveal what words cannot describe: 'the speechless terror' (Van der Kolk, 1996, p. 157) of trauma and the legacy of early or forgotten dynamics with attachment figures' (2015 p. 25). Too often this non-verbal communication is overlooked, not noticed in the busy-ness of life or misread by us, the grown-ups.

There is also complicated, adaptive grieving in the mix, currently on hold because of the challenges already outlined and other developmental vulnerabilities. How can grief be fully expressed and moved through when children and young people are doing all they can to protect their vulnerability? Instead it spills out over time or gets acted out. And those around them in the current situation wonder what on earth is going on - not aware of how haunted these children and young people are, by ghosts of their past. We will explore these and other significant challenges these particular children and young people face later on in the book (p. 62).

Recent history and the kids we lose

A few years back there was a big push towards inclusion across the UK, which I (and I hope you) believe is the right and proper way ahead in the 21st century. However, with hindsight, it was very foolish to just add vulnerable children in to mainstream classrooms without first ensuring the education staff in charge had everything they needed, in order to ensure true inclusion at every level. They - and the pupils - were left to flounder, not only with a lack of understanding around healthy child development and attachment theory but also around the developmental risks of having many ACEs and the disruption caused by relational trauma and loss.

Education staff had no idea what they were dealing with, and therefore did the best they could with what they knew. I was one of these: perhaps you were too. The only psychology training I received within my Bachelor of Education was reference to Maslow's hierarchy of needs and Piaget's learning theory. This really didn't prepare me at all well for the disturbed behaviours I witnessed and experienced over the years, in the classrooms where I was teaching! We weren't told how powerful and essential relationship was to the pupil's ability to learn, or how support staff would come to play such an important role, if they were encouraged to build genuine relationships: or the different ways of being that could support these children from a place of distrust into trust, into relationship.

In response to experiencing out-of-control behaviour, schools began to impose more and more controlling methods, in order to attempt to regain control. Zero tolerance is the policy so often referred to and used in the media and within schools. I don't believe that any teacher went into teaching to deeply wound a child or young person by their words or their actions, but unfortunately it can come to this, as difficult and complex dynamics around control can drive escalation.

WERE YOU AWARE...?

- We have children and young people in our schools right now who are not at all in the right state to learn, never mind undergo the increased anxiety provoked by SATs or GCSEs which are part of our expectations in our current English education systems.

- That if these particular pupils are made exempt from tests or exams, that this can negatively impact a school's performance data? So even those kind, attuned and responsive Headteachers, who can see that it's not helpful to put these pupils through the additional stress, know that they are treading a very fine line, in their ethical responsibility towards both the individual and the school.
  How have we allowed this to happen on our watch? We know that mental health and wellbeing is now on everyone's agenda, especially in schools. However, it seems that the implications of this have not been sufficiently considered - *yet*. In fact we're actually setting schools up to *overlook and marginalise* the mental health and wellbeing of their pupils, if they want to achieve good or outstanding Ofsted results. There shouldn't be such a direct, negative link. This is really not at all a wise trajectory.

- That some of the punitive actions being allowed in our schools at this time such as restraint, seclusion and isolation, with hardly any accountability or external monitoring, started off in psychiatric hospitals and institutions many years ago? The staff there felt out-of-control, not knowing what to do with the patients in their care. Most of us would see them as counterproductive. And are these techniques really appropriate for our schools? We have put our education staff in such a difficult position. Wouldn't the situation be different if our education staff are given the training, care and support that they need, in order to feel empowered, skilled and competent in the face of our pupils' distressed behaviour?

School to prison pipeline

There are many children who are currently in what's being described as the 'school to prison pipeline' (The Independent, 2019). What starts off as a well-meaning zero tolerance policy can quickly slip into restraint, isolation or seclusion which quickly activates escalated states of alarm, fear and terror in children (and adults). Being restrained or isolated are known to be an overwhelming and threatening context for human beings. Unsuprisingly, children in the documentary *The Kids We Lose* (*see* **References**) speak of 'getting madder' under these conditions, when the education staff's own misinformed intentions were to calm them down - a very serious misunderstanding of how bodies and minds function best. According to a developing field of research, there is now strong evidence to suggest a correlation between exclusions and the likelihood of dropping out of school, arrests and incarceration. A working paper published by the National Bureau of Economic Research (2019) reported the first causal evidence that strict schools do indeed contribute to the 'school to prison pipeline'. It was discovered that male minority pupils were most likely to be affected (nber.org/papers/26257).

We function best in the context of 'felt safety' and in relationship with other people. Attuned and responsive other people. Relationships with other people who are kind increases a sense of safety, so that what the neuropsychologist Stephen Porges refers to as the social engagement system within the individual's brain can be accessed, and they can recover a calm/alert state. We'll explore the nervous system in more detail later on.

These troubled children and young people usually already have a sense of feeling profoundly flawed and rejected: the disciplinary measures we currently use in school exacerbate this. Many of these pupils refer to themselves as 'bad' or even 'evil', as if there is something inherently wrong with them, when actually the vast majority have been wounded deeply by those who were supposed to care for them. They have often experienced intimacy betrayal.

The mimosa pudica and Porges' social engagement system

So many of them have a very fragile sense of self and poor internal controls (Bombèr 2007). I recently came across information about a little herb called the Mimosa

Pudica. It grows in South America and other hot climates. It has a very primitive 'nervous system' of electrical charges that trigger changes in cell water pressure at the base of its leaflets. This sensitive plant folds up its leaves and 'closes down' if it's touched. Please have a look at this fascinating plant, a quiet star of Youtube. I find it a really helpful analogy for those pupils of ours that I'll be talking about throughout this book. We can so easily 'close down' children and young people by our naïve responses to them. And yet really our task is to support them to remain open and engaged: we need to find a way to help them to stay connected to themselves and others - disconnection drives fear and shutdown. We will learn more about what fear can do in the next chapter, when we explore the use of discipline more deeply.

There is something potentially even more serious that we need to be aware of. If we continue naively activating more threat responses through our actions, we're perpetuating the creation of dangerous community contexts for all of us in the future. It simply isn't wise to activate the fight/flight/freeze systems within individuals or in our communities any further. Instead, we need to focus on learning about how to increase felt safety as a matter of urgency, so that these children and young people are able to quickly access or return to a calm or alert state. Threat or increasing challenge doesn't do this. Yet somehow there are many who strongly believe that the more we exert our power, authority and control, the more these children will learn.

> This threat further dysregulates the youth (pupil), moving her even further away from rational, cortical level of thinking and responses. Thus, the use of mechanisms of power and control like motivational procedures which attempt to manipulate a youth's behaviour is dysregulating, and can cause developmental damage.   Perry & Ablon 2019, p. 28

Zero tolerance is not the answer here. Zero tolerance actually increases risk … risk for the children and young people. And risk to us and our communities. We are designed for connection and function best as human beings in the context of relationship. I'm reluctant to even use the words to encourage you to imagine the opposite: they make me shudder. Disconnection, exclusion and isolation cause human beings to turn on themselves, and on each other. Connection drives safety for ourselves and each other. Disconnection drives toxicity, risk and danger to ourselves and towards each other.

> Much violence in our society is based on the illusion that life is a property to be defended and not a gift to be shared.   Nouwen 1997, p. 275

In her research studies, Dr Dowd (Burke-Harris 2018, pp. 119-20) has found a direct correlation between those being impacted by ACEs going on to being excluded from schools and ending up either as victims of crime or becoming the perpetrators of crime. In the UK one third of those carrying weapons have had weapons used against them (Home Office, July 2019, *An analysis of indicators of serious violence* Available online).

Tragically those who have had many adverse childhood experiences are likely to have compromised executive function (Bombèr, 2011) including poor impulse control and an inability to focus (just to clarify, I don't advocate for the use of ACEs scoring for children in schools). These two developmental vulnerabilities in particular are big obstacles for school systems.

> Healthy development depends upon a sequential mastery of functions; a dysregulated individual will be inefficient in mastering any task that requires relational abilities (cortico-limbic) and will have a difficult time engaging in more verbal-insight -orientated (cortical) therapeutic and educational efforts.
>   Perry 2020, p. 144

Currently, we expect children and young people to sit still for long periods of time, to remain quiet and to focus on curriculum, despite their internal 'alarm' systems being triggered by what they perceive as threats in their environment, often with no-one even realising. Sitting still and focussing are very complex expectations for pupils with developing and already compromised nervous systems. The challenge is how to somehow remain still, without shifting into a place of immobilisation, where they can feel trapped. Very difficult when they already spend a lot of time in their fight/flight nervous system, which involves being mobilised (actively ready for danger), rather than in their social engagement nervous system, calm and alert. They are misreading what they pick up from what's going on around them through the process known as 'neuroception' (p. 102) tuning into what they perceive as danger cues, threat, on high alert with no space to even think about our curriculum. Against the backdrop of so much trauma, all of this has implications on how we do school, especially how we interpret these particular children and young people: and, most importantly how we teach them, including the teaching involved in discipline.

But if we want to continue to increase the numbers of those on the fringes of our society, vulnerable to gang membership, criminalisation, radicalisation, then: *then let's not* take the time to consider what they have lived through, the toxic stress in the mix: *let's not* keep stress and shame at low levels for these pupils and *let's not* keep an eye on how they're doing and support them to come back to a regulated state. Instead, let's do everything we can to increase their experiences of alienation by punishing, segregating, secluding and isolating them. Terrified human beings can go on to terrify others. Human beings are designed to buffer the impact of so much that can and does happen in this world that is stressful for nearly everyone, one way or another, especially for children. But take that relational experience away and the potential of relational buffering away and anything is possible ... absolutely anything. The risk is too high. We will all pay for the result.

Finances?

What are the financial implications of facilitating good quality, rich, relationships with these children and young people and the different ways of being that we will explore in this book? Let's first consider that what matters is often not so much about increasing staff numbers but about the type of staff we have on board, and the way they relate to children and young people. Then, let's consider the financial implications of what I'm proposing to get it into perspective.

Here's an example from recent figures.

ON THE ONE HAND:

If we were to allocate a Key Adult (KA) to a child or young person (as per Bomber, 2007, 2015), then we would need to protect £13-15K per year for this work (the average annual salary is £12,081 for a teaching assistant (UNISON, 18/10/19).

If the Key Adult were to become Attachment Aware and Trauma Responsive by following a Trauma Informed Education pathway (see TIE for example, in **Useful Organisations**): including access to the Touchbase 7 day Attachment Lead course (@ approx £590), Theraplay® Level 1 (@ approx £950) and DDP Level 1 (@ approx £800) then approx £2300 as a one-off investment would also need to be protected.

Be mindful that this one person could also be the KA to a number of other children too.

So that's a total of less than £15,000.

ON THE OTHER HAND:

If we needed to move this child or young person (because of their behaviour) from mainstream school to an EBD school or a pupil referral unit in 2019, this could cost between **£18-20K per pupil, per year**. If the child or young person became disaffected there and end up being overseen by the youth offending service then **this would cost £33K to £38K per year**. If they end up in prison this would be **between £51k and £85K per year** (as per latest Ministry of Justice figures).

(Figures as of 2020)

Now, I'm no accountant! And even if some of these figures are approximate, it really seems a no-brainer to be preventative here. Investment in mainstream schools could save us so much in the UK, in the coming years. Now is the time to update our policies and practices. We simply can't afford not to, at every level.

The new wave

The approaches we use at the moment in our schools are clearly not working, a fact recognisable not only by reading exclusion data but also by the fact these approaches seem to be exacerbating the problems in our classrooms. Lower level behaviours are becoming more disturbed over time. Our behaviour units and pupil referral units are full of traumatised children and young people who may have been punished, excluded, labelled and medicated. Without intentional, alternative interventions by adults in mainstream, the outcomes for our most traumatised pupils are predictably poor. Something needs to shift, and I would argue that this doesn't mean excluding even more pupils, in the name of zero tolerance, by exerting more authority and control, but instead, considering how we could adapt and update our practice to meet and serve the needs of the pupils, who have been entrusted into our care.

We have traumatised pupils in the mix, adding to the stresses already in schools. It can feel like some pupils are purposefully oppositional, defiant, aggressive or withdrawn. But how the nervous system responds is out of our control, and theirs. There are involuntary responses, linked to safety or danger cues around them. So surely we need to learn everything we can about the terrain of trauma, to better understand how they see themselves, others and the contexts they find themselves in, so that we can respond in the most helpful way, for all our sakes? Wouldn't this be the most ethical response for our role? Our exploration in this terrain is supported by the work of researchers and practitioners such as Stephen Porges, Bruce Perry, Dan Hughes, Pat Ogden, Babette Rothschild, Jaak Panksepp, Gabor Maté and Daniel Siegel. In this book we'll look at the best ways to navigate the risks and ensure we have done absolutely everything we can to mitigate the circumstances that these children and young people find themselves in; to ensure that they have the best possible chance of recovery and being freed up to learn. And how to look after ourselves in the process. Doesn't that sound fair? Equal opportunities for all. No-one an outsider.

There is a way forward

I'm not talking about another project, another team, another intervention. I mean addressing the very foundations of how we relate, how we teach, how we discipline, how we function within the structure we call school and in terms of our family lives and wider communities, integrating inclusion into every fibre of how school operates. Change is difficult for all of us: it could mean giving up what we have become familiar or even comfortable with. Change brings new challenges and may leave staff unsettled for a while. So we need to support them at the same time as we find new ways to support our traumatised pupils.

It's not complicated; we don't need PhDs in this topic. In fact there are many easy wins along the way which can have a significant impact. I'm a strong believer that once the majority of school staff have the facts available, they will be creative with coming up with the solutions. We must get relationships on the map in school and then prioritise relationships first before anything else, yes, even the curriculum! *Nothing* must ever be at the expense of our relationship with the children and young people we are alongside. Nothing. No more good cop/bad cop approaches with children and young people. They need relationships with safe, predictable, integrated, mature adults. Relationships are key. However much someone has been wounded in relationship, bodies and minds function optimally and most safely through connection, not through isolation. And let's not be naïve. If relational trauma and loss is in the mix bodies and minds will have been impacted. If there's a pupil you know who's had many ACEs, sitting up, smiling at you, behaving compliantly, then you need to ask yourself: '*Where has the trauma gone?*' Trauma can sometimes lie dormant but it will unravel over time. That's the nature of relational trauma. We ignore or overlook it at our peril.

What we need is an updated framework that integrates neuroscience, pedagogy and psychology into the classroom. The practices of attunement, regulation and attachment must be in place and active before learning and cognition can occur. The way we engage, teach and discipline our pupils will make all the difference. They need us to be their strongest supporters, the ones who prioritise rich, relational interventions over everything else so that these pupils have the relational experiences they need to update. The mind and body is influenced by repetitive experience. What we need is the growth mindset that we often expect from our pupils. These pupils don't feel safe or grounded - yet. They can't utilise their exploratory systems - yet. *Yet* is a very powerful word and concept.

In crossing the terrain of trauma we'll see that there is a hugely significant neurodevelopmental order to follow with our interventions, in order to respect how human beings function best.

> Educational neuroscience offers a framework for exploring brain development, dampening down the stress response, and implementing strategies that engage and build brain architecture from the bottom up.   Desautels & McKnight 2019, p. 25

In school, we can invest all our time into our lesson planning, our delivery, our props and our resources, but until we realise that ACEs change the architecture of the brain, and trigger harmful inflammation in both brain and body, we remain stuck, and the children and young people in our care stay stuck. Today, we know what we need to do: together we can actually prevent the inevitable. We can support these traumatised children and young people to move from a place of despair and isolation into hope, resilience, strength, connection and growth. It is more than time to move beyond the simplistic and traditional view of rewarding good behaviour and punishing bad behaviour. Human beings are so, so much more complicated than that! How we *function best* as human beings, has to be considered. We will also discover as we travel further that our difficulties with these traumatised children and young people are not behavioural, but *regulatory*, and recognise how to respect biology so that we can meet both the regulatory *and* the relationship needs of our pupils.

Twelve steps for moving forward

1. In addition to SATS and GCSE results, Ofsted would measure the success of a school on its evidenced capacity to support the wellbeing of every child, to be the best they can be at the time, taking into account what they have lived through to date, using developmentally dependent and state dependent interventions as appropriate (p. 139).

2. In order for a school to receive Outstanding, it would have to have reduced all formal and informal exclusions, evidenced by presenting data revealing which pupils were now on part-time timetables, isolated/secluded, being sent home, not in lessons, off-rolled etc.

3. Anyone working with or alongside children would have Attachment Aware and Trauma Responsive training on an ongoing basis, so they know how to be and what to do in the face of distressed behaviours.

4. We would have relationship policies in place, rather than behaviour policies, which focus on respecting biology in all our policy and practice.

5. A Key Adult (Teaching Assistant) and Team Pupil would be mandatory for any child with a history of ACEs. There would be at least one Attachment Lead in every school ensuring everyone was kept up to date with the latest research on child development, attachment and neuroscience.

6. The school day would follow the neuro-sequential model for supporting hurting children **Regulate**, **Relate**, **Reason** and **Repair** in sequence, as discussed in, Chapter 5, **The Art of Attunement**.

7. All lessons would include sensory breaks as described in Chapter 6, **Regulate**.

8. All staff would attune to and respond to children and young people in their care in a gentle and calm manner, using repair as and when necessary. Threat would be viewed as a staff development and potentially disciplinary matter (Chapters 7, 8 and 9 on **Relate**, **Reason** and **Repair**): although, let's not blame teachers who are probably in a state of blocked care (p. 74) themselves! But work to support them to move out of it and back into empathic, attuned care towards their pupils.

9. Everyone involved with traumatised pupils to see themselves as stress and shame regulators by increasing safety cues, reducing possible stress triggers and increasing a child or young person's window of stress tolerance (see Chapter 4, **Respecting Biology**).

10. Those with specific responsibility to children who are known to have many ACEs to have regular reflective supervision sessions, facilitated by a trained trauma specialist.

11. Restraint, seclusion & isolation would be made illegal for children. Knowing a child's stress triggers and calmers would be critical. Swapping in with familiar others from Team Pupil (Bombèr, 2015-16) and staff taking time out in the midst of difficult dynamics would become standard practice.

12. Any type of move would need to be brought before an independent Panel, rather than the school's own council staff, to reduce conflict of interest and to add in further accountability (because of the risks, to both the child and our society, of impermanence).

Chapter 3

Reframing discipline

Faced with a range of challenging behaviours, caregivers have a tendency to deal with their frustration by retaliating in ways that often uncannily repeat the children's early trauma … It is standard practice in many schools to punish children for tantrums, spacing out, or aggressive outbursts - all of which are symptoms of traumatic stress. When that happens, the school, instead of offering a safe haven, becomes yet another traumatic trigger.   Van der Kolk 2015, p. 353

Currently in the UK, our behaviour model still seems to rely heavily on a behaviourist/ consequence or punitive/rule-based approach to understanding behaviour in homes and at school. These are underpinned by both our conscious and unconscious belief systems about behaviour. The following are based on James McTaggart's work in this area (personal communication) which clearly outlines the differences between punitive/ rule-based, behaviourist/consequence-based and what he describes as relational/ developmental based behaviour models. McTaggart sets it all out in a table but for the purposes of this book, I'm organising them in a different way. As you go through the list on the next page, tick those that you agree with and put a cross against those you disagree with. Ask around and see what family members and colleagues think. You may be surprised how many agree with these statements.

Behaviour/consequence model

We believe that we should use punitive/rule-based systems that use fear to manage behaviour.	☐
We believe that we should use behaviourist /consequence based systems that use consequences to manage behaviour.	☐
We believe that children and young people are responsible for their actions and need to take responsibility in order to learn.	☐
We believe that boundaries are needed to indicate right and wrong and to make our standards clear.	☐
We believe rules should be enforced without exception and clearly communicated.	☐
We believe behaviour is something to control and to manage.	☐
We believe consequences are sanctions and punishments and ways to shape behaviour.	☐
We believe that 'inappropriate behaviour' is wrong-doing, deliberate, learned, and voluntary.	☐
We believe that the causes of difficulties are a lack of compliance, insufficient discipline, learned poor responses, lack of appropriate reinforcement, wilfulness, callousness, arrogance and lack of self-control on the part of the child.	☐
We believe solutions lie in the child and in adjusting consequences.	☐
We believe children who don't manage should be excluded or fixed, helped and given an intervention.	☐
We believe policy effectiveness is measured by compliance and behaviour change.	☐

However, what if there were an alternative way in which we could interpret behaviour, and a different way to consider how we respond to it? What if:

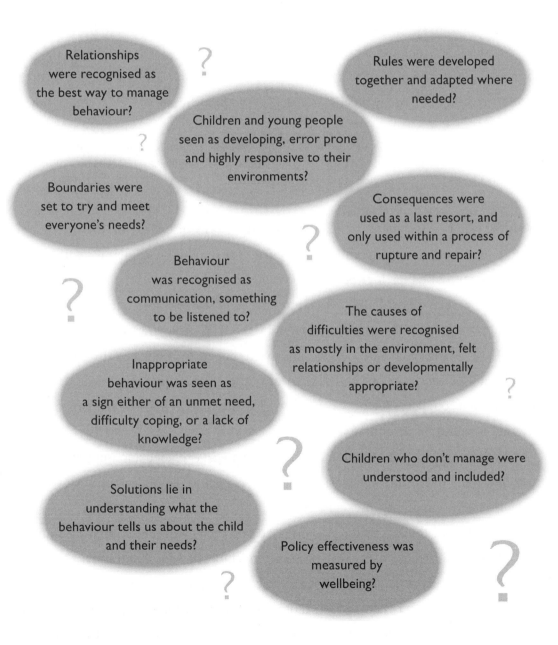

Relationships were recognised as the best way to manage behaviour?

Rules were developed together and adapted where needed?

Children and young people seen as developing, error prone and highly responsive to their environments?

Boundaries were set to try and meet everyone's needs?

Consequences were used as a last resort, and only used within a process of rupture and repair?

Behaviour was recognised as communication, something to be listened to?

The causes of difficulties were recognised as mostly in the environment, felt relationships or developmentally appropriate?

Inappropriate behaviour was seen as a sign either of an unmet need, difficulty coping, or a lack of knowledge?

Children who don't manage were understood and included?

Solutions lie in understanding what the behaviour tells us about the child and their needs?

Policy effectiveness was measured by wellbeing?

This second list is also based on James McTaggart's work in this area. Let's unpick it all some more … for far too long, discipline has been equated with punishment in the UK. But what does discipline actually mean? Where does the word come from?

The root word for discipline is actually *disciple,* from Old French, meaning *learner,* one who embraces the teaching of, follows the example of: and thus in the verb form, meaning to guide, lead, teach, model, and encourage (Knost 2013, p. 80). In other words, 'to discipline' really means 'to teach'. And punishment?

> What is the root word for punishment? The root word is *punire*. Punire in the verb form means to penalize, chastise, castigate, inflict harm, humiliate. There is no noun form of *punire* or its English equivalent, *punishment*.   (*ibid*)

With the rate of permanent exclusions climbing and re-offending on the increase in the UK, it seems that something in our current discipline system isn't working. It doesn't seem that either fear-based approaches (as advocated at the time of writing by Home Secretary Priti Patel (The Guardian, 2019) or zero tolerance consequence-based approaches in schools (as advocated by the 'UK behaviour tsar', Tom Bennett, (2019)) are having the desired impact that were hoped for. For healthy, appropriate behaviours, do we just need to escalate our zero tolerant policies; in other words, become even tougher? Or do we need to find alternative approaches closer to the original meaning of discipline?

Perhaps we also need to think about those who get excluded and imprisoned? We may find some interesting patterns. Maybe we can get to the bottom of what is going on here - and it's really not rocket science.

Personally, I think it's time we reframed and reclaimed the original meaning of 'discipline', so that those of us who promote attachment aware and trauma responsive principles can fully articulate what really needs to happen to enable troubled pupils to settle to learn, rather than add yet more rooms in the isolation suite or build more prisons. We know too much now to do anything else. So if discipline means 'to teach'…

Punishment

If you hear a senior manager speaking in school about a pupil needing to be disciplined, you could rightly assume he meant that the pupil needed to be punished in some way for his actions. In the UK this takes many forms, but usually involves some type of relational withdrawal (that is, removing relationships from the pupil) through time out, detention, seclusion, isolation, a managed move or exclusion. Replacing writing lines and the cane, this way of working has now become ingrained within our education system. Parents and carers too can expect that a child or young person will be removed, if they are displaying difficult, distressed behaviours. Regrettably, this approach continues to be prioritised by the UK Government as the best way to crack down on difficult behaviour, as noted at the time of writing:

> A package of disciplinary measures that include a renewed emphasis on exclusion and allowing teachers to use 'reasonable force' to improve behaviour … We [the UK Government] will back Headteachers to use powers to promote good behaviour including sanctions and rewards, using reasonable force, to search and confiscate items from pupils (including mobile phones), impose same day detentions, suspend and expel pupils …   The Guardian 27/8/19 [my parenthesis]

Somehow this seems a very naïve and simplistic solution to the complexities around us of being human and the very important need to communicate. If a pupil is distressed and is communicating this through their behaviour, then surely it would be more ethical to attempt to attune to and translate what they might be trying to say? After all, behaviour is communication; giving it a sanction or a punishment doesn't do anything about the underlying message. It would be a bit like suppressing a cough, rather than trying to find out if the symptom (the cough) was because of a simple infection or something far more worrying …

It also seems a very unfair and unethical approach to merely increase sanctions and rewards without really knowing who and what we are dealing with. What I mean by this is that the majority of those who are directly affected by these types of measures are those with additional needs, as described in the previous chapter. And, as we've seen, those with additional needs who have experienced toxic stress, and are developmentally vulnerable.

We all bring our own interpretations to the meanings of behaviour. What if the pupil in front of us wasn't deliberately trying to sabotage our lesson but had been triggered by something random, reminiscent of a past terrifying incident? What if the young person across the corridor is so distrustful of grown-ups, because of what's happening back at home, that they duck back behind the stairwell because they'd rather hide than engage with us? Nothing personal ... How would that affect how we behave towards them? Can we really envisage this young, suffering person is going to benefit from isolation?

Sometimes the kinds of measures used at the moment do seem to work in the short term. However, I would stress that that is just it - in the *short*-term. We don't see any sustained, meaningful change. We don't witness real learning. We may however witness compliance. I believe these kinds of measures work in the short-term only because of overt conformity, but not really out of free will, choice and new learning, especially if the use of increased fear, power and authority are in the mix. However, over time we will see the long term, often detrimental effects once traumatised children and young people start to unravel - what's happening at the 'roots' driving the behaviour we wanted to control has been left unaddressed, and the symptoms - the challenging behaviours - have got worse.

> Angry confrontations and punishment can at best temporarily halt unacceptable behaviours, but since the underlying alarm system and stress hormones are not laid to rest, they are certain to erupt again at the next provocation.
>
> Van der Kolk 2015, p. 353

These pupils really can't be left to navigate their emotional and physical dysregulation alone. Unfortunately we adults can really easily misuse our power and authority over children and young people, especially if we're feeling de-skilled, disempowered and unsupported in response to how the pupil is behaving. There is so obviously a power imbalance going on. We adults are usually stronger, taller, certainly older, and have more sway and authority than our pupils.

> Traditional discipline techniques are, in my view, a lazy way of dealing with misunderstood behaviour, which in most cases derives from a child's valid and unmet need.   Gillet 2019 (blog) p. 7

Let's really think about this so we can become more conscious about why we do what we do, and also perhaps challenge some of our own inner beliefs about discipline. Because we all have them: and in the face of extremely challenging behaviour, we may find ourselves inadvertently reverting to primitive, punitive responses that can horrify us when we're calmer. So looking at our beliefs in advance may raise our awareness, enable us to process our own experience and help us be in a more prepared and regulated (calm, open and engaged) state for any trying times to come.

Consequences / zero tolerance strategies reported as currently in use in UK schools

- Miss break or lunchtime
- Being shouted at in their face
- Sit in seclusion unit all day, only being let out to eat lunch
- Miss golden time
- Miss computer time
- In schools education staff can call time away from class 'reflection time' when really it is exclusion
- Sent to another classroom to reflect
- Excluded pupils' names on display in reception area
- Relegated from school's sports team if receive a certain number of behaviour points
- Time out
- Being on report: having to ask for a number out of 10 from each teacher
- Thinking chair
- Standing outside classroom
- Not being allowed to attend school disco if not enough behaviour points
- Missing a school trip
- Teacher looking in Yellow Pages to find another school for a pupil
- Being threatened with the police being called
- The police coming in and restraining a child
- Being restrained
- Teacher telling pupil they won't have any friends when they are older
- Being humiliated in assembly by being told to stand on a line painted on the floor

Anonymised comments from education staff

- There are 5 main rules - including rules about equipment and uniform. An example: students are expected to have a pen and a back-up pen and if they do not have these - sometimes a warning is given but sometimes students are sent to the isolation unit. We know of particular pupils in Y7 who have experienced big anxiety, particularly on a Sunday evening for forgetting equipment. This has had a significant impact on their learning.

- Students having to wear a lanyard around their neck if their uniform is not up to the expected standard - the lanyard reads something like '*I am sorting my school uniform*'.

- The isolation unit seems to be used in many instances as a consequence. It is either in a room or in little units with an adult to supervise - no direct teaching and often they are adults who are not known to the students. Students are sometimes there for a whole day. An example of this being used for a student who is adopted. It was requested by the parent that this was not used due to the level of distress that the student presented with. School agreed, however it was not communicated clearly to all staff. The student was placed in an isolation unit - from where the student sent text messages to the parent expressing the wish to self-harm, which they later did.

- A student with learning difficulties and adopted was sent into isolation for making noises. This is something the student does, when excited/stressed.

- The number of permanent exclusions have risen or students are put on a 'managed move' to another secondary school - with little transition support/planning involved.

- Students are told they are not allowed back to their main school. This seems to often happen a lot to students in Y10/11.

- There are examples of off-rolling - students told they cannot return to the school and taken off roll - yet not permanently excluded. Ofsted has become more aware of this.

- Local Authorities/Teams/Schools adopt several trainings and approaches which may conflict with each other. There is a lot of concern about Tom Bennett's ideas and the conflicts they create with AATR approach. Also emotion coaching, restorative approaches which do not always include the sensory regulation that we recommend.

- Some staff and leadership seem to have the need for 'consequences' and feel they need to be seen to doing something: *'Children can't get away with it'* etc - this language is particularly expressed at times of stress.

The mainstream approach in UK schools at the moment, recommended by a lot of teacher training providers, includes time out or walking away, so that behaviour seen as challenging isn't rewarded by our acknowledging it. There are also threats or punishment of the child in some arbitrary way, escalating our punishments if what we try doesn't work, under the justification that 'perpetuating a dominance hierarchy is somehow serving the greater good' (Gillet 2019 (blog) p. 2).

> Institutions that deal with traumatised children and adults all too often bypass the emotional engagement system that is the foundation of who we are and instead focus narrowly on correcting 'faulty thinking' and on suppressing unpleasant emotions and troublesome behaviours' ...   Van der Kolk 2015, p. 349

Tom Bennett advocates for consequences and suggests they are a 'conversation', although to my mind, a conversation is a two-way, interactive process. In his Independent Review, published in 2017, he writes:

> Consequences are a conversation. The school's culture's reply to the actions of the individual. That reply can either be to permit, to prohibit and discourage, or to encourage and praise. Without consequences, the conversation between the student's behaviour and the school's culture is lost.   p. 41

I would challenge what to my mind is a somewhat simplistic and power-based view, that even Bennett himself describes as 'the simplest method'. He has overlooked that human beings are complex creatures. There is so much that makes us do what we do. So complicated behaviour deserves a more complex response, which involves a 'state dependent' intervention, rather than a one size fits all (**Respecting Biology**).

If I'd been consulted, I would have written:

- A pupil's behaviour is communication, the beginning of a conversation. As education staff we need to involve ourselves in this conversation. A conversation is a two-way, interactive process.

- Before making a reply we need to support the pupil to communicate further, by increasing our felt safety cues (p. 70, p. 116), whilst also remembering their story (what they have lived through up till now, from pregnancy onwards).

- Next we need to actively listen, without adding in our own interpretation, translating what they might have said about what was happening for them if they had had the right words (instead of 'behaving' it). We may even wonder aloud together with them or say, '*Help me to understand (what's happening for you)*,' as it could be that once they start feeling respectfully heard, they may be able to join us in the translation process.

- Once we fully understand what has just happened by actively listening AND drawing on everything we know from the pupil's story, THEN it's our time to reply. We will need to determine whether any teaching is necessary. If there has been any kind of relationship rupture we will need to join in with some repair. And before any reason and repair is initiated, we will need to decide on the most optimal timing, so that the pupil can make best use of what we do and offer.

To me these would be the most helpful recommendations for education staff, for getting alongside traumatised pupils and those with disrupted attachments.

Tom Bennett advocates the use of three particular Rs in his document (2017) (overlapping with but not the same as the ones proposed in this book): *routines, responses* and *relationships*. Whilst these are all important, I would tweak their interpretations and flesh them out a bit, in line with Attachment Aware and Trauma Responsive practice.

Bennett suggests	I suggest
Routines	... that there must be consistency, but not rigidity (Siegel, 2015 p.227)
Responses	... that our responses must be relevant to the developmental stage and the state the pupil is in (Perry 2016, p. 32 & p. 48) (*and see* p. 143) and respectful of the pupil's value and dignity as a human being. Connection must always come first and whatever happens, all care must be taken so as not to damage the relationship (Hughes 2009).
Relationships	... ones in which the adults intentionally increase felt safety cues (Porges 2015)

I go further and suggest a completely different set of **Rs**, based on trauma and development specialist Dr Bruce Perry's sequence of engagement and processing (2004-2017), also integrating input from other sources and front line experience, because whilst to me the Bennett approach above is somewhat obvious and foundational, it doesn't really move us up a gear, respecting how we best function as human beings, when the going gets tough in class. We'll look at that from p. 95 onwards.

Engaging in *relational withdrawal* from traumatised children and young people where they are dysregulated, distressed, melting down, flooded with shame, getting out of control, with an already fragile sense of self and poor internal controls, is probably one of the worst things we could possibly do. Allan Schore states that 'affect dysregulation [the lack of ability to calm ourselves down] is seen to be the fundamental mechanism in all psychiatric disorders' (*in* Taylor et al, 1997, my parenthesis). If someone *can't* calm themselves down, they need someone else - a mature adult - to support them into that calm state, none of which is offered by the four empty walls of an isolation room.

Nor by someone with a still face keeping guard (*see* the truly distressing research by Tronick (2016) on the dysregulating effects of 'still face' - even the experimental research had to be stopped. Watch it on Youtube, and see if and how it affects you). True calm is not experienced through isolation. *Isolation is stress-inducing.* We seem to be creating more significant, complex difficulties for these children and young people as individuals and for our communities as a whole. It seems that policy makers and those who insist on behaviourist approaches don't recognise (yet!) that *we all* need co-regulation throughout life (that is, with someone calmer, empathic and more stable: Porges, 2019). So why would we put our most troubled and developmentally challenged pupils, in a state of extreme vulnerability, on their own? It simply doesn't make sense.

> Exclusions do not improve behaviour and take a harsh toll both on the excluded child's education and on society. Excluded young people are more likely to go to prison, be unemployed and develop severe mental health issues.
> CEO of Nurture UK - Kevin Kibble's response to
> DfE leak on new policy of school exclusions Nurture UK 29/8/19

Another important consideration to take on board before we go any further, is the fact that many children and young people who 'behave badly' have usually experienced some kind of attachment or trauma disruption and have a number of developmental vulnerabilities, not just difficulties with their affect regulation (their management of their own emotional and physiological state. You can find out more by having a look at The Trauma Tree *on the next page,* (Developed from the Family Futures© model 2011).

> We would never dream of treating a toddler as a failure for stumbling as they learn to walk. So why do we treat them harshly when they stumble through their emotional growth?   Gillett 2019 (blog) p. 7

The writer here is referring to toddler tantrums: but I think there are some very obvious parallels here with the traumatised children and young people I work alongside, especially as their emotional and social ages are compromised. These children and

THE TRAUMA TREE

(Developed 2011 from the Family Futures© model, with thanks)

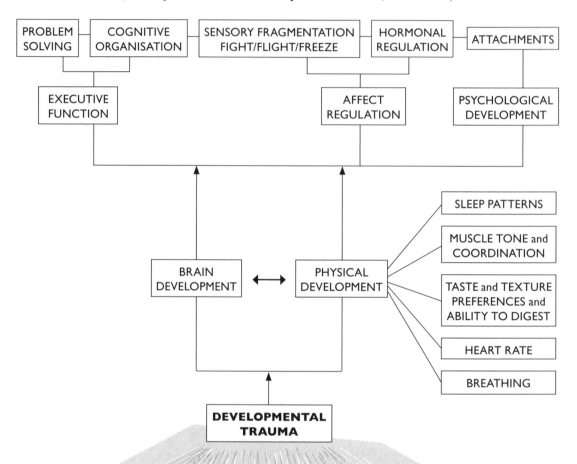

The Trauma Tree's 'roots' are in the
prolonged neglect, deprivation, loss, abuse, violence, upheaval
or any combination of these that the child has experienced in his or her early
childhood, fundamentally affecting the development of brain, body and the
relationship between them.

young people often present with much younger emotional and social ages, so we need to match our interventions developmentally to those ages, regardless of chronology.

It seems too often that our discipline is based on our adult wants rather than on the needs of a child or young person; we seem to have forgotten that differentiation, used when we're engaged with the curriculum, is necessary for learning about behaviour as well as how to self-regulate. What would happen if we could find a way to be alongside as fellow travellers through our relationship with them, having an understanding of child psychology and brain development and shifting our perspective? What might happen? I wonder if a new vision of school would open up?

It's also important to recognise that what we might consider as inappropriate at school probably served these children and young people well at another time and in another place, when their life was literally all about survival. Let's not forget that many expressions of their behaviour are, in effect, adaptive responses to what they have already experienced. Tragically, what happened in one specific relationship becomes generalised. It takes the body, heart and mind a long time to catch up with the present reality of the 'here and now' and another new relationship. This isn't an excuse for their behaviour, but a way of interpreting it, getting to what might underlie and be driving it: which surely needs to be taken into account when we're working out what to do? Are we being as thoughtful and intelligent as we are with the curriculum?

In other words, rather than creating an *excuse* for their often difficult and challenging behaviours, *recognising behaviour as communication* helps us be curious and work to understand what might be going on *behind* the behaviour, which then give us clues as to what might help, as we navigate discipline together.

Dynorphin

ACEs have many terrible consequences, amongst which is the blocking of the capacity to feel pain, sadness and joy. These children and young people feel unbearable pain. In order to bear 'the unbearable,' dynorphin, a natural opioid is released (Dr Jon Baylin speaking at the DDP UK Connects Conference (29-30/4/2019), a human, physiological response to traumatic experiences that means children survive through the ongoing state of pain, but somewhat numbed. This creates a chronic bad or flat mood, rather than the euphoric joy that endorphins allow us to experience. Along with blocking the unbearable and numbing positive emotional states, it also suppresses the attachment seeking and caregiving systems of neurological pathways in the child, so they they remain further isolated and at risk.

> *Anna arrived, sullen. Half-balancing on her seat she rocked back and forth, staring into space. As the teacher walked past her desk, he said 'Sit up and get started. I don't like the look of your attitude, Anna. You'd better get yourself in a different frame of mind or we're not going to be getting along today, I can assure you of that.'*

It's all too easy to feel irritated by children or young people with 'low mood or energy', who appear sullen and flat: and indeed their mood may be seen as disrespectful to authority figures and systems. Yet we can so easily misinterpret the presentation of traumatised children and young people, exacerbating the situation, simply by not knowing what's happening.

Threats over minor infractions

Survival was really an expression of the heroic nature of our body trying to save us.
Porges 2019, p. 2

A traumatised child who has already used 'heroic defences' (Porges, 2019) in order to build a wall to protect themselves will merely reinforce those defences whenever they experience any kind of threat. And sadly as well as ones they see but we may not be aware of, there are many potential threats in our schools at the moment, including education staff intent on ensuring these children are punished for anything they do that isn't expected or acceptable to them, from their own personal beliefs, experience and training in behaviour management. Here are a few:

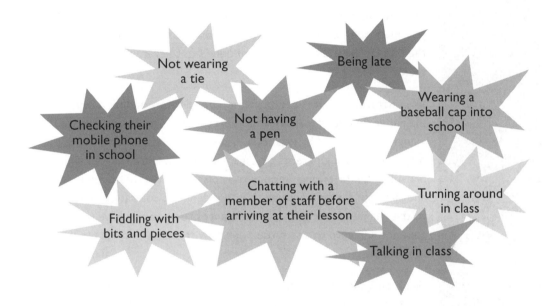

So before we look at how genuinely serious behaviours are addressed, let's explore what might be behind or driving each of these examples - let's think them through from an AATR perspective, considering what each behaviour might require in relation to the impact of ACEs on the ability to 'get it right'.

BEHAVIOUR	THINKING IT THROUGH FROM AN AATR PERSPECTIVE
Not having a pen	Having a pen requires pre-planning, organisation, and memory; these executive functions may well be impacted through developmental vulnerability caused by relational trauma and loss. In addition, it may involve having parents or carers organised and caring enough to provide a pen, or enough money to replace one that has been lost; and the pupil to have enough self-confidence to tolerate and admit to the shame of losing it.
Not wearing a tie	Wearing a tie requires pre-planning, organisation, and memory; these executive functions may well be impacted through developmental vulnerability caused by relational trauma and loss. In addition, it may involve having parents or carers organised and caring enough to provide a tie, or enough money to replace one that has been lost; and the pupil to have enough self-confidence to tolerate and admit to the shame of losing it. It also requires someone to have had the patience and care to teach the pupil how to tie it - and for the pupil to remember.
Being late	Being on time requires pre-planning and organisation; these executive functions may well be impacted through developmental vulnerability caused by relational trauma and loss. It can also require a child or young person to battle with apathy-inducing levels of cortisol, known to be high in traumatised children in the morning. In addition, it may involve having parents or carers organised and caring enough to help the child arrive on time.
Wearing a baseball cap into school	The pupil may experience toxic shame and wish to hide their face, as a result of a developmental vulnerability in their sense of self, caused by relational trauma and loss. In addition the cap may signal gang affiliation, as a means of keeping them safe; gangs are known to attract vulnerable young people, who may see them as a form of protection and attachment. The cap may also provide sensory comfort to a dysregulated pupil.

Checking their mobile phone in school	The pupil may have developmental vulnerability in the area of permanency, and their mobile becomes a transitional object, reminding them of important others with whom they are terrified of losing contact. They may well have already lost contact with people who were significant to them.
Checking in on a member of staff before arriving at their lesson	The pupil may have developmental vulnerability in the area of permanency and worked out that checking in with people they know helps them to remember the relationship and stay connected, despite the terror of separation or abandonment. Seeking proximity like this could be the pupil using the teacher as a secure base, so they can then take the risks required in learning (using their exploratory system).
Fiddling with bits and pieces	The pupil may have developmental vulnerability in their regulation system and are doing their best to try and soothe or calm their nervous system.
Turning around in class	The pupil may be hypervigilant, their stress 'thermostats' or alarm systems on 'high alert', fearful of unknown threats in their environment, because of what they experienced in another time and another place (see more on faulty neuroception, p. 102)
Talking in class	The pupil may have developmental vulnerability in the areas of their sense of self, permanency and/or regulation. They may have worked out that talking helps to soothe, helps them to 'be kept in mind' and helps them stay connected, despite the ongoing terror of separation or abandonment.

These seem such minor things: but instant punishment for any of them seems to omit any thoughtfulness about why some of our pupils need to behave in these ways. Relational trauma and loss go into the 'roots' of a developing child (Trauma Tree p. 48, *and* Bombèr 2011, p. 18), affecting their shoots and their fruits. Children are not blank canvasses. They are bringing into the now what they have lived through in the past, sometimes the very recent past, like this morning, before they left to come to school. And we're missing it.

Vulnerabilities in Executive Functioning

It's also important to remember that when a child or young person has had a considerable number of ACEs, that many, many areas are compromised, especially executive functioning (including higher brain functions such as organisation, memory, sequencing, cause and effect, empathy, mind-mindedness, reflection, logic, planning, impulse control, risk assessment and so on), which take time to develop and only do so properly when lower brain functions are in a state of calm alert alongside mature adults for considerable periods (Bombèr, 2011). It seems that those who've had a difficult start could be building up behaviour points (p. 42) in secondary at quite a rate through their disorganised style of attachment, for example, whist their additional needs and developmental vulnerabilities are not being acknowledged or supported at all.

Many schools are proud of their one size fits all model. Have a look at the FAQs on p. 90-3: some people might find my responses provocative. But when a pupil's fear or overwhelm system is activated in the school context, they are likely to move 'downstairs' into the lower part of their brain where there is no capacity for reflection or 'making good choices': only the capacity for reactivity - to defend and attack. This is the reality, so my sense is that this is what we need to work with and write into our behaviour policies, in order to accommodate it, so that we don't exacerbate an already traumatised situation for our most vulnerable pupils.

Now let's explore the more serious of consequences that our pupils can experience within our schools, by thinking about the use of seclusion or isolation, physical restraint and exclusions.

Seclusion or isolation

In the UK at the moment there are isolation booths, seclusion units and 'reflection rooms' in many schools (a 'reflection room' is a euphemism for a seclusion room). Seclusion, in relation to a pupil means to place him/her involuntarily alone in a room from which he/she cannot freely exit or from which the pupil believes he/she cannot freely exit. An isolation booth could be simply a small room, with bare walls, high-sided cubicles facing the wall containing chairs for the students facing inwards to a shelf at desk height: and a bare desk and chair for the member of staff … Or worse. As Paul Dix points out in a debate in 2018 (TES News), this 'is a long way away from a 'last resort': children isolated for the smallest infraction - wrong socks, rolling eyes, tutting or sucking a mint. They are caught in a no-man's land between a silent existence and exclusion'.

And then there is the matter concerning additional needs which I have already explored. Recently I was told about a pupil in secondary who has speech and language difficulties. The unfamiliar teacher had asked him what his name was: *'Philip'*. The teacher asked again: *'Philip'*. The teacher asked again: *'Philip'*. The teacher asked again: *'Philip'*. By the fourth time the pupil was naturally frustrated: *'Are you deaf?'* he muttered under his breath. For this - one whole day in seclusion. And my organisation has been told about an adopted pupil in secondary, with a background of neglect. She forgot her pen and back-up pen one day in year 7. She was sent to the seclusion unit as the school had a zero tolerance approach to behaviour. Her adoptive mother finds it very difficult to get her into school now. On Sunday evenings in their home now there is a lot more distressed behaviour.

Researching this book brought back a troubling memory for me. I had booked a meeting with a senior manager in a secondary school. The person apologised that he'd forgotten he was 'on duty' that day and would need to meet with me at the isolation unit in the school. Once we got there it appeared that being 'on duty' was more as if he were the 'guard' of a locked room that was cell-like, with windows so that the 'guard', the senior manager on call, could keep an eye on the pupil - the 'prisoner' in question. As you can imagine I was completely preoccupied and couldn't focus on the meeting at all. Questions about the pupil in the locked room flooded my mind as I sat there, becoming increasingly protective, angry and sick to my core.

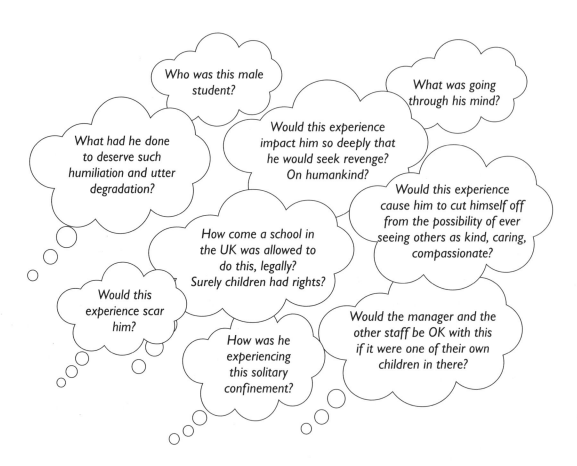

The image was so traumatic that I still remember it vividly today. I shudder to imagine what else is going on across the country nowadays. On our Attachment Lead course which is rolled out across the UK we hear too many tragic stories retold by those wanting change, but stifled by a traumatised system, where many in charge seem to have lost their capacity to be reflective. At the time of writing, Scotland is leading the way in terms of trauma informed and responsive practices within education (p. 63).

Seclusion banned

In late October 2019, there was an amendment to the 1989 Education Act in New Zealand (No. 80, Public Act 139AB). Seclusion is now illegal in any registered school or early childhood service: seclusion rooms are therefore now banned.

This is because they had noted that,

> Seclusion can be physically and psychologically harmful, and is not an acceptable tool in behaviour management.
>
> education.govt.nz (last reviewed 12/12/18) p. 1

Time out is permitted but it has to be the pupil's own choice, and he/she must be able to exit freely, for example wanting some space in the library. We must surely update our policies and practices too.

> Some kids get comments for small things like turning around in class. This can lead to isolation which is counterproductive because they don't get any work to do and are told to sit and not move all day.   (Anonymous but name supplied)

As Paul Dix (one of the founders of the UK *Ban the Booth* campaign) comments:

> Isolation booths were invented and replicated without debate or legislation. We need to limit punishment in schools to ensure that it does not become disproportionate; to make sure it is in line with our values, our laws and the rights of the child.   TES, 27/11/18 p. 2

I completely agree. I've even been tempted to switch my career path to the law as I so wish I had a stronger voice. Children need adults to be their advocates; they are completely dependent on us, the grown-ups. They don't have a voice in all this, and they so know that. For the pupils I am especially focussed on in my work this is yet another context of being powerless. And powerlessness is at the very essence of the original traumas they lived through. What hope have they got of recovery, if we apply this kind of sanction in our schools, which *should* actually be safe havens for those who have been used, abused, neglected, overlooked, tricked, groomed, manipulated … by grown-ups?

Physical restraint

Whilst there are some particular staff and schools who engage in very respectful and considered practice in the UK, there are others who use physical restraint far too often and in inappropriate contexts. This really concerns me. I've witnessed first-hand education staff becoming dysregulated themselves, especially in secondary.

At the same time, many staff are feeling overwhelmed and powerless. They are sometimes faced with risky behaviours in a context where they have a duty of care to both the child and the other children in the school. Too often education staff are not trained in the impact of relational trauma and loss upon bodies and minds, not only on the pupils we teach but on us too, the adults, as part of the relational dynamic. In addition, staff rarely receive clinical supervision, and so are at the mercy of projection, counter transference and unconscious processes between people, which can really muddy the waters (*see Glossary in* Bombèr, 2007). Some get entangled or enmeshed with the pupils in their care.

I'm concerned for pupils who have experienced relational trauma and loss, especially as one of our biggest 'asks' of them in our schools is to trust grown-ups, to relinquish control to grown-ups, to follow the lead of grown-ups. Because of what they've been through, they fear 'intersubjectivity' (relational connection between people), they fear being influenced by another person. They have the powerful sense they must remain in control at all costs. This isn't personal to the particular member of staff involved, though it can be felt and experienced this way; we're all humans and expect particular responses from the other people we relate to. This is one of the key developmental vulnerabilities of those who have experienced relational trauma.

Pupils who have experienced relational trauma can get very mixed up about time, in other words what happened when, and may also have significant difficulties with memory lapses and memories not being dated: some of the effects of living through trauma, since memories are laid down differently at the time of trauma, and are neither organised coherently nor retrievable in the usual ways (Centre for the Study of Emotion and the Law, *see* **Useful Organisations.**

See what you think as you read the following extracts. Be mindful that the legislation changes dependent upon the age and mental capacity of the child or young person. Extracts below and overleaf are from the DfE advice on *Use of Reasonable Force* - an online document from Assets Publishing Service, 2015.

DfE Use of Resonable Force 2015

WHAT IS REASONABLE FORCE?

- … schools generally use force to control pupils and to restrain them.
  Control means either *passive* physical contact, such as standing between pupils or blocking a pupil's path, or *active* physical contact such as leading a pupil by the arm out of a classroom.
- … Restraint means to hold back physically or to bring a pupil under control.
  It is typically used in more extreme circumstances, for example when two pupils are fighting and refuse to separate without physical intervention.

WHEN CAN REASONABLE FORCE BE USED?

- Reasonable force can be used to prevent pupils from hurting themselves or others, from damaging property, or from causing disorder.
- In a school, force is used for two main purposes: to control pupils or to restrain them.
- The decision on whether or not to physically intervene is down to the professional judgement of the staff member concerned and should always depend on the individual circumstances.

DfE Use of Resonable Force (cont...)

SECTION 93, EDUCATION AND INSPECTIONS ACT 2006 5

The following list is not exhaustive but provides some examples of situations where reasonable force can and cannot be used. Schools can use reasonable force to:

○   remove disruptive children from the classroom where they have refused to follow an instruction to do so;

○   prevent a pupil behaving in a way that disrupts a school event or a school trip or visit;

○   prevent a pupil leaving the classroom where allowing the pupil to leave would risk their safety or lead to behaviour that disrupts the behaviour of others;

○   prevent a pupil from attacking a member of staff or another pupil, or to stop a fight in the playground;

and

○   restrain a pupil at risk of harming themselves through physical outbursts.

The UK has been on a slow and confusing journey towards clearer and more consistent legislation but it still seems a work in progress. There is ambiguous guidance from different government departments, many of which are non-statutory. This unfortunately filters through to school policy and hence there is great variation from school to school.

These guidelines show clearly how our traumatised pupils can be set up to fail, since these recommendations don't take into account their fear of being controlled, of being trapped, of feeling powerless, of feeling intruded upon ... because of everything they experienced in the context of trauma and loss. There are also some ambiguous areas that education staff can interpret in many different ways: for example with respect to - *'destroying/damaging property'* ... should this apply to their work? Many of our pupils sabotage their work as a result of how they feel about themselves, another developmental vulnerability - a fragile sense of self. And *'disrupts'* ... fidgeting, making noises? Many of our traumatised pupils have dysregulation vulnerabilities. The document cited above states clearly that schools cannot use force as a punishment, but I have been given far too many examples in which physical force was used, which communicate loud and clear that there is something seriously amiss for these pupils.

And yet we must of course follow the Disability Discrimination legislation as well - so how does this work? I can assure you our traumatised pupils will interpret any of the above as *punishment*. For being them. Surely these pupils, with all their developmental difficulties, need a differentiated approach, to take account of their additional needs. Just because 'developmental trauma' is not - yet - listed in the DSM (the influential though highly controversial Diagnostic and Statistical Manual published by the American Psychiatric Association), surely no-one is so naive as to believe that if a child has experienced toxic stress, attachment disruption and trauma, there would be no consequences at school and at home?

I strongly recommend that we follow the lead of New Zealand who are demonstrating real leadership in this area. They are very clear about what is permitted. They have narrowed it all down to four clear points for the only times physical restraint is allowed to be used. To me this sounds much more reasonable.

- Breaking up a fight
- Stopping a student from moving in with a weapon
- Stopping a student who is throwing furniture close to others who may be injured
- Preventing a student running onto a road

p. 1, Education.Govt. New Zealand (last reviewed 30/10/19)

So restraint is only permissible by law when a person might be injured. And at the same time I think even more detailed advice needs to be drawn up as well, including my recommendations listed below:

* There must first be some attempt at connection with the child or young person by their Key Adult or member of Team Pupil (p. 163-4)
* Staff themselves must be regulated (calm, open and engaged). If not, they must swap in with someone from the pupil's small team of familiar adults
* Felt safety cues must be communicated by the grown-ups to reduce the pupil's sense of threat (p. 70, p. 116)
* The cycle of the 4 R's must be followed, in the right order, before any restraint is used (p. 149)

The eight main challenges for this particular group of children and young people

> You can take a child out of the traumatic situation, but rarely do children get out of the trauma themselves.   Post 2018, p. 34

There are many, many big asks for these pupils in our schools. Have a look at the next page for the eight main challenges we're going to focus on in this book when we're considering policy and practice around behaviour. When we think about these eight challenges, it's clear the ways in which our traumatised pupils respond could all be so misinterpreted by education staff who are not attachment aware and trauma informed. Misinterpretation can lead to punishment. This is why it's of such concern. Can you see how pupils could easily experience being 'flawed' when they're on the receiving end of our more traditional responses? And believing they're flawed cultivates the ground for more toxic shame to get established, which means increased distressed behaviour, which means more punishment, which means … and so the cycle continues … it's heartbreaking, and worse: unnecessary and preventable.

Progressive work

TES News (2018) quoted Dix: 'Can you really call a school 'outstanding' if its behaviour policy is reliant on punishment booths?' Thankfully, there are signs of hope. Up and down the country people are beginning to provide alternative practices.

Much pioneering and progressive work is happening in Scotland, in terms of attachment aware and trauma responsive practice. One such example is Executive Director of Education Services Maureen McKenna bringing an entire trauma informed agenda to every level of how they 'do school' (*Lessons from Glasgow*, Evening Standard, Jan 2020 *and check out the publications produced* by NHS Education for Scotland & Scottish Government (2018) *and the Scottish framework, see* education.gov.scot, **References**). I wonder what the impact would be, if all of us became more nurturing and trauma responsive in all our schools? (*and see* p. 136, 192).

I'd like to introduce you to an alternative way of being, a concept we can call *differentiated discipline*. Rather than the one size size fits all approach of zero tolerance, the emotional and social tasks and expectations we have of our pupils will be informed by the developmental stage, capacities and vulnerabilities of the pupil and their regulatory state at any given time. We're going to embark on a journey to map out the foundations that need to be in place first, for example, facilitating felt safety.

The Big Asks/Challenges in school	What will adults need to do?	What does the child/young person need?
Toxic stress As we've seen, ACEs create toxic stress. Toxic stress impacts everything, especially whilst the brain is so plastic and developing at its highest rate. It impacts brain structure, brain functioning, the immune system, hormonal systems and even how DNA is read and transcribed. It creates chronic dysregulation of the developing stress response system. This inhibits the development and functioning of the thinking brain (pre-frontal cortex). It also overstimulates the amygdala. The challenge is that schools can be hugely stressful places for many.	To become stress regulators	Low stress environments Increased sensory comfort Co-regulation involving encouragement and comfort
An overactive amygdala (p. 70) The brain's fear centre. When repeatedly triggered by chronic stressors it becomes overactive. We then see over-reactive or exaggerated stress responses even to low level stressors, like getting a spelling wrong. The stress thermostat thus gets short-circuited. Being reactive in school can result in punishment and exclusion.	To become stress regulators, and to be compassionate	Safe space Co-regulation Regular sensory breaks and sensory snacks
Faulty neuroception (p. 102) This will be explored in more detail in the next chapter, Respecting Biology. It's when everything inside is telling you that you have reason to feel threatened. We often describe this as misreading the situation, when in fact our traumatised pupils are reading the situation correctly but they are sensing it all wrongly, through a faulty lens.	Remain steady Not take things personally Increase felt safety cues (see p. 70 & p. 116)	To be kindly reminded where they are in time and space Grounding
Blocked trust (p. 23) When all your experience of close adults has meant being let down, being hurt, being overwhelmed or even being left in terror, you are not going to find it easy to trust adults in school, whatever their role or responsibility. We often describe this as being 'rude and disrespectful' when in fact our traumatised pupils have very good reason to distrust adults and the power and control we have over them, which too often in their experience, gets misused. How can they know we are any different, or may turn out to be!	Provide relentless care Use playful approaches (p. 200-212) Increase felt safety cues (see p. 70 & p. 116)	Patience, empathy and understanding Increased curiosity and acceptance

Fear of being influenced When trauma has left you powerless and decisions have been made on your behalf as a child that have not turned out well, it leaves the child fearful of others' intentions and motives, regardless of how simple the request. We can often describe what we see as 'disobedient' and 'controlling' behaviour.	Commentate how big an ask this is for the child or young person Use follow-lead-follow approach (Bombèr 2007)	Explicit understanding of why this is difficult Gentle challenge
Feeling exposed, needing to hide When you are hurting and don't want to ever be hurt again, it's wise to hide your true, vulnerable self and to not show anyone who you really are or what you really need. We may describe what we see as 'unreachable', 'compliant', 'clowning around', 'charming' or 'aggressive'.	Maximise any opportunities to soothe or comfort, however small and insignificant	To be surrounded by gentleness and strength together
Miscuing When you have had many experiences in which adults have abandoned you, let you down, hurt you or ignored you, you anticipate this will happen again, and you 'cue' others based on this expectation of the grown-ups, rather than what your real needs are. We often describe this as a child who 'couldn't care less', 'doesn't even notice our attention' or 'doesn't seem to show any care or empathy'.	Not take things personally. Go for body cues rather than solely verbal cues	Encouragement to test you out in regards to their needs and wants
Concepts 4-7 draw on DDP informed practice by Dan Hughes in Golding (2017b)		
Being stuck in their grief If you have determined never to feel small, weak, defenceless ever again, then how can you truly allow yourself to grieve deeply, so that you have opportunity to recover well? And yet our traumatised pupils have much to grieve. They have often experienced relational deprivation. They have had to say too many significant goodbyes, with no-one alongside capable of supporting them just to feel sad. *To grieve is to allow our losses to tear apart feelings of security, stability and safety and lead us to the painful truth of our brokenness. Our grief makes us experience the abyss of our own life in which nothing is settled, clear or obvious but everything is constantly shifting and changing. Nouwen 2017, p. 344* Can you see why grieving might be difficult for our vulnerable pupils, and likely to be avoided?	'Relational proximity' - a mature, empathic adult staying close by - is therefore a MUST for underdeveloped minds and bodies, resulting from developmental trauma and loss. They need us to provide emotional containment, encouragement, support, comfort, soothing, regulation, modelling and the instruction ... We are the ones, as adults with mature (or semi-mature!) thinking brains who can provide safe passageway through the chaos.	Compassion, patience, relentless care and understanding

Love vs fear

Perfect love drives out fear.   1 John 4 v18, NIV Bible

As a physician, specialising in neurology, psychiatry and psychology, Dr Gabor Maté points out (2019), Jesus, to whom this comment is attributed, was one of the greatest psychologists. What is love? Do we dare mention the word 'love' when referring to our classrooms, schools, pupil referral units, EBD services, youth offending services, prisons …? I feel nervous even mentioning the word 'love' in the professional context of writing this book.* But I am struck by how many people approach me at conferences and training events all over the UK expressing a depth of connection with hurting children and young people that can only be described as 'love', if we are to respect what is actually going on in the dynamic they describe.

However, in order to be mindful of safeguarding concerns, I will refer in this book more to 'rich relational interventions', as this implies that clear boundaries are held, as self-evidently they must be. Maté (2019) says that behind all his more complex works is the basic principle that if you treat a child well, they will treat others well.

Activating felt safety - the opposite of activating the fear system

Panksepp (2010) has made some important discoveries which must also inform our understanding regarding discipline. He states that all human beings have seven basic emotional systems that can be activated at any one time, all now visible within the brain, through neuro-imaging: *seeking, rage, fear, care, grief* (formerly panic) *play* and *lust* (Panksepp, 2010: here we'll focus on the first six, *also see* **Respecting Biology**). The focus of this book is on those who have experienced significant relational trauma and loss, often within and of close attachment relationships which can disrupt their systems.

My sense, from reflecting on Panksepp's work, is that we have been over-activating the *fear* system in the use of our current discipline model, within traditional parenting,

*Although my editor supports me in doing so

our schools and our justice system in the UK (sometimes consciously - see comments of Home Secretary Priti Patel as at 2019, *cited above on* p. 38). If we activate the *fear* system in a child we may initially get compliance, which can work well whilst we are trying our best to teach in an overcrowded classroom, where constant evaluation of our practice has become the norm. But this can quickly move our traumatised pupils into difficult states like fear and terror, which mean they become increasingly inaccessible; creating more distress for them, and building up more management problems for ourselves (p. 25). Fear driven compliance may suit us in the short term but can have negative long-term consequences for the child's welfare, functioning and life; and the community at large, later on. When we are in a fear or terror state as human beings, on what Dr Dan Siegel calls 'the low road', (Siegel, 2011) anything is possible. This is when inhuman acts occur, acts of violence and cruelty or risk-taking, in a blind, mindless way. When it's used without reflection, our short-term fix can backfire on us later on ...

This type of practice, including isolation, exclusions and managed moves, costs relationships, and fear is at its root.

Ironically, when behaviour gets really tricky and most difficult for us, this is the precise time these pupils need us most. And yet, against all the evidence from neuroscience, as I mentioned above, we withdraw, we strand and isolate them (*relational poverty*). Relational poverty increases the child's distress, maintaining the *fear* system on high alert and even strengthening it. Working in completely the opposite direction to where we need to go which really should be about keeping them close, *especially* when times are fraught; providing them with *relational proximity* - to us.

The latest neuroscience findings underscore and evidence what we've really always known: we are designed to function best in relationship. We also know that there will be behaviours and relationship 'ruptures' which challenge us and our relationships with our pupils to the core. So to follow the logic of what we now know, we must recognise that whatever consequences we use, we mustn't ever compromise or run the risk of losing our relationship with our troubled pupil - it needs to be fiercely guarded at all times.

THE VOICE OF THE CHILD
WHAT DO SCHOOLS NEED TO STOP DOING?

Stop being so strict about the small things, especially school uniform. Some days I would sit in lessons and feel so uncomfortable and start sweating but I was always scared because I wasn't allowed to say anything or even undo my top button in case I got a detention

They need to stop setting so much homework weekly so that the students can rest and spend time with their families

Shouting, it scares me

My brother's school have isolation. He spends a lot of time in there and hates it

Being made to go in another classroom when I'm angry - it's humiliating. When I was at my old school (with my brother - who does not live with me anymore) my brother would be violent and angry and his punishment was having to be sent into my classroom. It scared me and didn't help him. I didn't want to see that

People hurting my feelings when they shout

Shouting at children. Taking children out of class. Threatening to call parents

Schools need to stop putting students in isolation and there should be a time out spot where a child and adult can talk about what has happened. Isolation can make students feel they have done something bad and they need to be given time to hear their story

I think schools should not expel students as this can impact on their future

THE VOICE OF THE CHILD (cont …)
WHAT DO SCHOOLS NEED TO STOP DOING?

Have teachers who don't smile

No hurting in schools

I don't think students should be physically handled as they will react to this and could end up hurting the adult and this could lead them to being expelled

I think adults should not get into students' faces because this might make them feel they have nowhere to go and can make them react in a way they shouldn't and the teachers making it worse for them

Don't tell us off straight away infront of others

Overreacting to situations

Expecting students to go to lesson when they have clearly a lot on their mind (home problems) (peer problems)

Saying no to kids asking for the toilet

Stop expelling students, it can impact their future

Threatening to call parents

I don't like it when schools have teachers that shout. That used to happen at my old school and it didn't make me want to listen

Rewards I never get

Losing golden time and detention - you say it's thinking time but really it's detention

> The more healthy relationships a child has, the more likely he will recover from trauma and thrive. Relationships are the agents of change and the most powerful … is human love.
>
> Perry 2006, pp. 259-276

> Almost all of us have at least one additional exquisite sensitivity - a raw spot in our emotional skin - that is tender to the touch, easily rubbed, and deeply painful. When the raw spot gets abraded, it can bleed all over our relationship.
>
> Johnson 2011, p. 99

When a pupil's challenging behaviour is saying something about their hidden needs and when we are well resourced and feeling stable, in our best 'calm and alert' state, we will be able to think about and reflect on these (Golding 2017); rather than simply react to their presenting needs, which are often completely different. It will also enable us to engage in 'amygdaloid stories' - see below!

Amygdala whisperers and creating felt safety

When we 'drive out fear' within our classrooms and instead focus on facilitating felt safety, by activating our pupils' *care, play* and *seeking* systems (p. 66), we will, in turn, witness different, healthier and better-attuned behaviours. So let's become *'amygdala whisperers'* (Cozolino, 2013) - people who can 'tame' hurting children and young people into connection with us by ushering them into still, safe, kind spaces where they can be acknowledged, met and known.

The amygdala is the alarm part of our brain, based in the brain stem. It holds much sway over what we do, since we're neurologically biased to detect danger cues in order to stay safe and alive, a necessary part of survival. However, if it's going off all the time for our traumatised pupils, or in any case far too frequently, we need to convince the higher parts of the child's brain that it's safe to engage with us. We can do this by increasing our safety cues. And we do this by engaging in a powerful way of being and relating characterised by PACE, psychologist Dan Hughes' acronym for *playfulness, acceptance, curiosity* and *empathy* (DDP website - *see* **Useful Organisations**).

PACE needs to be embraced within our schools (Chapter 7 **Relate**). We also need to facilitate and prioritise alternative, therapeutic interventions which can be integrated into schools, without asking teachers to become therapists. These might include things not really much valued educationally at the moment … the arts, sport, pets, baking, mindfulness and working the land - all of which are recognised as buffering the impact of toxic stress. More on this on p. 116 and in Chapter 6 **Regulate**.

In fact, these things are already in place within the Youth Justice system in Spain and in Halden Prison in Norway. In these other parts of Europe where biology is more respected, the functioning capacity of human beings is being maximised. Organisations engaged in activating the *care, seeking* and *play* systems of others create a culture of felt safety. These institutions have seen incredible results.

Learning from Halden Prison

I was deeply moved after finding out about Halden Prison - a high security prison in Norway (*Breaking The Cycle*, 2017). This is one of the most humane prisons in the world, which has seen significant positive results from their practice (re-offending rates of between 20 and 25%) about half of that in UK prisons where the average re-offending rate within the first year according to the Ministry of Justice (2019) is nearly 48% (with the juvenile re-offending rate at 38.4%, slightly down on the previous year). I believe that we can learn so much from the Norwegian approach in our homes, schools and communities with regards to the meaning of discipline and how we might approach it in our schools.

Rather than using punishment, revenge or retaliation, those working in Halden prison focus on preparing their inmates for rehabilitation. They do this by creating *dynamic safety,* which in turn builds trust. The way they build trust is by having two priorities. The first is in respecting the value of all human beings, regardless of their crime, and the second is by enabling good communication between everyone. Those working in Halden prison keep in mind that any of their inmates could one day be their neighbour, and so see it as their corporate responsibility to 'grow' the kind of neighbours we would all want to live next door to. They have the future in mind. They're not just making it through the day, as we so often are in our homes, schools and communities in the UK. Halden Prison facilitates an environment in which inmates constantly have rich relational experiences with their prison wardens. They are aware that this is where the most fundamental teaching comes, through living life together, co-modelling appropriate behaviour. Experience always needs to come first. Surely this is the true use of the word 'discipline'?

Halden management are conscious of the fact that when people are dealt with badly there are often very poor outcomes, as in the high security prisons in the USA where there are weekly serious incidents. The USA rely heavily on punishment on every level (op. cit). In Halden over the last four years (2017) there has been only one serious incident. Important to note too is the fact that the staff actually *enjoy* working there! They don't feel their lives are at risk. They don't carry weapons, in preparation for threat, as opposed to usual prison practices. It is fascinating to hear how change is being brought about by those intent on adapting prisons. Some see finance as a barrier (places in Halden are more expensive than in the UK) but many realise that it is about changing perspective, with savings in the long run at every level from financial upwards - how do you put a price on a good neighbour making a new life for themselves? Here are some key recommendations from *Breaking the Cycle* (2017) that could well inform our own policies for discipline:

- Change the language for how we refer to people
- Change our policies on how we treat people
- Train our staff differently
- Have different expectations of staff
- Have a different perspective of what makes a successful day

The film highlights the intention not to churn out compliant prisoners who may go on to re-offend, but well-rounded individuals, who will be able to function well and contribute to society. Is it really rocket science to recognise how this list could make so much difference in our schools right now?

Let's try it:

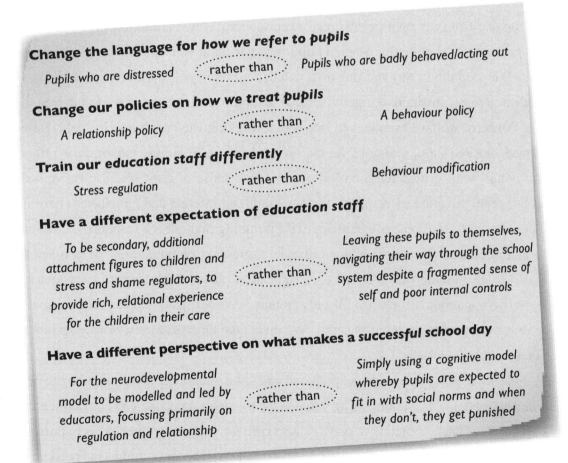

Change the language for how we refer to pupils

Pupils who are distressed   *rather than*   Pupils who are badly behaved/acting out

Change our policies on how we treat pupils

A relationship policy   *rather than*   A behaviour policy

Train our education staff differently

Stress regulation   *rather than*   Behaviour modification

Have a different expectation of education staff

To be secondary, additional attachment figures to children and stress and shame regulators, to provide rich, relational experience for the children in their care   *rather than*   Leaving these pupils to themselves, navigating their way through the school system despite a fragmented sense of self and poor internal controls

Have a different perspective on what makes a successful school day

For the neurodevelopmental model to be modelled and led by educators, focussing primarily on regulation and relationship   *rather than*   Simply using a cognitive model whereby pupils are expected to fit in with social norms and when they don't, they get punished

Our compassion tanks

Those who do not run away from our pain but touch it with compassion bring healing and new strength. The paradox indeed is that the beginning of healing is in the solidarity with the pain. In our solution-orientated society, it is more important than ever to realise that wanting to alleviate pain without sharing is like wanting to save a child from a burning house without the risk of being hurt.

Nouwen 2017, p. 186

I recognise from my own professional experience in schools that it's really hard, in the moment, to be empathic when a pupil is swearing at you, spitting at you, kicking you. We are human too and our own defence systems will naturally get activated. Our immediate, instinctive urge will be to defend ourselves: we've all felt driven to this. Some of us have even moved into something that Hughes & Baylin (2012) have termed blocked care, a way of functioning where we're simply existing (or rather surviving!) with gritted teeth on willpower and a sense of duty, because we've had so little reciprocation or response for our kindness, interest and empathy. There is a continuum to blocked care, starting with numbing and cut-off responses, through to more concerning responses, for example aggression or retaliation. If you sense that you are moving into blocked care right now, please don't be hard on yourself. Be self-compassionate: we are all only human. We all need support, and in some seasons, we need more intensive care. We must take blocked care seriously and look out for one another.

So we're going to have to get prepared and to be intentional about attending to our 'compassion tanks'. The first thing you need is to have a someone you can confide in, who has your back, someone whose role is to care for you whilst you do this important work - your own 'key adult' (Bombèr 2016, 2017). The next thing you need is a confidential, summarised list of the relational traumas and losses this particular pupil has experienced from pregnancy to the present day, remembering to revisit it from time to time when you're in a calm or alert state (after seeing your own 'key adult', perhaps).

All our Attachment Leads in the UK (trained by my organisation, TouchBase) (*see* **Useful Organisations**) use these kinds of Factfiles in their work. This will no doubt top up your compassion tank and remind you of pupil's roots, which as I mentioned earlier affects both the shoots and the fruits (p. 48). Compassion is a cooler state than empathy and occurs in the pre-frontal cortex, which means that it has the capacity to override self-defensiveness. That will mean that when something kicks off, as it will undoubtedly do, we will be able to use our reserves of compassion first. This will hopefully help us remain grounded and not take things personally. And then empathy will usually follow (Hughes & Baylin, DDP Conference presentation, 2019).

These children are going to need us to engage in an intentional, bold kind of caring, not wishy-washy feelings, merely led by emotions. Our emotions often get hijacked around traumatised pupils, so please don't rely on them! I recommend that you get to know what triggers your defensiveness, your own 'shark music' (Circle of Security, 2016): with that awareness, you'll be better able to 'rise strong' (Brene Brown has a book called *Rising Strong:* I find that phrase inspiring! 2015): in other words, to remain calm, alert and grounded, rather than acting from your own *fear* or *rage* systems.

Our schools have the capacity to be places of felt safety, emotional containers. We need more brave leaders who will step up and lead on this. There are some within our Attachment Lead Network, especially those in senior positions such as Headteachers: but we need many, many more to engage in this inclusive revolution to powerfully impact our communities both now and on into the future.

Felt safety decreases our pupils' alarm (*more in* Chapter 4 **Respecting Biology**). Quietening the amygdala wakes up other parts of the brain, including the hippocampus and the pre-frontal cortex, meaning learning can occur. Good news for the classroom! So let's further explore the benefits of the amygdala being quietened.

The benefits of being an Amgdala Whisperer alongside a traumatised pupil

STARTING TO BE IN THE PRESENT

As a pupil's alarm quietens, their hippocampus, the part of the brain related to time and space, is woken up. We know that these children are haunted by 'ghosts' from their past and recognise how we so often get caught up in their time warp, unwittingly behaving in uncharacteristic ways, because we have been swept up in their behaviour, feeling patterns and states. Getting stuck in the past is a symptom of trauma, and it's why we observe traumatised pupils frequently falling into time holes (Hobday 2001) through intrusive thoughts, flashbacks and night terrors. It's as if they are back there, re-living their experiences. They may not remember the first time, but it's as if they are repeating aspects of what happened again and again, in a traumatic state in which the capacity to actually hear or register the human voice is reduced. So it's essential to support these pupils to be 'present' and 'grounded'. If the hippocampus wakes up as a result of the amygdala being quietened, our pupils will have more capacity to stay present in the 'here and now'. Then they'll be far more able to listen to us as we teach curriculum and as we teach the boundaries of what is right and wrong (discipline) through our relationship with them (Chapter 8 **Reason**).

STARTING TO FEEL ...

As the alarm is quietened, some of their feelings start coming back, the feelings that were numbed or frozen in order to survive overwhelming states of tension and fear. This is when we might see our pupils starting to show us some of their sadness: we can provide them with comfort, even if all they can manage is seeng you tap your heart expressing how sad whatever they'd experienced might have been. Quietening the amygdala supports recovery!

STARTING TO THINK …

As the alarm continues to be quietened, not only will the child become more 'present' but their pre-frontal cortex will come on line too, otherwise known as the thinking brain, the last part of the brain to develop. This tends to only fully happen around the mid 20s in healthy development, so it's the most sophisticated part. When the child is able to access this 'top floor' of the brain, so much more is possible, that will enable the child to settle to learn, and help us as well. When this part of the brain is 'online', they can pause, reflect and consider. They can engage in the big asks of learning. They can tap into their exploratory system, whose operation we know is directly correlated to the workings of their attachment system (feeling safe means we can explore. Feeling unsafe means we can't). We need our pupils' exploratory systems, otherwise known as the *seeking* system, to be online in our places of learning! It's as if when they feel safe and their amygdala is quietened, the child's vision increases from a world of black-and-white to a world of different colours, textures and so on. In effect, they come back to life.

BEING ABLE TO PRESS PAUSE…

As education staff we need to be aware of the Default Mode Network (DMN) which gets activated when we are 'awake in our thoughts', doing nothing (Jonathan Baylin, DDP Conference presentation, 2019). This is when some very important processes happen like remembering, recalling, reflecting, daydreaming … Those who have experienced relational trauma have an underdeveloped DMN. A well-developed DMN means that our creativity increases (*ibid*). We can support our pupils to get stronger in this not only by overcompensating felt safety cues (p. 116) but by also giving them opportunity to pause with us. Just being side by side, together, no agenda, but just to 'be'. Sadly the pace is incredibly fast in our schools, with very little opportunity to pause, to reflect. Nicky Murray, a progressive and innovative

Headteacher in Scotland, whom I'll refer to again in my chapters on **Relate** and **Reason**, facilitates seven reflective check-ins for the pupils in his school throughout the day!

We can also strengthen the DMN by creating narratives together with our pupils of experiences we've shared with them, because when we listen to stories, that's where we go in our brains. So let's create 'amygdaloid stories', stories that quieten the amygdala and enable the DMN to get active! For example:

> *"It was such a big ask for you to trust one of your friends with your story. You had to find your brave part inside and you did. That brave part of you has been in there since you were small and has grown really strong over the years. You were probably surprised yourself by how big and strong your brave part had become, it's been quietly growing away through everything you've been through"*.

When we 'drive out fear' within our classrooms and instead focus on facilitating felt safety by activating the *care, play* and *seeking* systems, we'll see a different quality of behaviour.

> We never outgrow the need for community, interaction, appreciation, reassurance and support.   Knost, 2013, p. 2

So with all this in mind, let's now explore a framework we can use whatever our role, responsibility or focus, instead of our current behavioural model of discipline.

A MAP FOR AN ALTERNATIVE DISCIPLINE POLICY

I Familiarity

Nobody should be getting involved in any kind of teaching (discipline or challenge) unless they have a relationship with the traumatised child or young person involved. Ideally this should only be one of what I think of as Team Pupil - the team chosen to work closely with a pupil known to have a high number of ACEs (Bombèr 2016, 2017) or relational traumas and losses. Let's ensure their world stays small and they are surrounded by a small team of supporters, until they become more robust in terms of their sense of self, and until they have stronger internal controls, as opposed to having a fragile self and poor internal controls because no one helped them with co-regulation when younger. Practically this will mean that rather than whoever is 'on call' getting involved immediately, referring on to someone from Team Pupil to determine the next best plan of action.

It was English. I found Suzi hovering outside the classroom shouting expletives. 'It's boring. I hate the book. I have to just sit and do nothing' were some of her words, littered with swearing. Knowing I was Suzi's safe base I took her away from the classroom out into the space of the playground and pulled out a tennis ball from my SOS bag. Suzi knew it was time for squash ball. The game was aimed at channelling her hyperarousal into focus, partnership and some fun. We engaged in a repetitive and rhythmic rally that was calming, echoing the sound of a regulated heartbeat.

After about 10 mins of this, Suzi told me she didn't like the lesson, that she couldn't follow the teacher reading the book ... The Chronicles of Narnia.

Despite being in secondary, Suzi could just about fathom three letter words and so to be presented with a book like this was more than overwhelming. I said that I was there to travel beside her into the unknown and uncertain, to learn together. I asked her to forget the classroom for a minute and to challenge herself to try and work out with me what this book was all about. She accepted. We went to a quiet office and I presented her with a topical word search of the names of the main characters. In the midst of completing this word search, curiosity was reborn. 'Who is Lucy? What's with the wardrobe?'. As I started to narrate the storyline in an animated way Suzi lent in towards me, engrossed. Mesmerised. Her eyes glistened. I can only relay the magic in her eyes as being similar to that of a young child on Christmas Day recognising Santa had been. The innocence of the young girl who was so often assumed as a provocatively defiant teenager was available for me to see.

I grabbed at a beautifully illustrated version of the book, determined to keep the spark of her curiosity alive. 'Who's the white witch?' 'Where does she live?' 'What does her castle look like? 'She looks evil'. Suzi looked at the picture more intently and noticed she didn't have any eyebrows. 'It's her eyebrows, she has no eyebrows!' I asked her why that might be seen as scary. Suzi looked harder at the picture and contorted her face and her eyebrows, perplexed. "That's it Suzi, you've just done it! We use eyebrows to show how we feel!' She looked excited, wriggling her eyebrows showing me an array of different emotions. 'She has no eyebrows, so we can't see her emotions. She's emotionless!'. Although Suzi didn't make it into the English class that day, she travelled with me to a level of understanding about the main text of the book. She blossoms when we facilitate opportunities for regulation, relationship, reason and repair.

Nicola Yeandle - Attachment Lead, Eastbourne

2 Activating the care, play and seeking systems

Staff activating the *care, play* and *seeking* systems of the child or young person with their interactions and interventions in relationship (Panksepp, 2010, p. 537), is very different to the split of 'bad cop/good cop' (which tends to be the model followed, especially in secondary provision in the UK), by Heads of Year and their assistant pastoral leads. The approach I'm describing may seem a little naïve, considering some of the distressed behaviour in our schools at present. However, I have seen it work repeatedly, and it needs to be our direction of travel, based on how human beings actually function best. Current levels of aggression and exclusion rates in the UK suggest we're not getting it right - yet. This way reduces both.

> *Lee was messing around again in the corridors. Grinning, with a twinkle in his eye, Mr Hall sidles up to Lee. 'Hey! I can see you have lots of energy. Are you up for my challenge then? Let's see if we can beat our personal best at the plank … The HOY room is only a few doors away! Let's do it!!' Lee laughs. 'You won't beat me any day!' Lee heads to the HOY room. Everyone stops what they are doing for the quality minute timer to start! 'Ready, steady, go!'*
>
> *Lee does remarkably well, bows, and the members of staff clap. 'See you laters' as he skips off to his next lesson.*

As you can see, there's an order to all of this, throughout which we need to remain attuned to the pupil. We need to watch out for shifts in their body cues, their tone of voice, their breathing, their muscular tone … All of this will give us clues as to whether they are in the right state (yet) to learn. We must be flexible and not rigid in our framework, as there may well be times that we need to spend a lot of time investing in keeping ourselves regulated as grown-ups, increasing our safety cues, using sensory interventions with them and connecting with them at all levels. Whatever we invest in these areas, the better the overall outcome will be, so it really is worth it … however long this process takes. At the end of the day, we want the pupils in our care to *learn, to move forwards, to extend themselves* into new areas of development … and *to grow*. This is our primary goal. *This* is what this framework is for.

> Sending our children out into the world as adults with their needs met, with coping mechanisms in place for those times when the stresses overwhelm them, and with the knowledge of a safe haven where comfort is always available, when the world hurts them, is a powerful way to change the world for the better.
>
> Knost 2013, p. 53

3 Creating contexts in which pupils can thrive

According to an Ofsted report (2018, Point 16), 'We cannot have a zero tolerance approach … Our starting point should always the rights, needs and safety of the child'. The report goes on state that blanket approaches to restrictions on liberty must always be questioned, in terms of whether they meet individual children's needs or not (Point 22). In view of this and with knowing what many of our children have experienced in their early years when they were powerless, we are strengthened in questioning the use of isolation booths and other sanctions which restrict these children's freedom.

THE VOICE OF THE CHILD

HOW DO YOU THINK TEACHERS SHOULD MANAGE DISRUPTIVE BEHAVIOUR?

The teachers who knew how to engage with the students made learning fun. They didn't really need to use discipline with us because their lessons were always enjoyable

They should stick to what they say about consequences, so students know where they stand

Be supportive and not always focus on the bad behaviour but the good

Like my foster mum - a calm and quiet voice - no shouting

If you get angry, a fiddle toy to distract helps. Giving me some space. Low, deep voices make me nervous - I know when an adult is cross because their voice changes

I think teachers should let students calm down and have time then they will feel better. Teachers shouldn't shout as the students will respond in the same way and be more disruptive and then they won't be settled

They could have a space where they have a meeting and they could talk about what they would like to change or what has happened that they don't like and possibly have an adult to talk about what could be better or what the adult and child expects from each other

So let's look at what building a context for thriving looks like.

Creating a context for thriving

BUILDING RELATIONSHIPS OF TRUST AND UNDERSTANDING

Remember that for those who have experienced relational trauma and loss trust is going to be one of the biggest asks in school: our pupils are in a state of blocked trust, so they need you to be proactive - they need you to go 'find them'. They will need your compassion and kindness to give them endless patience, understanding and sensitive care. Use any form of communication possible. Be creative - notes, postcards, texts, emails, pictures, metaphor, small objects exchanged ... as well as words. Be mindful of their limited window of intimacy tolerance and please don't take their distrust personally.

UNDERSTANDING TRIGGERS AND FINDING SOLUTIONS

These particular pupils can be triggered by 'relationship' so be mindful of being respectful around this and realising it will often take time to tame them into genuine relationship with us. And do take the time to engage with their safe families to discover what other stress triggers might be too, because of what they've experienced. See yourself as a stress regulator rather than a behaviour manager and do all you can to keep stress at a minimum so that these pupils have the opportunity they need to practice managing small doses of stress first, in order to become more robust in the usual, everyday stressors of school life. I suggest solutions are *calmers* (the opposite of triggers), sensory interventions that familiar education staff (Team Pupil) engage in together with their pupils, not from a distance. Co-regulation leads to self regulation.

IF INCIDENTS DO OCCUR, DEFUSING THE SITUATION WHEREVER POSSIBLE

All education staff should view themselves as stress regulators. It's our responsibility to be the grown-ups leading in this area, being regulated ourselves and by facilitating regular opportunities for regulatory activities throughout the day. Be preventative. Integrate sensory breaks as a matter of course to keep stress regulated as you go, rather than just waiting until there is a build-up and then a possible pressure cooker effect.

When things do get tricky, I wouldn't distract. The pupil needs to know that you 'get it'. It's essential you communicate that you have heard whatever the pupil is trying to say, even if it's through difficult behaviour. Be a translator and have a go at reflecting back what you *think* the pupil might be trying to say, using emotions language. Match their *affect* … that is, saying *'You are letting me know you are so angry right now ...'* with a thoughtful face, staying calm and yet mirroring the emotion and intensity of their tone, the frequency and pace of their words and the body language appropriate for that particular emotion.

Reasonable adjustments and differentiated discipline

> Reasonable adjustments should be made to ensure that expectations of pupils who have special educational needs and/or disabilities are developmentally appropriate and fair. It would not be fair, for example, to isolate a child who has attention deficit hyperactive disorder (ADHD) or other special needs because they were not able to sit still when required to do so. Equally, for some children in care, the experience can reinforce trauma and/or result in an escalating scenario that leads to disciplinary measures for the child.   Point 40, Ofsted 2018

I was so encouraged to read the above in my research for this book! And to read in point 43, that the child's *experience* is what matters the most, rather than whatever we choose to call our sanctions within education. So I'd like to add in some important recommendations to flesh out the three above, from a trauma responsive perspective.

More recommendations for thriving

Regulation of the grown-ups

Education staff need to ensure they are grounded and not dysregulated in any way before engaging with a child/young person. There will be many times that the wisest course of action is to swap in with another member of Team Pupil, the other people working most closely with a particular pupil.

Increase safety cues

Pay attention to the felt safety needs of the pupil. As a result of being triggered your pupil can all too easily fall down a time hole (*see above*), so your first port of call will always be to increase your safety cues (*and see p. 116 on how to do this*).

Down regulate

Using sensory interventions, support the pupil to return to a place of being connected to their mind and body (Chapter 6 **Regulate**).

Connection

Engage in something collaborative together, whilst communicating loud and clear that you are 'with' them, 'alongside' them, 'for' them. Be explicit about the fact that you care about them, not just with words but with what you do whilst you are speaking. This is more likely to capture their attention. (Chapter 7 **Relate**).

Discipline

When the pupil seems to have been in the calm or alert state for a period of sustained time then deliver your succinct teaching point, using your best delivery, preferably using 'bits and pieces', not just words (Chapter 8 **Reason**). As Daniel Siegel recommends, 'Reduce words and embrace emotion' (2015, p. 227).

Repair

Facilitate an exit strategy and see it through *together* with the pupil (Chapter 9 **Repair**).

Felt safety. Meaningful connection. Differentiated discipline is the ethical way forward for these particular pupils. We have completed the necessary groundwork for understanding why we cannot continue with our current systems as this would be overriding what we now understand about what is happening for our traumatised pupils, which needs to be seriously taken into consideration, in order to honour difference and diversity. It's clear that the main priority is to facilitate felt safety, and that this safety comes about from being together, in relationship with responsive adults who can communicate acceptance and value to the core sense of self of the pupil which is still emerging and very fragile, because of everything they've experienced.

> People who feel safe and meaningfully connected with others have little reason to squander their lives doing drugs or staring numbly at a television; they don't feel compelled to stuff themselves with carbohydrates or assault their fellow human beings. However, if nothing they do seems to make a difference, they feel trapped and become susceptible to the lure of pills, gang leaders, extremist religions, or violent political movements - anybody and anything that promises relief.
>
> Van der Kolk 2015, p. 351

In the next chapter we will go into the latest neuroscience in more depth, so that we can think about what kinds of interventions would work best within these kinds of relationships, in these kinds of contexts, and most importantly when, as we will discover, its not just *what* we do that is important but *when* we do it - sensitive timing is essential.

THE VOICE OF THE CHILD (cont ...)

HOW DO YOU THINK TEACHERS SHOULD MANAGE DISRUPTIVE BEHAVIOUR?

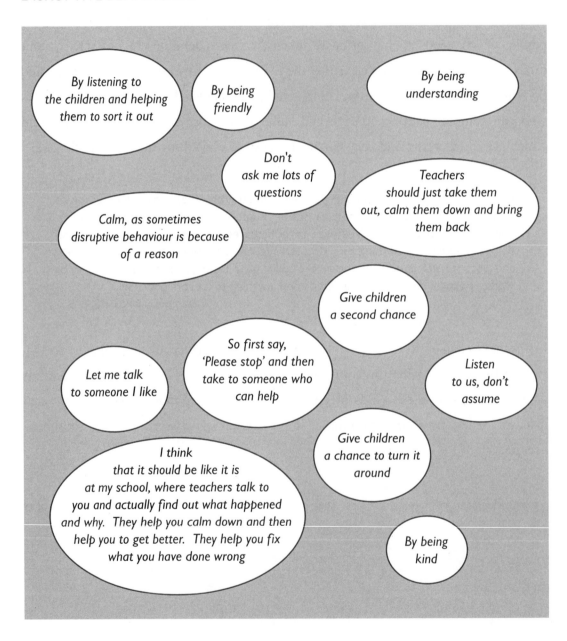

adoptionuk
for every adoptive family
in Scotland

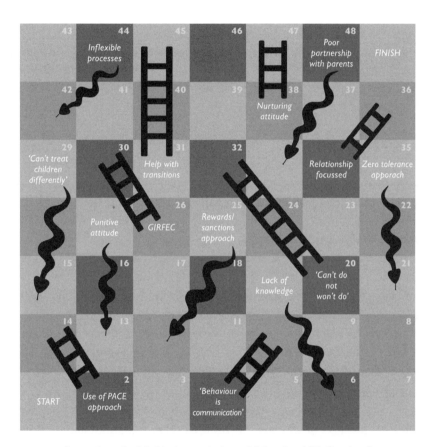

Reproduced with kind permission of Adoption UK, Scotland.

FAQs

Shift the frame, change the lens, and all the world is revealed, and nothing is the same ...   Burke-Harris 2018, p. 211

1/   What if the other children in the class ask why this child is being given different treatment?

Difference and diversity

- We need to set a whole culture of respecting and honouring difference and diversity, not just in policy but in practice, not just amongst the pupils but with the adults too. We are being watched! Everything we do must be inclusive of everyone. Our message needs to be:

    'I will treat you all with respect, and I won't treat you all exactly the same, since you all have different strengths and vulnerabilities. You can trust my judgement if I use different strategies with different pupils: my aim is to support all of you to be the best you can be'.

Psychoeducation

- Let's teach all our pupils about what stress is: the difference between everyday low-level stressors and *toxic* stress, how the nervous system responds and what we can do to soothe our nervous systems. When everyone understands what's going on they are more likely to be empathic towards others having a difficult time at the moment.

2/   How do I manage cynicism in other staff about all this?

Empathy

- Recognise that many staff feel hugely overstretched, overworked and disrespected as it is, so the thought of another way of working, strategy or intervention might just feel too much. Demonstrate sensitivity and understanding by asking them to help you understand why it's particularly challenging for them, at this time. Then empathise and communicate acceptance of their experience, and look for collaborative ways forward together.

Training

- Ensure everyone in the school has access to AATR work including the latest research in child development, attachment and neuroscience. Under the 2018 DfE Guidance, this is one of the responsibilities of Designated Teachers for example, so link up with them. The Consortium of Emotional Well Being in Schools recommends at least two days of whole school training in the first instance. There are a number of providers, including my own, Touchbase (touchbase.org.uk) which is part of TIE. I would recommend that two attachment leads get trained up too with more intensive training (traumainformededucation.org.uk) so that they can lead the way ensuring regular training for staff.

Differentiation

- Consider how the curriculum is differentiated within school. For example, you wouldn't do algebra with someone who couldn't count or didn't know the value of numbers. We have some traumatised pupils in our schools, with a fragile sense of self and poor internal controls, who are not ready - *yet* - for the usual whole school behaviour policies. So let's use this language when we're talking with colleagues, including those who are not on board with AATR approaches (yet!); doing so begins to nudge the school culture towards a tacit acceptance of differentiation around discipline, as well as within the curriculum.

3/ Isn't this just being soft? Surely school is the best place to learn that they can't have their own way? Aren't you just storing up trouble for later, when they are out in the real world?

- You are absolutely right - school is the best place to learn. So, let's ensure we make the most of this amazing learning opportunity! By being neuroscientifically informed we can ensure we get our timing right, so that traumatised pupils can actually hear us and utilise what we're offering them. Respecting biology means investing in our collective future. At the moment, we are indeed storing up trouble, as you put it, and yes, there could well be real difficulties out in the real world if we carry on in the same way. The choice is ours.

4/ Surely they need to understand that bad behaviour has consequences?

- I'm with you on this. Everyone needs to understand that all actions have consequences, for better or for worse. That's why we need to ensure that we build in sufficient reflective times and opportunities in order to make those connections, alongside the work of repair. Often there are natural consequences which are helpful, as they take the emphasis off 'being mean'. Traumatised pupils will need help regulating their states in order to be able to access their reflective capacity and so we will make sure this happens in our classrooms. Pressing the pause button will support this as well.

5/ Well, at our school no-one gets away with anything, and our pupils are doing well - so why should children elsewhere get away with things?

- I'm glad you feel your pupils are doing well. I wonder, however, how many are getting very good at hiding their true needs, in order to survive the system of 'no-one gets away with anything'. Fear and compliance may be in the mix. We really don't want to fuel the fear system, as it can lead to harm at a later stage - to self or others. And please remember that exclusions and managed moves only reinforce rejection and push the problems elsewhere - have a look at the evidence around the 'school to prison pipeline', on p. 25. Let's increase focus on supporting security, and on the seeking and play systems.

6/ What do other children say when they see one of these children getting off so lightly?

- This is a concern that is often raised at conferences when I'm presenting, so it's obviously a worry for some people. What we notice though is that in fact, children themselves are often quicker than we adults in realising that traumatised pupils need a differentiated approach. As long as we teachers are clear about *why we're doing what we're doing,* and confident in our interventions, pupils quickly pick up that we are not here to teach them all in the same way but according to what they all need. This demonstrates inclusive practice: most schools have actually signed up for it in theory but didn't necessarily have the tools at their disposal, until now, to actually know what it means in practice.

7/ So are you saying you should never tell off one of these pupils?

- Thanks for raising this. If you mean, am I saying *'We should never discipline these pupils'* - no, I'm not saying that. We will be disciplining them in a way that makes sense to where they currently are, so that they actually **learn** from the teaching used. If you mean raising our voices, yelling, shouting, humiliating or shaming or isolating, then yes: we will definitely not be using any of that kind of behaviour with traumatised pupils. Or with any other pupil, for that matter.

8/ What if they've hurt someone? Do we just let them get away with it?

- This is such an important question that needs our special attention. In *differentiated discipline* we address everything that needs addressing, including injury. We don't believe in a society in which humans go around hurting each other - that is not a civilised society. We will teach this very important lesson in a way that this pupil can understand, so they grasp the gravity of it and learn to respect and value life.

9/ How can teachers differentiate when that one child misbehaving is disrupting the whole class?

- Thank you for reminding us that sometimes it can seem as if it's just one child who needs a differentiated approach. But when we look more closely, we all know there are a number of needs within any classroom context: as human beings we all have our strengths and weaknesses. For example, someone in class may need a pencil grip to support him because of his poor fine motor skills. Someone else might need glasses due to poor vision. Someone else may need a different maths task as they can't negotiate number bonds yet. And so we go on … why should we only differentiate for physical and curriculum needs? What about emotional and mental health needs? Surely they also need to be respected?

10/ Won't school just descend into chaos?

- I'm so glad you raise this fear, I'm sure countless others have worried about this too. In fact, the opposite is true. What we learn and apply for the minority actually serves the collective whole. I find that dynamic fascinating and quite liberating. The way weaknesses can actually create real opportunities and possibilities for a better school system. As we continue to learn what works best for traumatised pupils and start to integrate it into our practice, it actually transforms education for everyone!
- It may feel unfamiliar at first, as we risk letting go of our traditional methods of control. That's why we need others around us, sharing the same approach and agenda, to help us stay steady for the journey through to a much greater sense of stability and security for all. So that everyone can settle to learn together. So stay connected!

VOICE OF THE CHILD

WHAT DO YOU THINK COULD HELP SCHOOLS FEEL SAFER AND CALMER PLACES TO BE?

Having teachers who actually care. Teachers might know their subject but they don't always know how to interact with children in a positive way and make them feel safe and comfortable

Adults that understand and don't shout

More adults

Knowing I had a safe place I could go to, like the library

Have a place I could go to hide

A school without people that judge you would be a safer place. I feel that the learning centre in my school is a safe, secure place to be

Sometimes being with my friends, having a calm box, and my Key Adult

Have a grown-up who likes me

A more flexible approach to how to educate individual students

Really listen to students

Some safe things from home (foster home). We have candles burning at home, smells of mango, apple and orange, the smell makes me feel safe. Fairy lights in my safe space or in the classrooms. Colouring books for when you need to calm. Relaxing music

My school has the Bloom Room which you can go to if you need to calm down and there is always an adult there to help you. You can do things like go in the sensory tent

Chapter 4

Respecting Biology

Twenty years of research has shown that childhood adversity literally gets under our skin, changing people in ways that can endure in their bodies for decades. It can tip a child's developmental trajectory and affect physiology. It can trigger chronic inflammation and hormonal changes that can last a lifetime. It can alter the way DNA is read and how cells replicate, and it can dramatically increase the risk for heart disease, stroke, cancer, diabetes - even Alzheimer's.

Burke-Harris 2018 p. xvii

Many education staff now know about attachment and recognise how this can be disrupted in the early years: many of us in the UK have been learning, sharing and developing this fundamental understanding for a while now through our training, presentations and publications. However there are still many who haven't as yet taken on the full implications of both attachment disruptions and relational trauma on the mind and body, or how this impact manifests in everyday classrooms. And most importantly, there's not enough understanding - yet! - of the practical implications of *respecting biology,* so that we can be helpful with our ways of being and interventions, rather than exacerbating the challenging dynamics of distress and disruption.

If they were widely understood, I don't believe we would be using the kinds of discipline I described early in the last chapter. In fact, I'm sure we wouldn't. Let's remember that practically everyone working in education is well-intentioned. But even with great intentions we can get it so wrong if we don't realise how easily we can be harmful and make things worse, or kick problems down the road where they will worsen with tragic inevitability. With the right information, we can make better choices! That's what we tell our students. So let's put it into practice by getting right up to speed with the latest understanding from neuroscience, so we can really use interventions that truly respect the biology of our traumatised children and young people. In this chapter we'll be taking a close look at how the nervous system, a key player in all of this, works, so that we can be clear about what's going on when times get tough.

By the end of this chapter we will have explored:

- The differing types of stress and how they impact us as human beings
- The Polyvagal theory, which will support us to understand what's happening within the nervous systems of our traumatised pupils at different times: what *neuroception* is, and why it's important
- The three different nervous systems that drive us as human beings
  - How we know when the social engagement system is operating in ourselves or someone else
  - How we know when the fight/flight system is operating
  - How we know when the freeze system is operating
  - The states we find ourselves in resulting from what's happening in the different parts of our nervous systems, and the possible defences we use when we are stressed, alarmed, triggered or challenged
- What the vagal paradox is, and why it's important; how neuroception can become faulty and the consequences for pupils
- What we can do to increase felt safety cues so that our pupils can move more easily into their social engagement system
- Increasing the window of stress tolerance
- How we can extend time spent in the social engagement system, and why it's important to do so

Our nervous systems are impacted by:

What's going on inside us
our nervous systems can be quietened or shaken up

The environment
it can be up-regulating or down-regulating

Others around us
verbal and non verbal language can signal either safety or danger cues

Other people's nervous systems
calming (regulating) or agitating (dysregulating)

The atmosphere
of safety or of threat

Familiarity or the unknown

Past experiences
happy or difficult memories

Trauma or loss
resolved or unresolved

Regulation experience
*whether we have ever had anyone support us to manage
big states, sensations and feelings*

**Whether we have a support network of
other people around us**

Stress

Visceral experiences affect the nervous system and our resulting behaviours. When our stress system is in good working order, it can help save our lives. When it's out of balance, it can shorten them. The way it becomes out of balance is when there has been a pretty much lethal dosage of the stress hormone cortisol, at some point, and what's most important is for us to recognise the timing and duration of the exposure to this stress hormone cortisol. If our traumatised pupils have experienced repeated or long-lasting traumatic episodes, when cortisol was surging through them (created in response to the stress of those experiences), it's likely there will have been seriously negative effects on their *development* as well as on the *state* their nervous system is in today. Hence why it's so crucial for us to trace back and know what our children and young people have lived through *before making any assumptions* about what they might or might not be doing in our homes, schools and out and about in our wider communities.

Let's explore the three different stress responses possible for us as human beings: a *positive* stress response, a *tolerable* stress response and a *toxic* stress response. It's important to note that bodies and minds have evolved to cope with positive and tolerable stress levels and responses, but not to manage toxic stress: enduring toxic stress is destructive.

The range of responses to stress

A positive stress response

This is a normal response to being human, experiencing low-level, everyday stressors. For example, the first day back to school after the summer break might mean a brief increase in heart rate and hormonal levels being mildly elevated (for both pupils and staff!). However, recovery is usually quite quick, and body and mind can come back to a place of equilibrium relatively speedily.

A tolerable stress response

This happens if there was a single incident of trauma or loss, for example the death of a much loved pet or a family member. If the stressor is time-limited, and if the child or young person has supportive adults around them to buffer the impact, then their brain and other organs will have the opportunity to recover. Before too long, the child or young person will be able to function in their life again, albeit still affected by or mourning their loss. One brave young lady I know who lost her beloved dad to brain cancer last summer somehow went on to take her GCSEs this summer just gone.

A toxic stress response

When frequent, prolonged, elevated or overwhelming stress is experienced by a child or young person through any kind of ACE through adversity, without adequate adult support. This takes much, much longer to recover from, impacting many different types of human functioning Burke-Harris (2018) states:

... this kind of prolonged activation of the stress response systems can disrupt the development of brain architecture and other organ systems, and increase the risk for stress related disease and cognitive impairment, well into the adult years.   *(p. 55)*

Please note too that positive and tolerable stressors become much more challenging when you have previously lived with toxic stress, as everything gets internally reconfigured to mean that you may be driven to respond *as if* you were again experiencing toxic stress, even with everyday, low-level stressors, like shifting from breakfast table to getting your coat and shoes on, or from transitioning from class to assembly. We recognise this effect in post-traumatic stress disorder, but it's important to remember that *developmental trauma* (in other words traumatic events or episodes happening whilst a child's brain is developing) has the same kind of threshold-reducing impact on stress responses.

HOW STRESS AFFECTS OUR BODIES

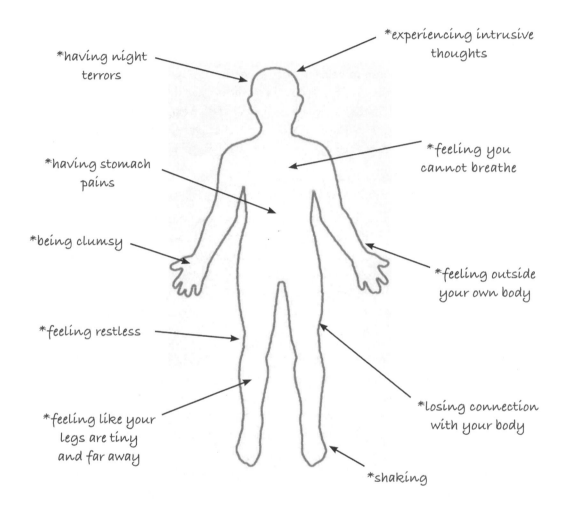

*having night terrors

*experiencing intrusive thoughts

*having stomach pains

*feeling you cannot breathe

*being clumsy

*feeling outside your own body

*feeling restless

*feeling like your legs are tiny and far away

*losing connection with your body

*shaking

Haines 2016, pp. 4-7

This list comes from the brilliant comic book *Trauma is really strange* by Steve Haines (2016) who helps us recognise that the children and young people in our care may not be able to verbalise what they are experiencing (and are unlikely to have a clue about the fact it's driving their behaviour or even where it came from). Some of this will be obvious and some will be hidden. This is how trauma presents.

I'm sure we could probably add other relational traumas and losses to this formalised list on p. 22 ourselves I'm sure, just as Burke-Harris has done in her particular context in the USA. The ACEs study (Felitti & Anda 1998) is an immensely helpful starting point for those of us trying to understand and make sense of what we need to do in our schools to support hurting children and young people.

It's significant *when* the ACEs happened, and *what* (if any) *protective factors* were around at the time for a particular child or young person - the best example of which would have been a mature, caring, empathic adult. It's really important to note that most of our fostered or adopted pupils have high ACE scores and have low protective factors in the mix. So they will have experienced toxic stress, *without* the protection, regulation and comfort of 'good enough' parents at a very early age, some even within the womb. Early events leave deep imprints that increase the complexity of healing and finding safety. Let's also not forget those who *have not* been moved into care, but who have also suffered high ACEs. We know that ACEs will have impacted their brain development, relationships, hormonal systems, immune systems and their DNA as well. So we're not just looking at labels here; we're trying to understand any pupil who has experienced relational trauma or loss. And of course there's a big link between trauma and attachment, since trauma disrupts attachment, causing numerous difficulties and challenges (p. 1).

> Trauma occurs when an event creates an unresolved impact upon an organism.
> Levine 1997 (in Haines, 2016 p. 3)

What's important to consider is how our traumatised pupils can be helped to stay grounded in the face of intense sensations associated with the body and mind's fear responses and being triggered again, and more so, in the future. That's one of the focal points of this book, written to help you free the particular children and young people you work with to function in all areas of their lives, despite everything they've lived through, and the severe consequences of these disturbed situations, which were outside of their control. And to support us to understand the need to use differentiated discipline because of their fragile sense of self, poor internal controls and faulty neuroception.

The Polyvagal Theory and neuroception

Stephen Porges has taken the therapy world by storm by giving us a theory with which to understand the behaviours we see presented in the context of trauma. Here I'm going to integrate the theory into the educational context, to help us understand its significance for our practice in schools. Porges' Polyvagal Theory (2011) describes how visceral experiences affect the nervous system and our resulting behaviours. According to Deb Dana (2018), the theory is basically the science of feeling safe enough to function and to live, or, in other words, to feel safe enough to tap into your exploratory system so you can learn. It explains how social interactions are essentially negotiations in helping minds and bodies find safety.

> The science of feeling safe enough to engage in life and take the risks required in living.
> Dana 2018 (rhythymofregulation.com)

At any given moment, we are all constantly evaluating our environment and other people at an unconscious or gut level (though not cognitive), for cues signalling danger or safety, in order for our nervous system to 'set' our priorities for adaptive strategies at a physiological level. This sensing is named by Porges as *neuroception*, and is very different to perception. Neuroception is a sense we are not even aware is functioning, as it is outside of (and too quick for) our conscious awareness. As human beings, we have systems in place for survival, and we're predisposed to cues including behavioural cues from others, which flag up different degrees of safety, danger and threat - it would be very dangerous if we weren't. More on neuroception later on in this chapter, but for now please simply remember it's linked to felt safety - or the lack of it.

The vagal nerve plays a significant role in Porge's work. The vagal nerve is often called the *wandering nerve* as it's one of the longest and most significant nerves in the body, joining up with all the major organs along the way. Different parts of this nerve can get activated or deactivated at any one time, meaning that it's possible for one of three very different systems to be switched on at any one time, *according to how the environment has been 'read' for safety.*

Depending on which system is operating within you, Porges suggests:

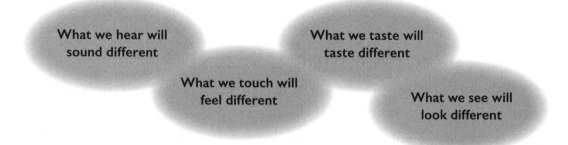

What we hear will sound different

What we taste will taste different

What we touch will feel different

What we see will look different

Three different nervous sysytems

So, let's set the stage for understanding what's happening inside traumatised children and young people, by first considering what's possible in all our nervous systems. For a long while, people understood there to be *two* main systems operating within our autonomic nervous system: the parasympathetic and the sympathetic systems or pathways. The parasympathetic system being the more comfortable, linked to resting and digesting: and the sympathetic one being linked to mobilisation when something was not OK - fight or flight! However, Stephen Porges (2011) proposes that there are *three* possible systems at work, within the autonomic nervous system as a whole. He found that in fact the parasympathetic is made up of two possible systems, and the sympathetic system has one, three in total.

The three systems are hierarchal in terms of responses. There is the *social engagement* system, the most sophisticated and developed system: secondly *the fight/flight system*: and thirdly the most primitive and least developed *freeze* system.

I'm going to outline them so that we know what they are and what they might look like in reality. Dana (2018) has created a ladder to support adults to increase their self-awareness (*we use it at* TouchBase - *see* **Useful Organisations**), encouraging us to consider how our experience of ourselves, others and the world can change. If you had to give your experience of each system when it's activated in you a symbol, a colour, or a name, what would you call each one? One of my young adult clients calls the 'freeze' a grey mist that comes over her. She calls the fight/flight a dark red. She calls the social engagement system her happy place! How would you describe yours?

THE SOCIAL ENGAGEMENT SYSTEM

If the body senses felt safety the ventral vagal nerve of the parasympathetic branch gets activated. This is linked to the social engagement system. In the social engagement system - our brain stems, limbic systems and neocortex are all 'online' and active.

If this system is activated, these things happen in our BODIES:	Middle ear muscles can tune into medium frequencies, for example the human voice Breathing is deep and easy Our hearts beat regularly at a healthy speed We can access our words easily Speech is fluid Our tone of voice will be modulated Digestion can take place Our temperature is regulated We are able to be still or active
If this system is activated, then the MIND responds with being:	Mentally and emotionally present Attentive Attuned Responsive And has a sense of time and the future

If this system is activated, and we realise our need for dependency	We call on someone we can depend upon to help us - a response some call 'to friend'. We're more likely to do this when we're in a healthy space emotionally and mentally, in this calm/alert state. We are designed for dependency and so respond really well to this kind of support.
In the CLASSROOM we might observe a pupil:	Giving relaxed and engaged, intermittent eye contact Actively listening Focussing, despite possible background sounds Concentrating Using good working memory Making contributions associated with the task in hand Relaxed and with a comfortable body posture Involved in reciprocal conversation and discussion

Basically being in this social engagement system means our pupils are in just the right state for learning! It's a system directly linked to felt safety and acts as a brake on the sympathetic system, inhibiting the fear response. In this system we can have a sense of where we are in time and space and we can reflect - using our pre-frontal cortex - sometimes referred to as the 'thinking brain'.

A brief exercise:	If you recognise this system in yourself, what would you call it? What colour would you give it? What would be the best metaphor for it?
Complete the sentences:	I am _____ Others are _____ The world is _____

THE FIGHT/FLIGHT SYSTEM

If the body senses a 'threat,' another part of the ventral vagal nerve gets activated. Threat can come in the form of many different kinds of alarm triggers. We are all so different and so much is based on what we have lived through up till now, projected onto the current situation, as well as or even instead of the actual situation. A gesture, a mannerism, a smell, an atmosphere, a particular look, a mood … or even fear, shame or guilt inside ourselves, can all equally activate a threat response.

> Fear, shame and guilt often make us shy in our isolation and prevent us from realising that connection with other human beings can offer us a way out into restorative healing and freedom.   Nouwen 2016

This active defence system of *fight* helps us to move into immediate action to resist whatever we perceive as threatening, whereas that of **flight** helps us to get away from the threat as a matter of urgency. The sympathetic branch of the nervous system has now come online, and is mobilised. This system is directly related to alarm. If we're in our fight/flight system - the neocortex starts going 'off line', becomes increasingly inaccessible.

If this system is activated, these things happen in our BODIES:	Middle ear muscles tune into very low or very high frequencies - predator sounds, overriding human voices Our breathing becomes fast or shallow Our heart can beat very fast We can't find our words Speech is altered. Our tone of voice will change - low or high pitched Stomach will feel churned up Temperature will be affected - very hot or very cold Movement

If this system is activated, then the MIND responds with being:	Preoccupied Hypervigilant Aggravated Edgy Aware of a sense of feeling trapped or cornered Only able to think in terms of the next second or minute
In the CLASSROOM we might observe a pupil:	With a flushed face or a pale face Hyperventilating Scanning Having overreactive responses Using defensive talk 'Get away from me ...' Having aggressive outbursts Exiting Running away Hiding

In the fight/flight system resources such as oxygen, blood and sugar are diverted to the big major muscle groups and the brain. Primitive reflexes can take over. You sense that you are in an emergency.

A brief exercise:	If you recognise this system in yourself, what would you call it? What colour would you give it? What would be the best metaphor for it?
Complete the sentences:	I am Others are The world is

THE FREEZE SYSTEM

Occasionally, a third system can be activated and is basically the last port of call for human response in the face of toxic stress. This is the system most familiar with those who have experienced many ACEs. The ventral vagal nerve has in effect an 'evil twin' (though a necessary one), called the dorsal vagal nerve. It's located in the parasympathetic nervous system, as is the social engagement system, but whilst that system enables us to be resting and digesting, the freeze system, the most primitive system of all, immobilises us *without fear*. In the *freeze* system both the neocortex and limbic system go offline with fear.

If the system is activated, we are in a fear or terror state and move into defence, two things may happen:

Either **hyper-freeze**, which creates the sense that we have 'stepped outside' our body and mind so that we don't feel the impact of whatever is happening to us. In this active defence we might take on other personnas or use risk-taking behaviours.

Or **hypo-freeze**, or **flop**. This immobilised defence system is our last port of call, when everything else has failed. We simply surrender to the threat, as this seems the best option. We might just be frozen to the spot, unable to move. This defence may also kick in when we have moved into a fear or terror state.

If this system is activated, these things happen in our BODIES:	Middle ear muscles tune out so we can't hear anything Breathing becomes very shallow or can stop altogether Our heart can slow right down, moving into shut down We can't speak We can't sense our body at all - can feel like watching on Poor postural control Weak tone Very still Fainting episodes or going unconscious

If this system is activated, then the MIND responds with being:	Dissociative states - anything from just thinking nothing, blanking out, becoming immobilised through to unconsciously adopting another persona: speaking in a different voice, writing in a different handwriting. Memory may be selective or difficult to access
In the CLASSROOM we might observe a pupil:	Day-dreaming Rocking Making odd sounds Using a different voice With different persona coming into play for example, being a cat, a superhero, a baby ... Spacing out Not being with it Being floppy Unable to stand up Collapsed Risk taking

You may be curious about the range of responses listed as possible here, including some seemingly, quite polarised behaviours. Body psychotherapist Babette Rothschild (2017) has a useful chart for more detail of the varieties of response in all three main systems I outline in this book (see **References**).

For example, Rothschild refers to two aspects of freeze - *hyper* freeze and *hypo* freeze, and goes into further detail. If the body moves into this system, it's in a state of fear/terror. The children and young people in our schools who have been impacted by trauma will be very familiar with this system, and if we observe this state in them, it will give us a lot of information about their experience; and it's the time when we need to be most protective, attuned and responsive to them. It's directly linked to a sense of powerlessness and being threatened.

A brief exercise:	If you recognise this system in yourself, what would you call it? What colour would you give it? What would be the best metaphor for it?
Complete the sentences:	I am Others are The world is

For our purposes in schools, the most important part to recognise in all of this is that the *'choice'* of system in operation is *involuntary*. Each system is linked to whether there is a sense of felt safety, or not. We are constantly checking out our environment for safety, threat or danger cues, our bodies and minds trying to work out the most effective system to be active at any given time. And what is equally important is to note is that we as adults can act intentionally to support others, including our traumatised pupils, to soothe and regulate their states of distress, and re-activate their social engagement system. This is essential and encouraging news for schools.

STATES

So at any point we could notice our pupils being 'driven' by one of these nervous systems because of the shift in their states. According to Perry's work (2013) there are five states that all of us can be in at any given moment, those of *calm, alert, alarm, fear and terror*. Each state relates to a specific nervous system. If we are *calm* or *alert,* we will shift into our social engagement system. If we are in *alarm* we will shift into our fight/flight system and if we are in *fear* or *terror,* we will shift into freeze (p. 108).

So when a traumatised pupil's state of dysregulation is being expressed through the kind of behaviour that traditionally meets with zero tolerance discipline, there couldn't be a more important time to use what we now know and do everything we can to move the pupil into a state where they can have a deep experience of felt safety.

The vagal paradox

Despite our defences usually helping us as human beings, Porges also suggested something called the 'vagal paradox' (2008). The two defences described above as hyper- and hypo-freeze can turn in on us and cause us harm when we are in the fear/terror state. For example, and although instances are incredibly rare, we could hurt ourselves really badly because we're in a dissociative state, or stop breathing in hypo-freeze state. A girl I knew threw herself down the stairs in school, a very high risk behaviour which occurred because she was in such terror, almost literally 'out' of her body and mind. The Vagal Paradox helps us understand the gravity of the rare situation in which someone moves into a profound state of freeze - we must provide urgent support, especially of course if the pupil actually stops breathing.

We will now consider neuroception in more detail, and why it's important that education professionals know about it, followed by how we can increase felt safety cues. Finally we'll look at how to sustain our pupils in their social engagement system for just that bit longer … and then just that bit longer again … and why this is so vital in school.

Neuroception explored a little deeper

What can complicate matters significantly for a traumatised child or young person is that when you have experienced toxic stress, everything is shaken up in both body and mind. Toxic stress re-sets the thermostat (*so to speak, and please revisit the Trauma Tree on p. 48 which describes all the areas that can be shaken up*).

There are many, many possible developmental compromises or vulnerabilities as a result of having lived through toxic stress. And one of the most significant developmental vulnerabilities that traumatised children and young people have to contend with is faulty neuroception. Basically their neuroception has been altered in such a way that they now see threat everywhere, *even when there isn't a threat*. It makes sense that everything is topsy-turvy now since they *have* experienced overwhelming threat, emotionally, mentally, physically and/or sexually with someone else or with more than one person, in a different place, at another time. It's become a survival strategy to now make the general assumption that there is threat everywhere, and that everyone is a possible threat.

So faulty neuroception is an inability to detect accurately or not whether the environment is safe or whether a person is trustworthy (Porges 2011). It's easy to imagine that faulty neuroception can create all kinds of difficulties for the individual themselves and those they come into contact with. There are so many possible stressors during a school day and in everyday functioning at home or out and about in the community. For a child or young person to be able to feel safe and to keep the emotions, thoughts and defensive responses associated with past relational traumas and losses away (Ogden 2015) is a *huge* ask. So you can see why they are going to need us to support them with this!

Porges believes that faulty neuroception can be a factor in many different medical disorders including anxiety, autism, reactive attachment disorder, amongst others (Porges, 2004). This is an interesting development and discovery and I'm sure extremely controversial too. If it were taken on board, it could have far-reaching implications for treatment plans in future years. Am I so bold as to say that I personally believe that faulty neuroception is at the root of most of the exclusions in the UK? I am. From my experience, our traumatised pupils' experience of threat being everywhere, from everyone, runs through so much of what's happening on the frontline in our schools.

Maté (2019) discusses how many generalised behaviours like anxiety are linked to not having experienced the necessary relational buffering that many could have done with (children and adults!) when we were younger. Relational buffering is when you have kind, caring and supportive others around you, who function as attachment figures, sources of safety, security and stability in your life. In children this would need to be adults. Gabor explains how displaying anxiety is an attachment alarm to the adults caring for a child or baby: if it's not attended to, and the child or baby soothed, then the *specific* context in which anxiety was left unattended can quickly become *generalised* to other situations. This also makes me see so clearly the impact of faulty neuroception as a player involved in generalised anxiety.

I'm sure we can all think of a child or young person who demonstrates faulty neuroception. They are the ones who move into threat responses *very* easily and quickly, despite our honourable motives and the best of intentions to support them. Just to clarify: there may be times when it's *appropriate* for them to move into a threat response, for example if the pupil is being bullied. However, I'm sure like me you can think of times when you smiled, were generous towards a pupil and they have completely rebuffed you! Again like me, I'm sure at the time you were shocked by their response, especially if you had purposefully been trying so hard to support them. It's distressing to be on the receiving end of faulty neuroception, as well as being distressing for the one experiencing the threat. The threat feels very real, as if there were a lion in the room. It's far from comfortable for the body or mind to be moving into the fight/flight or freeze systems, so no one would do so out of choice!

It's important to clarify that all of us can become alarmed, challenged, stressed or triggered in everyday life and move into our flight/fight system, not just traumatised children or young people. Whilst a healthy person can move smoothly between the social engagement system and the fight/flight system, and out again (especially with support), the traumatised person can remain stuck further in alarm, fear or terror states and does not know *how* to move back to a place of safety - the social engagement system. They get stuck. That's where we need to come in, as mature adults!

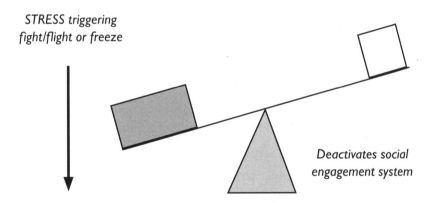

STRESS *triggering fight/flight or freeze*

Deactivates social engagement system

As babies and children growing up, we're all meant to learn about this recovery process, how to bring ourselves back to a state of equilibrium in the context of a relationship with a foundation of safety, stability and security. We were meant to learn it back at home with our primary attachment figures as we developed, especially within our early years.

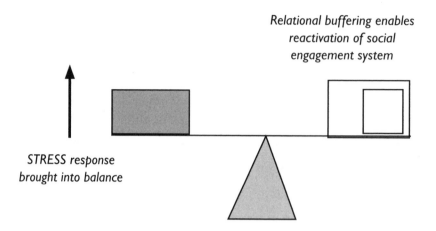

Relational buffering enables reactivation of social engagement system

STRESS response brought into balance

This is what we mean by receiving 'good enough' care, which we can internalise for support going forwards. However, when those people who were meant to be your source of comfort can also turn into your source of terror, attachment becomes far more complex, and you end up with a deeply insecure way of interpreting everything that's going on around you, including the intentions of others. Words - like being told to *'Calm down'* - are not going to reach you or make a difference (p. 76) because your capacity to hear and understand the human voice is vastly reduced. Being asked why you're behaving as you are, is not going to help, because the thinking part of yourself has gone offline. Being shouted at, or isolated, is not going to help you learn to self-regulate. Attachment theory and the polyvagal theory complement each other so well, in terms of making sense of what we see in the distressed behaviours in our schools right now, and helping us recognise how we should respond.

We need to focus on remaining grounded, regulated, in our own social engagement system, consciously overriding the sympathetic system of our own alarm states. If we're not able to maintain our sense of balance then we must swap in with someone else from Team Pupil. Our aim is to maintain relational proximity with the pupil in our care, not to engage in relational withdrawal. When things are really kicking off, our pupils need us close by.

How are you doing, reading through all this information? Is your mind whirring, or bringing up images of particular pupils you've worked with, or wondering about the state of your own capacity for accurate neuroception? You're not alone. All these things take time to assimilate. The key things I hope you'll be taking away are that:

* Our nervous systems can shift at any point dependent on how safe we feel

* Through being regulated ourselves we can become a regulated resource for the others around us, including traumatised children who are moving into dysregulation

* Traumatised children, young people and adults have faulty neuroception in the mix which means they can pick up on cues they interpret as threatening when others don't

* We need to provide relational proximity, keeping close to the pupil, and staying connected with the individual who is in fight/flight or freeze state, and increase our felt safety cues

* We can observe body cues to decipher which nervous system is 'driving' a pupil

* Once we know which nervous system a pupil is in we can work out and use the most appropriate state-dependent intervention, rather than a one size fits all approach

* It is possible to shift states ands systems using sensory interventions. We need to rely less on cognitive interventions, and increase our sensory interventions to respect biology and reach our pupils.

Increasing felt safety cues

I would now like to introduce you to some ways to support a traumatised child or young person into *feeling safe*, despite their sense that they are threatened in some way. Let's call it giving them felt safety cues, and I'll divide them into two sections: a way of being for us and the physical space. First we'll explore how to facilitate really fundamental safety cues, before considering how to support our pupils to 'exercise their vagal tone' so that they can be recover more quickly from incidents of raised stress. We'll thus be able to strengthen their capacity to activate their social engagement system quickly, after moving into one of the other systems.

If we can embrace and embed this kind of caregiving into school life, it will truly support these particular pupils. However there will also be times when we need to compensate for their sense of threat, by drawing further attention to the felt safety cues than usual.

> The neuroception of familiar individuals and individuals with appropriately prosodic voices and warm, expressive faces translates into a social interaction promoting a sense of safety.   Porges (2008)

How we are

FACES

Educators with warm, open faces and warm eyes immediately create felt safety with other pupils and other adults. Ensure you move your face a lot! And smile! The muscles in our face are closely connected with the muscles in our middle ear connected to the ventral vagal nerve. When we don't feel safe, muscles around eyes and in our cheeks change very quickly. We may just be thinking or preoccupied with something but our whole face will change as a result. Children and young people who are hypervigilant will spot these subtle changes: to them they signal threat or danger cues. Those with still, neutral, faces will also create increased difficulty with pupils with faulty neuroception, who will default to perception of threat in the absence of other interpretation: so be careful which adult you match them with. Genuine smiles can relax and reassure the brain. It's not necessary to become Pollyanna, but even with cynical adolescents, warmth conveyed through your face can make all the difference, for example through brief smiles used intermittently.

A 16 year old I work with spoke of needing to keep her eye on a college tutor the whole double lesson, because of her still face. She said, '*She freaked me out. I had no idea what she was up to or what she was going to do next*'. Let's be mindful of what messages we're putting out, consciously or unconsciously, which can be so unsettling for our traumatised pupils.

TONE OF VOICE

Educationists who vary their tone of voice, particularly those appropriately utilising a sing-song way of speaking with younger children, will easily create felt safety. Monotone voices can create a lot of trouble for pupils with faulty neuroception, who may interpret it as threat (like a lecture or criticism). If you have difficulties with this, I would recommend booking yourself in to listen to a professional story teller: we can all learn a lot from their skill at making a narrative riveting.

BODY LANGUAGE

Educators who have open, warm body language will enhance felt safety in the pupils around them. Those who fold their arms and puff themselves up to appear bigger and stronger will increase the level of perceived threat around for these pupils and so their distress will continue.

SURRENDER

Educationists humble enough to apologise when the relationship between them and their traumatised pupils doesn't go well will increase felt safety for them (**Repair**, p. 250).

We need to recognise that we are the grown-ups and take responsibility for leading in the area of relationships, modelling appropriate responses to what comes our way. It's not appropriate to take comments or behaviours personally or to react out of a hurt place. Let's go to someone we trust, another adult, to help us process hurt or any other feelings: not the pupil. We're all in school for the children, not ourselves. Staff who carry on determined to make a point and to prove their control of the situation will end up increasing the threat experienced by traumatised pupils. Their relationships will suffer as a result.

RELATIONSHIPS FIRST

Educators who realise that whatever happens, relationships have to be protected, will increase felt safety for their traumatised pupils (p. 189, **Relate**). Those who focus simply on tasks will leave these pupils vulnerable to threat responses. If the work doesn't get done, but your relationship with the pupil remains intact, then this will be an investment into the brighter days ahead. Relationships provide essential buffering for those who have already experienced toxic stress. Perhaps, as the song goes, by bringing ourselves into relational proximity with the traumatised pupil, we really do '… say it best when we say nothing at all' (Donald Alan Schmitz & Paul Overstreet Sony/ATV Music Publishing). Our words will mean so much more once we've gone sensory, in relationship, first.

BEING PLAYFUL AND NOTICING

Not taking ourselves too seriously will also help! Just adding basic childlike playfulness and humour in the mix (p. 193). Never sarcasm, which easily backfires for those with a faulty neuroception. We need to convince our pupils' biology that they, our pupils, are safe. Noticing out loud can help this too. Noticing a member of staff's friendly, warm eyes. Noticing a member of staff's warm voice. Give these pupils a relational experience so they know what felt safety is, but also be witnesses for one another. We need to invite our pupils to notice and check out evidence for there being safe adults around them; as humans, we are all evidence-seeking creatures. Felt safety is possible if we are all intentional about increasing our safety cues.

B Where we are

INCREASE SENSORY COMFORT

We want these children and young people to notice their states, sensations and feelings, and a good way to help them with this is to give them different sensory cues to 'awaken' them and make them sit up and notice their environment. Consider seating: best to think about providing a position that offers the pupil wide vision. Traumatised pupils *may* respond best to being at the back of the class or to the side near a wall, so that they have good vision of everything around them, and they can check out their environment: they may well be driven to do so by their heightened hypervigilance.

GIVE CHOICE

Offer two or three choices about where they are positioned in class, to give some control back to the pupil.

HAVE AN EXIT CLEARLY MARKED

It's important that these children and young people know where the nearest exit is, and may well not wish to sit with their back to it, for obvious reasons. Ensure the exit pathway is easy; our traumatised pupils need to be able to exit quickly if necessary, so make sure there are no obstacles in their way and there is a clear way out. I know of a secondary pupil who was hemmed in in a busy hall with a visiting speaker, talking about abuse and neglect. She felt trapped and her anxiety increased dramatically, a real trigger for her. She needed to be able to leave easily.

PROVISION OF A DEN-LIKE SPACE

These children and young people do appreciate a space they can retreat into if necessary. A space they can withdraw to, maybe even hide away. They can either create their own together with you or you can set one up for them. They need to be able to set the pace for togetherness and separateness - the dance of attachment - especially whilst building trust.

KEEP ONLOOKERS TO A MINIMUM

Ensure these children and young people are never crowded by adults, especially if feelings are running high after an incident, for example, or something unstructured and unusual is happening at school (for example, an end-of-term event).

RESPECT PERSONAL SPACE

Ensure you are mindful and attuned to their intimacy tolerance window. This may mean you being seated at quite a distance in order to communicate with the pupil. Consider asking them how comfortable they feel with the distance.

ENABLE THE PUPIL TO GET GROUNDED

Sometimes a traumatised child confuses the past and present, what happened and what is happening and so watch out for this. If you think that a child might have fallen down a time hole or is dissociating, do ensure you increase and overcompensate your felt safety cues immediately, using your presence as they may be very frightened, and support them back into the grounded here-and-how, Use something like - 5, 4, 3, 2, 1: *'Name 5 things you can see that are blue, 4 things you can hear, 3 things you can feel, 2 things you can smell and 1 thing about you'.* This task, steadily delivered gently bit by bit (not all at once), interrupts the activation of fight/flight and can support them to notice bodily signs of safety.

Increasing the window of stress tolerance

If you've read any of my other books, or learned elsewhere about attachment and trauma-informed practice, you may well be familiar with the fact that traumatised children and young people usually only have a limited *window of stress tolerance*. Their 'overwhelm button' can get quickly activated not only because of their faulty neuroception, but also because they have not received much oxytocin along the way to dampen down the stress caused by everyday stressors. Their window of tolerance doesn't need to remain limited. We can support them to extend it by:

- Giving them a Key Adult and a small team to watch their back and be their best supporters (Team Pupil p. 163)
- Ensuring all the adults remain regulated (calm, alert, steady, grounded, empathic)
- Giving the team the responsibility for being the stress and shame regulators, not the child or young person
- Increasing opportunities for fun through ... playful interactions, gentle child-like humour, collaborative activities, being on the lookout for anything funny and mentioning it! (**Relate** p. 189)
- Increasing sensory comfort in the environment both around the child or young person and also providing things for them to use personally, for example giving them a special sensory pencil case with some fidget bits and pieces in, a 'calm purse' (p. 184 *and* Bombèr 2007).
- Giving the team responsibility for facilitating regular sensory interventions for the child or young person as and when they need them (p. 141)

Extending the time spent in the social engagement system

This is where nurturing schools can play such a significant part in the recovery of their traumatised pupils. Drawing on Porges, what we're working to do is to strengthen their vagal tone. We are well placed in a school context to be relational, and facilitate different types of educative opportunities.

Arranged around the star on the next page are ten different types of educative opportunities to facilitate on a regular basis, in school, together with a consistent, trusted adult ideally from Team Pupil (the team around the child or young person). I spent quite a time in the academic year 2018/2019 travelling around the UK introducing education staff to these experiential exercises: the feedback was consistently positive. I always suggest you try them for yourself first. It's so important we adults experience them before we share them with our pupils! Since we are the lead regulators. We need to know what they all feel like, so that we can genuinely believe in what we're sharing and teaching. I'll go through each of them in more detail in the **Regulate** chapter (p. 151).

The practical strategies and practices are intended for the pupil and adult to do *together*, not in alone or in isolation. Our traumatised pupils need rich relational experience in the mix, lots of quality moments of real human connection with mature adults. Connection is the most fundamental of all human needs, and because this has been adversely so impacted for them in their early lives, we must pay paramount attention to honouring and protecting connection if we are to really help them learn and make the most of their lives in our schools.

A further interesting initiative has been the Safe and Sound Protocol, developed as a result of Dr Stephen Porges work on the Polyvagal theory (*see* The Listening Project *in*, **Useful Organisations**). Music is listened to through headphones, and elements from a movement repertoire are used together with a therapist or educator working alongside children or young people to decrease stress and auditory sensitivities.

Strategies for extending time spent in social engagement

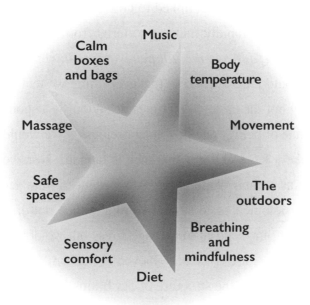

This protocol was first used in the context of autism, but is now being used in the context of relational trauma as well.

Through the process of exploring and experimenting with all these things, we can support the particular pupil we are working with to start developing their own unique anchor (p. 184-5). We all need one of those when the going gets tough! Co-regulation can lead to self-regulation: but many of the traumatised children and young people we work with simply won't have had opportunity yet to explore or practise any of this with anyone. Now is the time!

When little people are overwhelmed by big emotions, it's our job to share or calm, not join in with their chaos.   Knost 2013, goodreads.com

In summary

Which of the three nervous systems described above kicks in at any given time depends on the state we experience, linked to how safe we feel: our neuroception is at work, picking up cues and rapidly making patterns from them, of security or threat. *So we can never state definitively that all behaviour is intentional.* Nor, as cognitive approaches imply, would it be true to say that everything we feel (and do) is led by our thoughts. It's simply not the case. Sometimes behaviour is a spontaneous response to our physiological state of being, 'decided' unconsciously. We wouldn't punish children for reflex action, like a leg kicking if the knee is tapped. Nor should we punish our pupils for behaving as if their world is not safe; because it may feel unsafe, for them, and that is not a physiological state anyone can be argued out of. We have a number of possible defences at our disposal to manage stress but we don't have any conscious choice over which ones we use if we have moved into alarm, fear or terror. In fact the more we move downwards in the structure of our brains (because we're so frightened) the more inaccessible we become to reason, logic, argument and so on.

Those who have a trauma history can get stuck because they've been emotionally hijacked. They have picked up on a cue their nervous system has rated as threatening. So they need *us* to provide them with an exit strategy back to their social engagement system, until, through us and with us, they can learn to do this for themselves. In school, this presents us with a real insight into how to go forward with our traumatised pupils.

How accurate our neuroception is will impact our states, and in turn our default nervous system. Tragically those who have previous ACEs often have faulty neuroception in the mix which exacerbates their difficulties in functioning in so many aspects of their lives. However, there are ways in which we can compensate with multiple, enhanced safety cues for our traumatised pupils, so that they have more opportunity to spend time in their social engagement system. We can also become stress regulators by paying attention to our own nervous systems, by remaining close alongside and by engaging children and young people in sensory interventions.

As Porges makes clear, we are 'merely' trying to move these children and young people from a place of *vulnerability* to a place of *accessibility*. When a child or young person picks up danger through neuroception, which then activates their fear circuitry, it will stimulate animal defences which can involve fight, flight, freeze or shut down. It's essential we recognise what's happening and re-establish their ability to socially engage at these times.

> Connectedness provides the neurobiological mechanism to link social behaviour and both mental and physical health.   Porges 2019, Slide 5

On a hopeful note: Dr Pamela Cantor who set up Turnaround for Children in the USA (*see* **Useful Organisations**) has proved that by respecting biology, training education staff and providing compensatory regulation and relationship, it's possible to see positive changes. From 2011 to 2014, exclusions have been halved! Classroom climate, productivity and engagement have increased by 20% and severe incidents have decreased by 42%. Do look into her work!

And from the UK as well, we're already starting to see really positive outcomes.

Respecting Biology │ **EVIDENCE FROM PRACTICE**

Our support is well established now and we are clear of its advantages. It certainly keeps our community safe. It is consistent and learners trust its application. As a result we have a significant reduction in any form of physical interventions, which is hugely reassuring. We are literally hardly needing to hold at all now.

Lyndsey Brown, Headteacher with two Attachment Leads in the school, Bradford

We aim to help the children with difficulties by being stress regulators rather than behaviour managers. In terms of success for example, we have two pupils who started with us in year 3 who really struggled and were in overwhelm on a daily basis. Through using the tools and the strategies that we learned with these children they now have very few incidences of overwhelm and where they do, they recover much more quickly.

Aimee Cave, Assistant Head & Attachment Lead, York

In this chapter we have considered what it is that makes us truly human, what makes us do whatever we do. Our nervous systems hold a lot of sway! Traumatised children and young people are not disturbed - *what has happened* has been disturbed and disturbing. Because of this they experience the full range of states and all three nervous systems, a capacity each one of us possesses as a human being. It all depends on what we have lived through to date and what we are living through in the moment as to where we will end up in our nervous system at any given time. We have learned that what happens in our nervous system is involuntary.

Now we know how our nervous system works we are going to look at attunement. We need to know how to tune into what's going on so that we can facilitate the most helpful ways of being and choose our interventions wisely. Let's consider the essential art of attunement.

Chapter 5

Rediscovering the Art of Attunement

The body speaks clearly to those who know how to listen ... The multifaceted language of the body depicts a lifetime of joys, sorrows, and challenges, revealed in patterns of tension, movement, gesture, posture, breath, rhythm, prosody, facial expression, sensation, physiological arousal, gait and other action sequences.

Ogden 2015, p. 25

Now that we are clear about how our nervous systems operate and the importance of state-dependent interventions, it's important that we explore attunement. Even if we've been trained in *'what is good for a child',* we must never overlook what's going on right in front of us at any particular time. The body gives so much away. For example, even if a pupil is being compliant in joining in with an activity, you may notice a particular look in their eyes, or their body tensing up. If you were to see something like this, it would be important to switch or adapt what you're doing.

Whatever we do, *it's essential we communicate our utmost respect at all times.* If we don't, it can lead to disastrous consequences as we saw in the previous chapters. So if we are to be effective in our teaching both curriculum and about behaviour, it's essential that we become experts in attunement. We need to be sensitive in our timings (*please see the chapter on sensitive timings co-written by the author with* Dr Dan Hughes, *in Settling to Learn,* 2013). I'll extend those basics further here in terms of everything we now know.

From the work of Dr Bruce Perry, we understand that whilst it's important to recognise a pupil has had many ACEs, we also need to think about the *relational health* (p. 144) of the child or young person we are supporting (or parenting). We know that a child or young person with a high number of ACEs *and* relational poverty will very likely have poor outcomes at every level and that rich relational buffering can provide the social air they need, in order to breathe, and breathe well, even after the most horrific of circumstances. *And attunement is going to be a key part of that buffering.* So let's first consider:

> Who is around this child or young person?
> What is the quality of those relationships?
> Do those around the child or young person spend attuned time with him or her?
> Does the child/young person experience feeling seen and heard?

The capacity for attunement of the people round the child or young person is the *best predictor of favourable mental health and wellbeing.* Attunement isn't just about warmth of care, or sensitivity to need, but how we respond and the timing involved, sensitive timings based on the interpersonal cues from the child or young person. Is the adult, for example, matching timbre, volume and pace of how we speak, so that their communication and way of being resonates and connects with the child or young person? (Trevarthan 2014). This is also named as 'the power of showing up' (Siegel, 2020). How many teacher training and parenting courses currently emphasise how to draw on the wisdom of the body to facilitate the process of attunement and to support change? Without this, the adults are left mostly dependent on the child or young person's verbal narrative (how they respond, or don't, what they say) or their own (possibly inaccurate) sense of what's happening between them and the pupil. However:

> The story told by the 'somatic narrative' - gesture, posture, prosody, facial expression, eye gaze and movement - is arguably more significant than the story told by words.   Ogden 2015, p. 13

Somatic expressions communicate the child or young person's *experience and understanding* of the situation they find themselves in, their *expectations* of themselves and others, and *what meaning* they are making and attaching to all of these. They may respond with a minimal, *'Dunno'*, but there's so much more going on than the pupil can articulate. So it's essential that we take the time needed and give the necessary thoughtful attention to consider not only what's being said in words, but to what is *also* being conveyed *beneath* the words, through the body. Because, as psychiatrist Bessel Van der Kolk (2015) so succinctly puts it: 'The body keeps the score'.

I'd really like to highlight that it's *always* best to tune into body cues, in preference to verbal communication, with our traumatised pupils, because of the psychological challenges I've outlined in the preceding chapters, such as blocked trust. What we hear isn't necessarily the real or full picture! I'm always asking staff to go beyond what we're being shown overtly or presented with. Remember we're often miscued by our pupils' defence systems, consciously or unconsciously. Also notice especially when there are contradictions. Our bodies find it hard to hide or to lie.

"I'm fine. I don't need any help!" The sleeves of Lena's jumper are now in tatters as she has chewed the cuffs down so much.

Stella (13) was asked how she was. 'Fine', she said, looking away. She seemed flat in her feelings, her eyes looked very sad and her body had no postural control. I gently whispered that I wasn't sure she was that fine, as her body was letting me know that maybe she was upset about something ...

Morgan's fingers are constantly in his hair, picking, picking ... sometimes he makes his scalp bleed. If he's challenged, however gently, he simply glazes over and looks away, but his fingers will soon find their way back.

What is attunement?

Attunement describes how we can tune into, read and then respond to someone else's state and needs at any given time. These needs could be social, emotional, mental, physical or spiritual. A person who is well-attuned will respond with the most appropriate tone of voice, facial expression, body language and verbal language based on their best sense of what is going on in the other person. In order for someone to be able to use attunement, they need to have experienced it themselves in the past: they need to be in a state of *calm or alert* (that is, in their social engagement system p. 26), and they need to have a good supply of kindness, compassion and patience.

As Trevarthen (2014) states, we're born wired for connection: in other words, born to be social. From birth, we look for companionship with people. Babies are born needing the security of attachment (ideally with a mature adult) for safety first, and born curious, and it's this drive to connect and curiosity that paves the way towards connection. So the attachment system in each of us for safety, security and stability must be attended to first and then, when it's been attended to and is settled, the exploratory system can then come online, linked to extending oneself outside the known and familiar ... to be curious, to seek, to explore, to take risks and so on.

These complementary urges support the child or young person to experience being secure, as well (when they are secure and with people who attune to, enjoy and engage with them) as being an object of delight, to experience responsiveness, to learn about facial expressions, to get a sense of their value and worth as a human being, who others are and about the world around them. *Being attuned to is the foundation for empathy.* Relational interactions bring regulation (of the survival urge to connect) and are rewarding, as well as bringing increased social learning (through curiosity). Regulation when faced with everyday, low-level stressors. Rewarding, as our oxytocin (the feel-good hormone) levels are being topped up by gentle, consistent loving care. And learning is best when we learn through and alongside one another. So we have to feel safe and settled in order to be able to learn - learn the curriculum, about the world, and about behaviour. So internalising safety depends on first being attuned to by an empathic, mature adult.

When an adult attunes to a pupil they are communicating that the pupil is safe to be with them, because they can read and respond to what the pupil needs, as they go. With this felt safety, the pupil is then able to take the risks necessary for learning. I think we sometimes forget the risks and asks school involves! All the more risky if you have a fragmented sense of self, a developmental vulnerability from having lived through relational trauma.

What happens when we *don't* have all this? We remain alone, dysregulated, and we are oxytocin deprived. We may seek out other means to try and support ourselves with our regulation and reward needs. Later on, when older, there may be a real possibility of addiction difficulties in the attempt to meet our own regulation and relational needs, if in the past we've had to cope with so much alone (*and check out* Gabor Maté's *work on this*, 2019). And so the unhealthy cycle continues ... as Perry (2014) comments, 'Relationships have a key role in global health, creativity and productivity of a group'.

How do we attune to another person?

We can't assume that everyone is good at this or even knows what to look for! Those who have experienced a parent or carer who was attentive and responsive to them will probably know how to do it, and it may feel instinctive, even though it was learned from that parent or carer. Being on the receiving end of attunement from a mature adult, in a genuine relational experience, is the most effective way to acquire this ability. But even then it may help if we look more closely at what the different elements are. It's a skill that can be learned, and you're probably already doing much of it, so this is to help you continue to develop your capacity. Start with giving full attention, and being curious. Notice the actual, practical movements of the person in front of you. Wonder what they might be feeling, what might be happening in their physical,

ATTUMENT, MISATTUMENT AND EVERYDAY STRESS RESILIENCE

Tronick & DiCorcia (2015) who work in the highly esteemed Child Development unit at the University of Massachusetts do not believe that resilience is a trait that develops from an individual's experience with extreme adversity. They believe that resilience is actually a regulatory or coping capacity that develops from an infant's experiences with everyday stress, and that this capacity to manage everyday stress in later years is supported by a mother's reparatory sensitivity to relational ruptures throughout the early days, weeks and months of a child's life.

The mother's ability to attend to her infant's signals and to respond appropriately is instrumental to the development of stress regulation and of resilience. (p.125)

Tronick & DiCorcia specify that the mother's most important ability is that of relating to what happens following misattunement or mismatches in the dyad (pair made up of the parent and child). Misattunement must be followed by repair; the parent must have the means to

emotional and mental inner worlds, what they need. Use all your senses to get in touch with what's happening for them. Wonder to yourself what the person in front of you is really trying to say through both their mind and body.

Quality moments

Life is very rushed and we all seem to live at an incredibly fast pace nowadays. It's hard to see even close friends regularly, and everyone seems really preoccupied. And of course we're also surrounded by technology. So we'll need to be very intentional about making time for quality moments with each other, times when we are fully present, fully attending to the other person. Think about pressing the pause button as soon as you meet up with the particular child or young person you're working with. Be physically present. Be emotionally present. Be attentive, attuned and responsive. We all have lots to do, we all have racing thoughts. But let's practice *being in the moment* so that this child or young person really has an experience of feeling fully 'seen' and 'heard'. Given mindful attention. I wonder what would happen if these children and young people experienced many quality moments like this throughout their day? In his research, (2014) Bruce Perry and his team found that many of those who had experienced a significant level of ACEs (for example children in care) didn't have that many positive interactions during a day, putting them even further at risk. But what if they did? We could actually increase their relational buffering and have positive impact on their capacity for resilience! How amazing is that?

The benefits of VIG

Now you may be thinking '*How can I get better at this? Are there any tools out there to help or do I just need to work it all out on my own?*' Well, I'd like to introduce you to VIG. Some of you may have already come across it but many still haven't. VIG stands for Video Interactive Guidance. In education, we can learn a lot from those who belong to AVIG UK (*see* **Useful Organisations**). AVIG UK are experts in spotting attunement, since developing this capacity is the main purpose of this method. They have an increasing body of evidence behind them to prove its effectiveness in promoting healthier attuned relationships. Practitioners use video clips from films of authentic interactions between two people, a parent/carer and their child, a member of Team Pupil and the pupil, a couple ... to enhance communication within these relationships.

VIG works by actively engaging the adults (parents/carers/education staff etc) in whatever it is they would like to change, for example, creating a better quality relationship between them, to reduce aggressive outbursts, to increase communication. They are asked what their hopes are, what areas they'd like to work on, and the adult and child are then filmed for around five to ten minutes at a time, when they're feeling relaxed and getting along. Then the best moments of adult attunement to the child are chosen by a VIG 'guider' from the film, creating two to three minutes of video footage of the adult already doing something positive (in the area they have stated they'd like to improve), to watch with the adult and to discuss together.

The use of VIG (which is based on Professor Colwyn Trevarthan's theory of intersubjectivity and Jerome Bruno's mediated learning) promotes attunement, empathy and wellbeing in children and adults. It's recommended in the National Institute for Health and Care Excellence (NICE) guidelines. This type of work transform the child's stressful states into non-stressful states.

This is what they say best facilitates everyday stress resilience, the kind we are interested in, for our schools, where there are so many everyday opportunities for stress - for all of us, but for already traumatised children especially. These range from a child's friend choosing to play with another pupil at break time through to the risks required in learning something new.

So maternal sensitivity can really support or hinder the growth of resilience (*ibid*). Thus if the child has experienced neglect for example, then of course he is not going to be able to manage the everyday stressors of school life, without additional support. Think about all those who've grown up to be adults who didn't have this co-regulatory support in their classrooms, in their schools.

So, so tragic. We all know what dysfunctional regulation can look like and what it can result in - we just need to open our newspapers. But it doesn't have to remain this way any longer, not with what we now know. For their sake and for the greater good, we can strengthen our pupils' resilience in our schools.

If reparatory sensitivity is what is needed, then our

really helps the adult 'learn the child' and learn about themselves. It is a very respectful, positive and hopeful way of working on sensitive areas where the adult is left feeling empowered and having the sense that they can make a massive difference to whatever it is they hope for in their relationship with the child.

AVIG UK focusses on what they consider to be the five principles of attunement: being attentive, encouraging initiatives, receiving initiatives, developing attuned interactions, guiding and supporting

When they watch the video, the adult who has been filmed is asked what they notice, and they are supported to scan the footage for any instances of those five elements. According to Kate Miller at Connected Moments (*see* **Useful Organisations**) the five principles can be broken down, as shown here.

5 Key Principles of Attunement

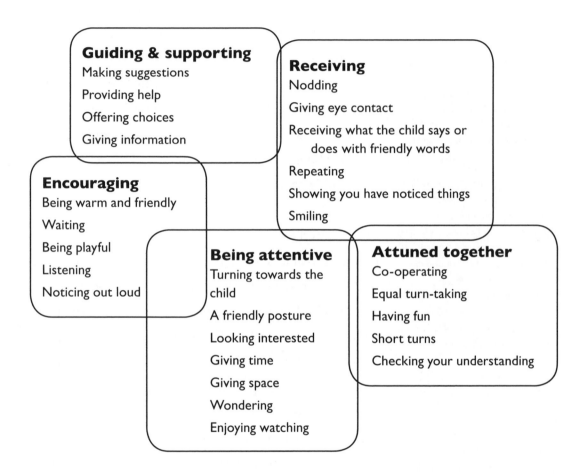

Guiding & supporting
Making suggestions
Providing help
Offering choices
Giving information

Receiving
Nodding
Giving eye contact
Receiving what the child says or
      does with friendly words
Repeating
Showing you have noticed things
Smiling

Encouraging
Being warm and friendly
Waiting
Being playful
Listening
Noticing out loud

Being attentive
Turning towards the
child
A friendly posture
Looking interested
Giving time
Giving space
Wondering
Enjoying watching

Attuned together
Co-operating
Equal turn-taking
Having fun
Short turns
Checking your understanding

With kind permission of Kate Miller (personal communication)

Before we go on any further, have a look at these five lists and highlight the areas in which you think you're already strong, in green, and those that you are not so practised at, in orange. See which ones you think you don't do much of at all, yet. Be curious about this. How come you've learned to relate this way? Where or from whom did you learn that? When interacting with traumatised children and young people, be mindful which of these elements you're using, and be intentional about practising small teams (of additional attachment figures) need to be practising attunement, responsiveness, sensitivity and repair whenever possible, and especially at times of relationship ruptures, relational mismatches and dysregulation. We have an ethical responsibility with what we know and must act on this.

Successful regulation accumulates into regulatory resilience, which emerges during early development from successful coping with the inherent stress in typical interactions. These quotidian stressful events lead to activation of behavioural and physiological systems. Stress that is effectively resolved in the short run and with reiteration over the long term increases children's, as well as adults', capacity to cope with the more intense stressors. (ibid. p. 124)

Our pupils can't manage this alone. They need us to get alongside them and facilitate the necessary regulation, relationship, reason and repair together with them, which they need in order to navigate this hugely important developmental task; and in order to grow resilience, so that they can recover and function well at home, in school and out in their wider communities.

some of the orange ones, to find out what that's like, in the interests of becoming more attuned. You can also practise attunement with colleagues, partners, friends and strangers, and learn a lot about yourself in the process - there's no limit to where attunement has value! And it's important we're curious about why we ourselves do or don't do whatever we do, before we can be wholly curious about the children in our care. Self-reflection of this kind is never wasted.

VIG SESSIONS

If at all possible, I strongly recommend asking someone who is trained as a VIG guider to get alongside you and the child or young person you're working or living with, to facilitate VIG. Encouragingly, in Scotland, an attunement profile which draws on adapted attunement principles as developed by AVIGUK, is now being used in schools. It allows all education staff to explore how they attune to the pupils in their care, with each other and together with parents/carers (education.gov.scot, 2017). So whether you are a member of Team Pupil or a parent/carer, this would be so worthwhile. VIG guiders can support you to identify the quality moments where you are truly connecting with the child or young person, and they with you, using the indicators listed above. This is not only encouraging, but can also serve as a reminder of what *is* possible and what *might* be possible: yes, even in those difficult parts of the recovery journey together (*and please see contact details for* AVIG UK *in* Useful Organisations). In Scotland, as part of GIRFEC (Getting It Right For Every Child), adapted attunement principles as developed by AVIG are being used within whole school nurturing approaches (2017 Education Scotland).

Attuning to states of being

Attunement involves being observant and responding. Babette Rothschild's extremely helpful chart (Rothschild 2017, p. 121) gives helpful clues as to what body cues to look out for, to help identify what state an individual might be in. By 'state' I am referring to what Perry (2017) describes as, *calm, alert, alarm, fear or terror.* Let's remember that the different states relate to the three different systems that Porges refers to as the social engagement system, the fight/flight system and the freeze system. Being at ease or at rest, calm and alert, can activate social engagement (associated with *play, care and seeking/being curious*) (three of Panksepp's emotional systems, p. 66). External and internal stressors can activate threat responses such as *fear, rage or grief* which tend to be associated with *social disengagement.* So if we are going to engage in *state-dependent interventions*, (that is, choosing our interventions according to our recognition of which part of the nervous system is 'driving' the pupil and underpinning the state they are in) as opposed to a one size fits all approach, then we're going to need to really know what we might see as characteristic of each state.

CALM state	The pupil is in the neo cortex area of the brain, and can think abstractly. They can consider the past, present and future and have a sense of extended time.
ALERT state	The pupil is in the sub cortex area of the brain and can think concretely. They can consider past, present and the immediate future and have a sense of hours and days.

ALARM state	The pupil is in the limbic area of the brain and can consider the past but the present only in terms of hours and minutes. They are emotional, and their capacity for thought is reduced.
FEAR state	The pupil is in the mid area of the brain and can consider the past to an extent and the present only in terms of minutes and seconds. They are reactive and their capacity for thought is significantly reduced.
TERROR state	The pupil is in the brain stem and has lost access to their sense of where they are in time and space. They are reflexive and are no longer thinking.

drawing on Hambrick & Brawner 2017

For example, if the pupil we are working with is in a socially *disengaged* system - fight/flight/freeze - then we can intentionally activate safety and inner nurturing which can start the process of enabling them to access their social engagement system. Lots more on how we do this in the following chapters, but for now, in a really simple way, you can try it on yourself! When you are out of sorts, try:

♥ Stroking a pet ♥ Gazing at a picture of someone close ♥ Giving yourself a firm, gentle hug ♥
♥ Turning the temperature up so it is warm ♥ Wagging your eyebrows! ♥
♥ Smiling ♥ Changing your body posture, standing or sitting with open hands ♥
♥ Deliberately breathing slowly ♥ Meditating ♥ Having a massage ♥
♥ Mindfully eating (gentle chewing activates the ventral vagal) ♥ Asking for a hug ♥

Ian & Ross (2011-2012) p. 10, Fig. 6

We must learn the pupils that we teach. We need to observe the cues that can tell us what state they are in so that what we do to support them into learning can be state-dependent. I don't know whether it's because I have one (whose name is Maisie), but I do think dogs make it very obvious what state they are in. Dogs allow us to think very visually about the different parts of the nervous system. So using the visual of a dog, let's consider the states again, building on what we learned in the **Respecting Biology** chapter.

State dependent interventions

Know the stage (developmental) and watch the state (of regulation).

Perry 2020, p. 148.

For our purposes in education, I've simplified and adapted some elements from Rothschild's chart (2016/2017) - and added some dogs that remind me of Maisie in different moods! (*see overleaf and perhaps read alongside* pp. 104-9). The body gives us so many visual cues about what part of their nervous system is in operation (and you can ask simple questions, for example regarding temperature, for example of hands). Once we're mindful of the pupil's state, we can decide how to respond.

By the way: I am not at all implying we continue telling our pupils to 'calm down' to change their states - but rather support them through state dependent interventions! All being told to 'calm down' does is to exacerbate the state they are in, often moving them further down into lower regions of the brain, where connection with others is lost. We must 'actively' listen, so they feel 'heard'. Feeling heard in this way gives a sense of being respected and valued. We can give them feedback about what we can see going on with their bodies as well, in a non-judgemental, un-intrusive way, open and willing to be corrected if they say we're wrong, but maintaining our position of concern and care. This not only communicates that you can 'hear' them but that you're also willing to support the growth of their own self-awareness. So that one day, they'll be able to tune into their own body cues and know what to do to support themselves. Until that day, let's get alongside and attune …

Once we know the territory we find ourselves in, when a pupil has experienced attachment disruption or relational trauma, and we are practising attunement, knowing

ADAPTED FROM ROTHSCHILD (2016/17)	PRIMARY STATE	AROUSAL	MUSCLES	EYE AREA	SKIN TONE	HANDS & FEET	CONTACT WITH SELF & OTHERS
LETHARGIC							
Parasympathetic I	Apathy	Low	Slack	Pupils smaller, lids may be heavy	Variable	May be warm or cold	Withdrawn
Lee (8) slumped over his desk. *Molly (14) sat curled up in the corner of the library.*							
STATE DEPENDENT INTERVENTION: activate by gently increasing energy levels							
CALM							
Parasympathetic II	Safe, clear thinking, social engagement	Low	Relaxed/toned	Pupils smaller, eyes moist, eye lids relaxed	Rosy hue, despite skin colour	Warm	Likely
Lee (8) sitting up, smiling and chatting playfully with his friend Bill sitting next to him. *Molly (14) sitting in her chair talking and laughing with her Key Adult.*							
STATE DEPENDENT INTERVENTION: continue teaching							
ALERT							
Sympathetic I	Alert, ready to act	Moderate	Toned	Pupils widening, eyes less moist, eyelids toned	Less rosy hue, despite skin colour	Cool	Possible
Lee (8) looking at his book with a puzzled expression trying to work something out. *Molly (14) with her hand up, asking a very relevant and helpful question.*							
STATE DEPENDENT INTERVENTION: continue teaching							

ALARM Fight/Flight

Sympathetic II	React to danger	High	Tense	Pupils very dilated, eyes dry, eyelids tensed/raised	Pale hue, despite skin colour	Cold	Limited

Lee (8) Increased fidgeting and then gets up to pace the class room
Molly (14) Asks to go to the toilet as she feels unwell

STATE DEPENDENT INTERVENTION: Put on the brakes by switching to a sensory intervention

FEAR

Sympathetic III	Await opportunity to escape	Extreme overload	Rigid (deer in headlights)	Pupils very small or dilated, eyes very dry, lids very tense	May be pale and/or flushed	Extremes of hot and cold	Not likely

Lee (8) starts climbing the furniture to get out of one of the higher, bigger windows, completely oblivious that he is putting himself in danger
Molly (14) throws open the classroom door and then throws herself down the stairs, risk taking but without much consciousness, laughing manically at the bottom.

STATE DEPENDENT INTERVENTION: Slam on the brakes by switching to a grounding intervention

TERROR hypo freeze

Parasympathetic III	Body is closing down	Excessive overwhelm induces hypo-arousal	Flaccid	Lids drooping, eyes closed or open and fixed	Noticeably pale	Cold	Impossible

Lee (8) is frozen to the spot staring, seeming oblivious to all going on around him
Molly (14) faints in the corridor

STATE DEPENDENT INTERVENTION: medical emergency, call paramedics

Please note: This state appears in Rothschild's chart. She is referring to an extreme and exceptionally rare instance of when the body starts to shut down. Death itself is rarely reached. The worst I have come across in a school context in relation to this state was a secondary pupil going into flight, running out into a corridor and then collapsing; paramedics had to be called, and she recovered well. I'm including this so we are all aware that under what are perceived to be extreme conditions, our nervous systems can override everything if significantly overwhelmed: medical attention is required (this is what Porges refers to as the vagal paradox, see p. 110) what to look for, so our interventions can be state-dependent, we can move on to the order of *when* best to use our interventions and what these might be! I'll be addressing that in the next section on key learning from Dr Bruce Perry, and introducing the structure of the rest of this book.

With this approach, differentiated discipline becomes an integral part of learning how to settle to learn in school, learning how to self-regulate. It's not a brick wall to crash into - or through, in the case of exclusion - if, because of what has happened to you, and how it's adversely affected your development when no-one fully attuned to you or your needs, you go off course.

A NOTE ON THE WORK OF DR BRUCE PERRY

The regulatory networks that originate in lower brain areas have widespread impact on upstream systems in the brain and downstream stems in the body.   Perry & Ablon 2019, p. 15

I am deeply grateful to Dr Bruce Perry for everything I've learned from his published works, his clips online and his talks in the UK. His work has significantly impacted my practice for more than a decade. Something that I will never forget from one of his talks many years ago was the need for all our interventions to be:

Rhythmic

Relevant

Relational

Repetitive

Respectful

Rewarding

As a practitioner, these 6 Rs have become the core elements of all my work out in schools and with families. Dr Perry went on to develop the much respected Neurosequential Model®, that offers cost-effective ways to integrate core concepts of developmental psychology and neurobiology into practice and can provide the necessary ingredients for a

... neuroscience directed, intentional and effective trauma informed intervention,   Perry & Ablon 2019, p. 30

This is the umbrella for the three interrelated programs that he has created:

- NMT®   Neurosequential Model of Therapeutics
- NME®   Neurosequential Model of Education
- NMC®   Neurosequential Model of Caregiving

There is extensive training available through the Child Trauma Academy (see **Useful Organisations**) in each of these three models. In brief, a web-based assessment tool called NMT® Metrics (Hambrick & Brawner, 2017) maps out a child's history including both the ACEs and what he refers to as the Relational Health factors that the child has lived through and with. Those using Perry's models create online 'brain maps' using this information (web based NMT® Clinical Practice Tools application). They help create an estimate of both the timing and the severity of possible risk around the child, because it's not only important what someone has lived through but *when* specific experiences happened, and whether there was anyone around to buffer those experiences in some way. For example, a child who has lived through and with emotional abuse with their birth mother from the age of two onwards, but may have had a really nurturing grandmother and a couple of very responsive teachers at some point along their life journey, may not be considered as much at risk as someone who experienced neglect from pregnancy onwards and there was no-one in their possible support network who was actively present to attune to and respond to their needs.

The information gleaned from these brain maps guides *'the selection and sequencing of developmentally appropriate (and age-acceptable) interventions.'* (Perry 2020, p. 144). All the interventions are intentionally designed to duplicate what should have happened first time around, in other words, moving up from the brainstem sequentially into the higher regions of the brain. This is also referred to as a 'bottom up' approach. Please read the grid from the bottom line going upwards, ie bottom up, so you're following the sequence of the brain's development, from most primitive to most sophisticated.

Function	Part of brain	Location	How we can be
Reason	Pre-frontal cortex	Top floor!	Reflective
Relate	Emotional/limbic brain area	Ground floor!	Reactive
Regulate	Brain stem area	Basement!	Reflexive

Perry (2020) states that preliminary data received from schools where those trained in NME® have been working are very promising. I haven't trained in NME® as yet myself but have completed the first excellent introductory day, and plan to do more (you might also wish to consider doing so).

> Many report fewer critical incidents, increased attendance, fewer teacher sick days and improved standardised test scores.   (*ibid* p. 150)

Interventions

Perry & Albon (2019) state that most interventions with these children and young people tend to use top down approaches, in other words, getting immediately cognitive. I can second this, in both the education and therapy contexts where I've worked over the years. We're far too quick within education to attempt to engage the pre-frontal cortex, the thinking brain! They go on to describe how in order to respect biology, a bottom up approach is necessary, as described here,

> Any effective approach must instead follow this sequence of engagement: regulate, relate, and then reason. One must start by regulating the youth (a brain stem activity) before the youth will be ready to engage relationally (a midbrain level activity), before they can finally be invited to reason (a cortical activity) to try to solve a problem collaboratively. *If one violates this sequence or does it out of order, it is unlikely that there will be access to the cortex.*
> Perry & Ablon (2019, p.26 [my emphasis]

They explore why so much attunement is needed, so that if a pupil becomes dysregulated at any point the teacher needs to circle back and re-regulate the pupil, rather than merely continuing on regardless. That 'sensitivity to, and adjustment for, an individual child's stress tolerance is critical' (*ibid* p. 25). That's why there's a chapter on the art of attunement in this book, and you'll find the word cropping up a lot as well!

When we encourage teachers through training in attachment aware, trauma responsive practice to interpret what they see through a trauma lens, it creates more opportunity for growth in the pupil. There are benefits for the teacher too, as it helps to remind us not to take the behaviour personally. We recognise that these pupils are haunted by ghosts of the past and have developmental vulnerabilities as a result of this past. We can see how we get caught in the pupil's time warp, rather than being on the receiving end of something thought through and premeditated in the cortical regions of the brain. This understanding enables us to support ourselves to remain regulated - to be calm and focussed around our traumatised pupils. Regulated teachers bring calm, as opposed to further chaos, in an already shaken-up mind and body of a previously traumatised pupil.

> Viewing challenging behaviour through a compassionate rather than an affronted lens helps adults access their cortexes when responding to such behaviour.   Perry & Ablon 2019, p. 29

The best practice for learning

Perry (2020) believes there is the possibility of a school creating therapeutic opportunities throughout a school day, if the school is trauma informed and the education staff understand the impact of relational trauma and loss (p. 147). He recommends sensory breaks before cognitive tasks, not just at the end of the day, but at regular intervals, five minutes here, ten minutes there, teaching in between. The NMT® recommendation process starts with considering who is around a child or young person because 'the quality and permanence of this relational milieu is one of the most essential elements of successful outcomes' (*cited in* Perry, 2020, p. 147). He goes on to comment that ' ... the best predictor of current functioning in youth is current relational health, not history of adversity' (p. 149).

Perry & Ablon (2019) describe how educating and changing a brain to learn social thinking skills, attention skills or flexibility is always best achieved within a rich, relational context together with primary (for example with their parents or carers) *or* additional attachment figures, like education staff who have a strong connection already with the children and young people (p.21). The importance of togetherness, relationship and collaboration, is critical. So this is why creating Team Pupil is such a big part of this kind of work in our schools. And interestingly empathy, through the use of reassurance and reflective listening, is viewed as a means of regulation.

In terms of discipline, Perry & Ablon (2019) describe how we must always avoid the use of power and control, and use regulatory strategies instead. This is what most of this book is about - regulation and relationship. They point out how any kind of learning requires predictable, patterned and repetitive interactions and that any trauma informed approach must allow the pupil some element of control. Perry (2020) goes on to add anything that is primarily rhythmic, repetitive and sensory, listing music, dance, yoga, drumming and various sports, can be included as regulatory interventions which could provide this.

So in the rest of this book we're going to explore bottom up approaches: because even though it might seem appealing to go for top down approaches in education, because we want these pupils to think and to reason with us, we *must* respect their biology, in terms of the right order to reach their thinking and reasoning.

IN SUMMARY the best way to reach these particular pupils is by using the neurosequential order mapped out by Dr. Perry, that of **Regulate**, **Relate** and **Reason**. Dr Perry brings in a fourth intervention called *reflect* at the **Reason** level. However, I'm going to add in **Repair** as my fourth **R**, at the **Reason** level, for the times we need to teach behaviour (discipline), and there is a need for a restorative opportunity. I find this **R** very helpful in supporting our traumatised pupils who battle with toxic shame. And from time to time, we'll need to go back to **Regulate** again, before progressing; we can change states at any time, so we need to keep attuning to which part of the nervous system is operating from moment to moment. So perhaps we could most helpfully think of it like a circle, with the possibility of going back to an earlier stage where necessary - you'll see these circles at the start of each of the next chapters.

I'll be integrating Perry's recommended principles and practices with everything I've been learning from both frontline experience in education in the UK as well as current research. And you'll find first-hand evidence on the effectiveness of this way of working from educational professionals throughout the book, as well as more direct comments from the children and young people we all want to support.

Are you up for thinking differently, and experimenting with your current practice? If so, you really are reading the right book! Our traumatised pupils don't need more of the same. They need something different. So here we go.

Chapter 6

A Way of Soothing **Regulate**

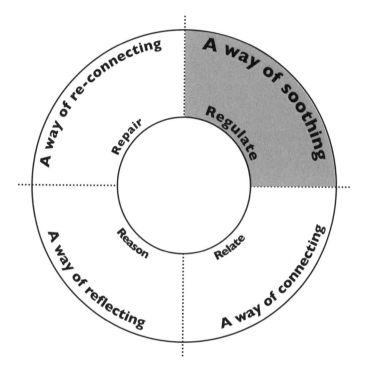

Sadly our educational systems, as well as many of the methods that profess to treat trauma, tend to bypass this emotional engagement system and focus instead on recruiting the cognitive capacities of the mind. Despite the well-documented effects of anger, fear, and anxiety on the ability to reason, many programs continue to ignore the need to engage the safety system of the brain before trying to promote new ways of thinking. The last things that should be cut from school schedules are [choir], physical education, recess and anything else involving movement, play and joyful engagement.   Van der Kolk 2015, p. 349

We can alter the caregiving environment so that it will appear - and be - safer for children and less likely to evoke mobilisation or immobilisation responses ... We can also intervene directly with children, exercising the neural regulation of brain structures, stimulating the neural regulation of the social engagement system, and encouraging positive social behaviour.   Porges 2004, p. 24

The art of regulation

I believe that **Regulation** is the essential **R** for laying down firm, secure 'foundations' when we're working generally with traumatised children and young people, and especially at times of crisis. We need to give them regular, relational experiences with us day to day which are regulating, in order to teach the pupils in our care who have experienced toxic stress, ways to soothe and quieten the lower parts of their brains. They need the experience first through co-regulation, and then, over time, they will learn how to self-regulate.

We know that these pupils are going to have developmental vulnerabilities in the area of regulation; so our responsibility is to get skilled up in this area so we can be preventative in moderating the level of stress the pupil is experiencing at any one time, to give them space to learn. Rather than carrying on regardless and the pupil experiencing the pressure cooker effect later on in the school day or in the family home, having to bear the brunt of the stress build-up on their own, manifesting in behavioural difficulties, let's ensure there are sensory breaks integrated throughout the school day. This will protect the dignity of the pupil and will make all our lives a lot easier. I honestly think if we truly applied this principle, our exclusion levels in the UK would be dramatically reduced. Are you up for the challenge?! What is there to lose? We have *everything* to gain, on behalf of the pupil's future education trajectory and for the wellbeing of the whole school community and of course the family.

I've learned how important it is that traumatised children and young people understand what's going on inside themselves, through some psycho-education. Louisa Aspden's '*Help! I've got an alarm in my head*' (2016) is really useful: we give it out to every child and young person we work with in TouchBase.

And the time to start learning these skills is not when dysregulation is at sky-high levels. The time to lay down new neural pathways so that our pupils can begin to know what calm actually *feels* like, is when a crisis is *not* happening. After all, it would be bonkers to practise fire drills during an actual fire ...

That way, when things *are* getting heated, those pathways will be increasingly more accessible and we'll be in a better position to help our pupils move toward them. Until that happens, until we are confident that they actually know how to calm themselves down and regain self-control, we need to differentiate our emotional and social tasks and expectations, when these pupils are presenting with challenging behaviour. Because when it comes to those moments of challenging behaviour that might otherwise invite zero tolerance discipline, co-regulation, together with us, their core team of education staff, is the only biology-respecting way forwards.

The difference this makes | **EVIDENCE FROM PRACTICE**

With regards to regulation ideas for some of the youngest children, who have experienced early childhood trauma (and are not yet ready to allow their adult to lead them into their sensory integration recommendations), we have found we need to be more creative. Heavy work tasks around the school (such as sweeping, hoovering, cleaning windows or tables, emptying bins, collecting the post, delivering fruit or errands, setting up the dinner tables and sorting supplies etc) are incorporated throughout the day to provide the calming sensory breaks, whilst boosting self esteem too.

Similarly, for the most stressed of our young children, key adults observe them carefully for any brain-stem calmer activities they are seen to already engage in. Very often children will intuitively engage in repetitive, rhythmic activities which can then be consciously woven into their day and enjoyed by both the child and their key adult! Activities such as, playing percussion instruments, listening to music, singing, dancing, trampoline, bikes, space hoppers, climbing, sorting tasks, winding masking tape around cardboard tubes, colouring, cutting/sticking, hammering, walking, rocking, hole punching etc.

Daniel Thrower, CEO & Attachment Lead, Anne Oakley,
SEND & Attachment Lead at The Wensum Trust, Norfolk

> One of ours uses white noise from a website in a room with sensory bits and pieces in. For example, hanging over a gym ball for ten minutes or so. He is then able to settle back into class.
>
> Attachment Lead, Brighton

> Sensory circuits in the morning and after lunch really sets the pupil up for the morning/ afternoon.
>
> Attachment Lead, Brighton

> Using the tricycle outdoors gives him a sensory experience that regulates him.
>
> Attachment Lead, Brighton

Child trauma expert Dr Bruce Perry has enabled us to understand that the brain is like a layer cake, developing from the bottom up, inside out, and that to respect biology we must honour this order in all our interventions with traumatised children and young people. So let's look at how to reach and connect with a pupil's brain stem and mid brain, whilst things are going haywire: with the sensory motor brain first, the deep centres where unconscious, defensive, primitive responses kick in. The way we'll do this is by offering soothing comfort and reassurance, not just with our words but with all kinds of sensory communication, the only way to make genuine contact with our pupil when this particular part of the brain is driving their behaviour. This first step will form a crucial part of our differentiated discipline practices - such a very different approach from going in with immediate sanctions.

The psychology of trauma is complex. Physiology is relatively simple. In trauma, the old parts of the brain are fixed in defence systems of fight, flight or freeze, as we've discussed. As Van der Kolk states, 'in order to change, people need to become aware of their sensations and the way their bodies interact with the world around them. Physical self-awareness is the first step in releasing the tyranny of the past' (2015, p. 101).

So in this chapter we'll be looking at what tells us we need to provide regulation: what we need to do, and then particular evidence-based activities we can use to support children and young people to become grounded and present, so that they can sense their own body in the present time and space. We'll explore how to support health and wellbeing (including through diet and exercise), and then we'll move onto more detail as to what this looks like in practice in our various settings.

Signs of dysregulation in our classrooms and corridors

Firstly, let's consider the bodily signs of dysregulation, how we can tell it's going on and what to look out for presenting itself through hyper-arousal, hypo-arousal or a mix of the two, breathing difficulties, listening difficulties and through the expression of physical ailments.

> Let's consider Lee. Zipping about the classroom. Can't sit still. Into everything. Opening drawers. Pulling items out. Climbing onto the ledge to shout through the top window to someone outside. Fingers in sockets …
> Are you exhausted yet? I can assure you I am!
>
> And Katie. Slumped over her desk. Poor postural control. Very still. Almost porcelain doll-like. A stare and a painted-on smile when you go near. Sluggish in her movements. Taking ages to do anything. Are you frustrated yet? I am!
>
> Or Adnan who one minute is whizzing backwards and forwards, ducking and diving as if wanting to play a game of chase with the teacher and then collapsed in a heap in the reading area, almost listless and then up and about again laughing manically and using big movements to connect with his peers.
> Are you confused and finding it hard to think clearly? I am!
>
> Zoe is staring ahead. There is a sadness and a heaviness about her. From looking like she is holding her breath she starts panting and then before you know it she has had a full blown panic attack.

Zach doesn't ever seem to hear what you're saying. He seems completely oblivious and you find yourself repeating yourself on numerous occasions which is infuriating. He seems to hear everything else that isn't relevant in the classroom context, for example the tap being turned on next door or the bird singing in the trees!

Bashid is complaining of tummy ache and aches and pains in his legs. He is yawning loads but when you ask him how he slept last night he says fine. You've started wondering whether there's a link between his yawns and his anxiety levels, as you've noticed they seem to increase when there's some independent writing to do.

Lots to notice but difficult to manage, eh? Even harder if we have no understanding of the impact of trauma and loss and and their impact on the body. From the examples above I'm sure you can see how easily some of these behaviours might have been read as:

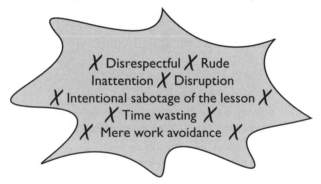

X Disrespectful X Rude
Inattention X Disruption
X Intentional sabotage of the lesson X
X Time wasting X
X Mere work avoidance X

I could go on but I'm sure you get the idea! These behaviours could easily lead to disciplinary measures in schools. Many of our pupils are misinterpreted due to a lack of understanding and training in this area.

The body and mind are entirely interwoven aspects of each other, and their innumerable elements constitute a complex adaptive system.   Rose 2016, p. 8

Issues presented in class - pupils' bodies communicating dysregulation

WHAT'S HAPPENING	WHAT WE NOTICE
*HYPER-AROUSAL	This is when we observe an increase in energy levels. Some might describe the child or young person as seeming quite 'hyper'. There is usually a lot of movement: for example the pupil can't sit still but is wriggling around, is getting up and about and so on.
*HYPO-AROUSAL	This is when we observe a decrease in energy levels. Some might describe the child or young person as quite 'flat'. There isn't much movement, for example the pupil might remain in one spot and seem unable to do anything.
*A COMBO	This is when the child or young person moves in between hyper and hypo arousal presentations as described above, in quick succession.
*BREATHING DIFFICULTIES	This is when the child or young person breathes rapidly, maybe even hyper-ventilating, catches their breath, feels they can't breathe or has shallow breathing. (*Obviously do take breathing difficulties very seriously, checking in with a health practitioner if usual breathing doesn't quickly resume).
*LISTENING DIFFICULTIES	The middle ear muscles don't function properly when a pupil is dysregulated. Without functioning middle ear muscles these pupils are hypersensitive to low frequencies (background) sounds. They have difficulties prioritising the human voice. Auditory hypersensitivities are commonly associated with trauma histories.
*PHYSICAL AILMENTS	The body can groan in all kinds of ways when a pupil is dysregulated.

Trauma comes to the medical room

I believe one common misunderstanding in schools highlights the need for education staff to understand the impact of trauma and Polyvagal Theory as essential to our practice. A few of my students complain regularly of aches and pains, particularly stomach ache. They tell me during their therapy sessions how often they've been turned away from medical rooms, HOY rooms, student services and inclusion bases, or told they are time-wasters. But they're adamant that they really do have aches and pains. They complain of what they experience as staff insensitivity, in commanding them back to class with exasperated looks and impatient tones, or at worse, punishment.

It would make sense if these particular students have aches and pains. They have lived through and with such toxic stress. Far too many have a high number of ACEs. Their nervous system has been left all shaken up. The enteric or intrinsic nervous system (ENS) is known as the brain of the gut or the *second brain* (Society Neuroscience, 2018). This is because it can act independently of the brain and spinal cord, the central nervous system (CNS). It evolved *before* the CNS. Did you know that this gut area has the largest collection of neurons found in the body outside the brain? Fascinating. It gives endless feedback to our brains. It's increasingly being understood as a very significant organ in processing our emotions and contributing to our 'intuition'. So we need to take stomach issues especially seriously for our traumatised pupils who have experienced or are living with toxic stress. As Van der Kolk states (2015), referring to adults,

> Traumatised people chronically feel unsafe inside their bodies. The past is alive in the form of gnawing interior discomfort, their bodies are constantly bombarded by visceral warning signs, and in an attempt to control these processes, they often become expert at ignoring their gut feelings and in numbing awareness of what is playing out inside. They learn to hide from their selves.   p. 96

Children and young people are often more in touch with their 'gut feelings' than we are as adults. So let's support them to stay open to trying to read their own body cues, as this is the healthiest response in the journey towards recovery.

As we saw in the **Respecting Biology** chapter, the vagus nerve connects the guts and the brain: 90% of the information collected there goes upwards from the gut to the head. It's largely the guts that inform the brain, *not the other way around*. This has implications for whether behaviour is intentional or non-intentional, directed by or resulting from something sensed/felt or thought. So let's be respectful and take expressions of discomfort seriously, and indeed, empathically.

In addition to emotional dysregulation expressing itself somatically, there are now hard facts about heightened propensity to illness for children and adults with a high number of ACEs. Karlen, a Swedish researcher (*in* Burke-Harris 2018, p. 73) looking at children or young people with three or more exposures to early toxic stress, found an increase in cortisol levels and more susceptibility to colds, stomach flu and other viral infections. Burke-Harris (2018) also correlates toxic stress to increased inflammation and hypersensitivity for example, allergies, eczema and asthma and even auto-immune disease. So we need to take physical ailments seriously in schools rather than assuming these children and young people are time-wasting complaining of their physical ailments. It's clear that those impacted by ACEs often experience compromised mental health and wellbeing, and a compromised immune system.

Our traumatised pupils lacked sensitive, attuned and responsive care, so they need a double dose now; in order to experience protective buffering, so that they're not thoughts afterwards. This process is too fast for conscious thought.

Look at the impact of a still face (p. 47) - a perfect example of the body taking precedence over the brain and the pupil becoming dysregulated. That young woman doesn't feel comfortable in busy, public spaces with the possibility of unpredictability and noise. Imagine this same young adult in a busy corridor at school in between lessons: the chaos of those times is a recipe for disaster.

We had to work on quietening these alarms going off inside her body in order to support her to function well. The only way we could do that was through sensory input. If I were to attempt to get cognitive, and to tell her to think it all through in her brain, she would have given me an incredulous, disparaging look: '*What? You have no idea!*' If she'd understood the brain science, she would have explained that it wasn't a matter of willpower, of making the right choice. She would tell me it ran deep. That her mind was reading her body. It was *so* powerful, she had actually felt at the mercy of her body response a lot of the time.

at potential risk of the more serious and life-threatening diseases at a later stage of life. In addition to appropriate medical care, understanding and empathy go a long way to soothe, calm and contain minds and bodies.

I also advocate that these students need us to offer healthy, sensory comfort options to soothe and calm these pains and aches for themselves. I know of a colleague who is already being proactive in this, offering blankets to be wrapped in, hot water bottles, hot drinks or menthol rub and ice packs. Having a supply of simple things of this kind in school is such an investment for these students, costing so very little. Sensory comfort goes a long way to support and soothe bodies.

I'm not saying keep these pupils in the medical room all day long. But assessment and acknowledgement of what might be happening, and some communication of the kindness and nurture these students need in order to recover from what they have previously experienced - novelty surprising the brain - is what's needed now. Surely this must be part and parcel of how all our staff treat all our pupils?

So let's engage in quality moments, through which our traumatised pupils feel seen and heard and where they experience us validating, not discounting, their experience:

'*Your body is trying to tell us something; I wonder what that might be?*'

What messages are we communicating to our pupils and students when we engage in mind-body interventions in this kind of way?

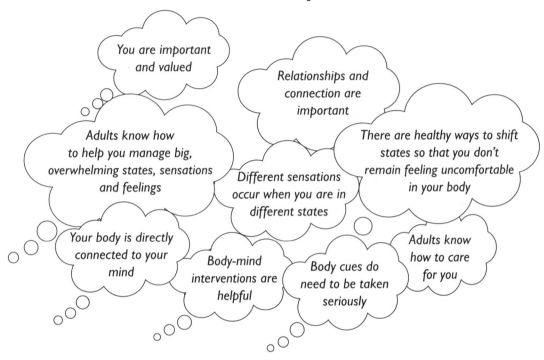

You are important and valued

Relationships and connection are important

Adults know how to help you manage big, overwhelming states, sensations and feelings

There are healthy ways to shift states so that you don't remain feeling uncomfortable in your body

Different sensations occur when you are in different states

Your body is directly connected to your mind

Body-mind interventions are helpful

Body cues do need to be taken seriously

Adults know how to care for you

What might we be preventing?

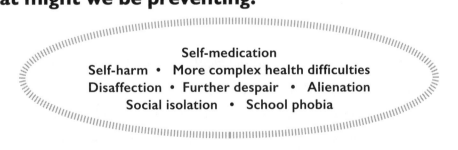

Self-medication
Self-harm • More complex health difficulties
Disaffection • Further despair • Alienation
Social isolation • School phobia

Many of the older students I support are not aware of what's going on in their bodies, never mind their minds! I'll never forget a student hitting his arm whilst he told me cheerfully that he 'was over' his dad's mistreatment of him. He had no idea what he was doing with his arm until I pointed this out (gently and sensitively), much to his

> Our bodies can override our thinking. In fact the bodies are the epicentre for thinking! So we really need to understand this if we are going to effectively work with pupils who have experienced trauma and loss. We must get to grips with the science!
>
> *The brain is body, as are the nervous, hormonal, muscular, digestive, circularity, and respiratory systems; all of which being mechanically and energetically responsive and adaptive in times of emotional conflict or trauma, individually and systemically.*
>
> *Rose 2016, p.7*

surprise! Let's not assume all our pupils are 'grounded'. When a child or young person comes to me with an ache or a pain, it seems to me that this is an educative opportunity too good to miss.

Surely we need to be supporting them to tune in to their bodies and their minds: isn't this half the battle? If we can encourage self-awareness and collaborative action, then we can support our students to take alternative pathways towards health and wellbeing. Then they'll be in a position to thrive, not to be at the mercy of toxic stress. If we want our pupils to be in control of themselves, and calm, we need to help them know what this means and how to do it. It's really not rocket science!

Let's look at how we can help quieten and soothe the lower parts of our pupils' brains, so that we can support our pupils to deactivate their constant alarms going off, in response to the threats they believe surround them.

Picture one of your traumatised pupils: the different outcomes there could be for that pupil going to the medical room: being given a kind word and a hot water bottle, or being told off.

Which is going to help them more, short term and long term?

Which will help them to better tune into their needs?

Help them trust adults?

Help them actually get back to learning?

HEALTH: SIX MAIN AREAS REQUIRING SPECIAL ATTENTION WHEN A PUPIL HAS A HIGH NUMBER OF ACES AND OTHER RELATIONAL TRAUMAS AND LOSSES

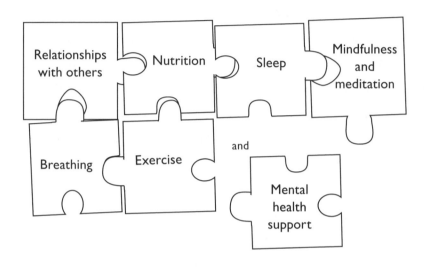

I'm going to outline why each of these is so important and what we can do. Then you'll find a **Living Well** template to use with your pupils to start planning for going forward together.

RELATIONSHIP WITH OTHERS

First and foremost and respecting biology, we need to ensure these children and young people have strong, relational buffering, initially with adults, to receive regulation. For several years now I've been supporting educational staff to do this by creating a team of four of five members of school staff around each pupil: we call it Team Pupil.

The key person in this team encouraged to form the strongest attachment to the child or young person (apart from their family or carers) is the 1:1 Teaching Assistant or mentor, the Key Adult (*my Attachment Aware Schools Series,* Bombèr 2016-17, *outlines and boundaries the different, unique roles and relationships of everyone in this team*). Name your team (with the pupil). Take a photo of the team. Meet together as a team. Do something special as a team together with the child or young person, for example share a snack or lunch together every now and then. Re-group as a team to remind the pupil through actual relational experience (not just in words, or in a text etc) that you are all there as *their supporters* (more on deepening and enriching these relationships in the next chapter, **Relate).**

NUTRITION

Burke-Harris (2018) explains how higher cortisol levels that result from toxic stress drive children and adolescents to crave high sugar and high fat foods. She recommends making some changes to their diet, substituting lean proteins and complex carbohydrates instead, describing how this can improve the body's ability to regulate itself, boosting the immune system and improving brain function.

What we eat and drink and when can really impact our bodies and minds. Dr Marilyn Glenville, a leading UK nutritionist, talks of the significance of nutritional psychology/psychiatry, stating that 'diet is an important modifiable risk factor for mental health' (2019). She describes what can impact us for better or for worse, and how particular aspects of diet can actually enhance mental health and wellbeing if the child/adult has experienced toxic stress as a result of trauma and loss. She outlines how mental and physical health are fundamentally connected, and how nutrition has the potential to influence the impact of trauma. At the International Congress of Attachment and Trauma in London, November 2019, she stated:

Oxidative stress, inflammation and changes in the gut microbiome are some of the physical effects of stress which can be reduced by changes in the diet. Prolonged stress can deplete the body of essential nutrients and using nutritional support can combat the negative effects of stress. Also the chronic activation of the fight/flight response can be reduced by changes in patterns of eating, food choices and timing of food.

Glenville is running a clinical trial at this time to continue researching in this important area. Habits having a negative impact on our mental health and wellbeing may include:

- Eating a lot of processed foods
- Eating a lot of carbohydrates and sugary foods and drinks
- Not drinking enough water
- Not having breakfast

And habits having positive impact on mental health and wellbeing may include:

- ✔ Eating breakfast
- ✔ Drinking plenty of water regularly
- ✔ Eating a good mix of fruit and vegetables of different colours
- ✔ Vitamins including: B vitamins especially vitamins B5, B6, B12, vitamins C and D
- ✔ Minerals - magnesium and chromium
- ✔ Amino acids - tyrosine and l-theanine
- ✔ Eating slow release foods
- ✔ Turmeric
- ✔ Good quality Omega oils, especially Omega 3
- ✔ Probiotics
- ✔ Eating small meals regularly

Glenville has developed a recommended supplement programme, from natural products, for those who have experienced toxic stress as above: Mental Health Wellbeing support, Omega 3 support, Advanced Probiotic and sleep support (marilynglenville.com). At TouchBase we recommend these for the children and families we support, under the supervision of The Natural Health Practice - NHP (*see* **Useful Organisations**).

All this has implications for breakfast clubs, nurture provision, snack boxes and school dinners. In other words, if we want to improve behaviour, we need to consider what we're giving these children and young people to eat. For example how about swapping the white bread often used for toast in breakfast club to granary or wholemeal bread? Or swapping a school dinner of pie and chips to grilled chicken, sweet potatoes and green vegetables? As we know, chef Jamie Oliver did try and challenge the content of school dinners but his recommendations haven't been followed through in most of the schools I come across. When asked why not, schools generally cite financial hardship, an area really worth addressing when we know the financial costs of dealing with escalating dysregulated behaviour and exclusions. For those children and young people with parents or carers experiencing the impact of poverty you could consider the support of Transforming Lives for Good (TLG - *see* **Useful Organisations**) as they run Make Lunch. TLG Make Lunch Programme enables and equips churches to provide free, hot and healthy meals for children and families who would otherwise go hungry.

SLEEP

Burke-Harris (2018) describes how toxic stress increases the risk for every sleep disorder there is, including nightmares, insomnia, narcolepsy, sleepwalking and psychiatric sleep disorders like sleep-eating. This is a particularly concerning area as sleep disturbance seriously impacts health and wellbeing: good sleep enables our 'immune system to upgrade, using the downtime to calibrate its defences' (p. 103). So we need to support our traumatised pupils with even better 'sleep hygiene' than that recommended for the average population. We all know the kinds of things this involves - we should be doing them ourselves! (and - are you?!)

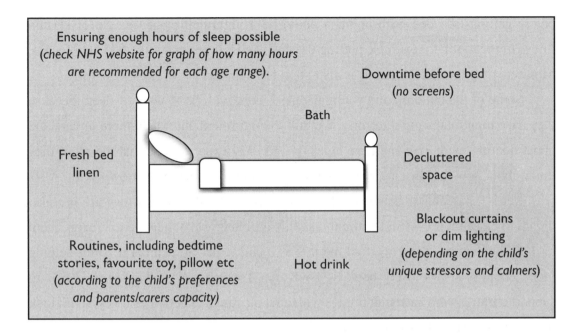

Ensuring enough hours of sleep possible (*check NHS website for graph of how many hours are recommended for each age range*).

Downtime before bed (*no screens*)

Bath

Fresh bed linen

Decluttered space

Blackout curtains or dim lighting (*depending on the child's unique stressors and calmers*)

Routines, including bedtime stories, favourite toy, pillow etc (*according to the child's preferences and parents/carers capacity*)

Hot drink

Obviously we can't control sleep hygiene as educational staff! We need to find ways to work with parents and carers to support them to support the children and young people in their care to improve their sleep. One way this has been done in schools is to link families up with the Natural Health Practice (NHP) (*see previous page*), which supplies natural supplements to help individuals sleep more soundly (*check out their Sleep Support, see* **Useful Organisations**). We have also found that supporting families with healthy IT hygiene really shifts things too. One of our TouchBase staff, Suzi Lambert, has written up IT guidelines for the whole family!

We can also weave sleep hygiene into our psycho-education with young people. I often talk sleep with the young people I work with one way or another! Most say they've never been able to sleep very well. My first port of call is to check out whether they feel safe in their room. Often they speak of shadows or sounds or dolls/teddies that look spooky at night. Together we consider if there is anything they could do differently (if younger, we have this dialogue together with their parents/carers) to increase felt safety. It may be parents/carers checking the space first together with the child, 'a safety tour' before getting into bed each night: it could be a nightlight or getting rid of certain things in the room, for example putting the dolls and teddies under the bed out of sight! Monster spray (perfumed water) is also good for 'monsters' - works every time!

Some of the children and young people I work with don't want to sleep, because they have nightmares/night terrors. We talk them through and I help them understand about floating memories and time holes (p. 76). My experience is that the more they know about how the nervous system works, the safer they feel in their own skin. Also, whatever is 'shareable is bearable'. I also let them know that if ever they are in a bad dream to close their eyes in the dream, as this will help wake them up and bring them back to their room. Someone told me this as a child and I remember it really helping me!! There is also a lovely book by Dr Karen Treisman, *Neon the Ninja* (2018), to support children who have nightmares with a whole range of activities to try, so do look into it. Wonderful ideas in there!

I usually get my pack of essential oils out as well, and ask them to choose what they'd like to try (always mindful of allergies). We discuss which smells they find calming and which alerting. I encourage them to experiment with different oils on their pillow, on their radiator and in diffusers. The calming ones are for sleep. They go away and try out their chosen scent and often report better sleep. Many traumatised children and young people have a heightened sense of smell, so this is often a good way in. However, there are some who need more than this. We discuss the use of breathing exercises and visualisations to help them calm. We try out different exercises and apps together. If they find it hard to visualise we go online and experiment again with different possible environments for their bedroom! We explore different soundscapes - the sea, a tropical storm, light rain, white noise ... they choose. Again they can try them out throughout the night and they too often report better sleep!

All that being said, however, if a pupil arrives in school exhausted or becomes exhausted during the day, I think we should allow them to sleep: I've had to do this from time to time. I wouldn't recommend this in front of the whole class but allow the child or young person a private space to curl up with blankets and cushions. I feel it's important to communicate loud and clear how valuable and crucial sleep is for their mental health and wellbeing. Obviously, if this becomes a regular occurrence, then it will be helpful to think preventively together with the family. If it's still problematic, then I would suggest meeting up together with trauma-informed practitioners in the health sector to consider what other options might be possible.

In addition to the strategies above I strongly recommend considering the following:

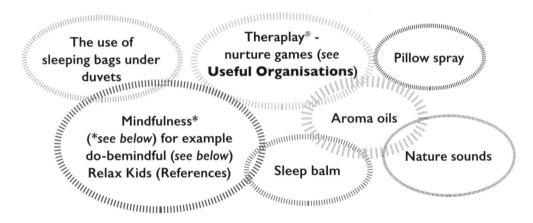

And what's clear is that it's not just the oil or the visualisation or the tropical rain that helps; it's expermenting with these things with an encouraging adult who is interested in what will make life better for you, who acknowledges your sleep problems with empathy: it's about being enabled to make your own choices, being given control over your experimentation and exploration, and having that adult be keen to hear what *you* find works best for *you*, what *you* find out for yourself: an adult who trusts and affirms and is interested in your choices, and delighted when you start feeling better. That's co-regulation, that's relational buffering, that's secure attachment. All the things our traumatised pupils and students didn't have, and need so much.

And not only that: look how, through these interventions, the pupil is learning about and becoming more confident about learning. They are developing curiosity;

they are having concrete experience of making plans, carrying them through, being interested in the results, adapting according to what they find - becoming scientists in fact! And practising the brilliant executive function skills they need for learning. Why on earth would anyone choose instead to simply tell them off and give them a demerit for yawning in class?

MINDFULNESS AND MEDITATION

Burke-Harris (2018) describes how studies have shown that meditation and mindfulness decrease cortisol levels, enhance healthy sleep, improve immune function and decrease inflammation (p. 112). We can do this in all kinds of ways through mindfulness/meditation exercises, games and activities. A couple of story books that we really like at Touchbase are *Imagine Eating a Lemon!* (2018) for the primary phase, and *Quiet the Mind* (2012) in secondary. There are also many different Apps available, so experiment together and find one or two that might be appropriate and helpful. Within our team we use Headspace, Calm and Living From Rest for both ourselves and the children we support as there are sections for children and young people too! Some further ideas include:

- On **do-bemindful.com** you'll find an initiative for teachers, parents and children. It begins with ensuring teachers are well supported and regulated, as they complete some online training in mindfulness first, fitting it in as and when they can, so that they can be mindful teachers. Then they have the option of having the resources to support the pupils they work with. This initiative provides many beautifully illustrated cards to engage pupils' imagination and their own mindful practice. You can even facilitate groups for parents and carers, as part of creating a mindful community. I had a taster when I was in Scotland: loved what it involves! (see **Useful Organisations**).
- On **bbc.co.uk** there is a section called: *Seven Techniques for Helping Kids Keep Calm*. We really like the cloud spotting exercise!
- On **copingskillsforkids.com** there are lots of ideas. We really like Hoberman Sphere breathing: you can get these colourful spheres from many toy

shops - they can be used for training adults in how the nervous system works too. Each of our training teams has one for their kit on the road!

- On **biglifejournal.com** there are five fun mindfulness activities for children
- On **calmforkids.com** there are lots of great ideas!

**Do however please note that we need to be very aware that going to or focussing on still, quiet spaces within a room or inside themselves can be extremely uncomfortable for many pupils who have experienced relational trauma and loss, because of intrusive thoughts, flashbacks of unresolved issues and unprocessed, floating memories of overwhelming stress. These traumatised children and adolescents may even find it too scary just to sit quietly and close their eyes, so it should never be insisted on collectively in class or individually. *Mindful practices*, such as mindful eating, mindful watching or mindful walking can be much more suitable (that's why we at TouchBase like and use do-bemindful.com as it offers so many different creative types of mindful practice to experiment with). Mindfulness can be very helpful, but it's not a universal panacea for everything, nor for everyone.

BREATHING

You may remember from the **Respecting Biology** chapter that our nervous systems react in an involuntary way. We know that we can't directly change how our major organs, such as our heart or liver, function, in any given moment (though we may be able to reduce our heart rate, with practice). However it's important to remember that we can control our breath. And controlling our breath can positively impact everything else! An important and readily available route to improving vagal tone (p. 122).

The resting heart rate of those who have experienced relational trauma and loss can often be compromised, so we need to experiment with alternative ways of breathing together with our traumatised pupils. There are so many different techniques and games out there so just get looking and have a go! (*See also above, in the Mindfulness section and also the downloadable breathing exercise cards available on* childhood101.com). In order to quieten and slow down our breath, exhaling for longer can help to override our fight/flight/freeze systems and return us to our social engagement systems, back in contact with ourselves, each other and the world, out of panic and terror, rage and freeze. So we need to invest in breathing!

EXAMPLE 1:	Breathe in for 4, hold for 2, breathe out for six, hold for two.	Repeat!
EXAMPLE 2:	Blow out your fingers as if they are candles on a cake, whilst counting out loud to 10.	Repeat!

EXERCISE

The sensitivity of dopamine receptors in our bodies becomes significantly impacted when we experience toxic stress (Burke-Harris 2018). This means that we need more of the good stuff in order to feel the same amount of pleasure as an individual who hasn't experienced high levels of trauma might. Really unfair, but unfortunately, true. To an extent this explains what's going on in the addiction world. Burke-Harris comments that moderate physical exercise can regulate the stress response in those who have faulty dopamine receptors now, and also reduces inflammatory cytokines. She recommends at least *an hour a day of physical activity* that builds up a sweat. She explains that exercise isn't just good for muscles but for our brains as well! Apparently exercise helps 'increase the release of a protein called BDNF which basically acts like Miracle-Gro for brain and nerve cells' (p. 110). This being the case, it's important to experiment with the child or young person to find out what they like and can imagine doing on a very regular basis. You'll find additional ideas to complement this later on in this chapter in the form of sensory breaks.

MENTAL HEALTH

There are many children and young people who have experienced relational trauma and loss who will need additional mental health support from specialists in this field at different times in their lives. If a child or a young person has experienced relational trauma it can often be helpful to facilitate dyadic therapy rather than individual therapy. I strongly recommend those listed on the Theraplay® and DDP UK Connects Network (Dyadic Developmental Practice, a practice created by child psychologist Dr Dan Hughes, and practised and promoted in the UK by the DDP UK Connects Network), (*see* **Useful Organisations**) for those who have been wounded in the context of relationship, through attachment disruptions and relational trauma (pp. 197-212 in **Relate**). Both these approaches involve dyadic work between child/young person and an adult, facilitated by specialist therapists. All practitioners in schools can integrate ways of being from Theraplay® and DDP informed practice - for example, using PACE (p. 200) in all interactions in school, including in differentiated discipline. These approaches are available to all and are worth learning about (*see* Trauma Informed Education (TIE) **Useful Organisations** *for how to get trained up in this*).

It's very important that we keep supporting our colleagues to interpret behaviours and consider interventions through a trauma lens, given how much misunderstanding there still is at the moment. Whenever I'm involved in any meetings about pupils that we know at Touchbase, especially if it involves a discussion regarding their behaviours (more often than not!), I share the Trauma Tree (p. 48). Be the one who keeps the awareness of trauma alive. The one who provides the most accurate lens. The one who gently challenges any attribution of blame within the systems round the child, to reduce the likelihood of splitting. The one whose respect and empathy for everyone involved keeps the adults' socially engaged brains online, so that they can think clearly together about the needs of the child and young person in their care.

Living Life Well

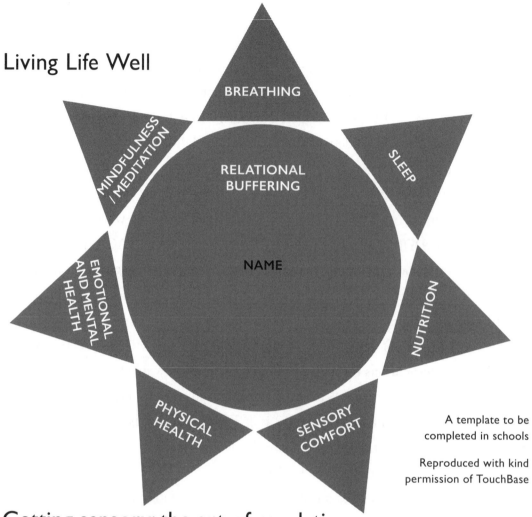

BREATHING

MINDFULNESS / MEDITATION

RELATIONAL BUFFERING

SLEEP

NAME

EMOTIONAL AND MENTAL HEALTH

NUTRITION

PHYSICAL HEALTH

SENSORY COMFORT

A template to be completed in schools

Reproduced with kind permission of TouchBase

Getting sensory: the art of regulation

Talking can be an important part of healing and recovery, but as a whole organism we don't truly change until our bodies comes to life, coming out of danger mode. The only way to get the body awakened is to go sensory. In the rest of this chapter, we'll explore what sensory interventions look like. But at the most basic level, we really do need to get more gym equipment into our schools - and not just in the gym! In corridors, in form rooms, in reception areas, in classrooms - in the staff room - everywhere! Two of everything! It may just be that someone is getting dysregulated and needs to get on a rower for ten minutes or an upright bike for ten minutes. Even better if someone from Team Pupil can jump on one too, side by side. After all, we have mirror neurons so we can download calm from our Key Adult - or our colleague, when times get tough for adults too. And co-regulation leads to self-regulation!

In the **Respecting Biology** chapter I identified ten possible areas to work on, to introduce and strengthen vagal tone and meet the regulation needs of our children and young people. They all facilitate fantastic opportunities for neural exercise!

Environment

Consider what you could do to make your environment - home/school/other context as comfortable as possible. There's so much we can do with any or all the following, even better when we can involve the children and young people in choosing.

Textures	Temperature	Layout	Areas for privacy
Sound levels	Colour	Lighting	Displays	Smell

Body temperature

Toxic stress can move an individual into the fight/flight system, where they can then either get stuck or move further down into the freeze system (p. 108). Body temperatures can often become hijacked, with the child or young person either becoming very cold or very hot. So having a variety of resources to hand which can support the pupil get back to a more comfortable temperature is very helpful.

FOR THOSE WHO ARE COLD, *consider*	blankets, hot water bottles, wheatbags heated in the microwave
FOR THOSE WHO ARE HOT, *consider*	ice packs, ice to suck on, a wet flannel, a frozen bag of dry rice

Sensory snacks

It will be really important in our schools to either provide sensory snacks and drinks or to ask families to send pupils in with sensory snack boxes (we may need to invest in a fridge-freezer in the inclusion department!), obviously taking allergies into consideration. Depending on the child or young person's presentation we'll need to work out whether they look like they need alerting or calming, as we all present with either hyper- or hypo- or a mixed response when moving into our fight/flight systems. If the pupil moves into a hyper- and hypo- mix, in other words shifting between the two in quick succession, then only use calming snacks and drinks.

FOR THOSE NEEDING CALMING, *consider**	Snacks: toffees, chewy health bar, frozen strawberries, nuts* Drinks: hot chocolate, cuppa soup
FOR THOSE NEEDING ALERTING, *consider*:	Snacks: crunching on ice, frozen peas, an orange, an apple, celery Drinks: citrus drinks, drinking from an orange through a paper or bamboo straw

please seek advice regarding allergies

Music

We can co-regulate pupils with two different types of social engagement behaviours - face-to-face behaviours such as facial expressions, gestures, prosodic vocalisations (tone and musicality), listening and reciprocity *and* through links with music! Music can be used as a portal, for example lullabies, when we are babies. And when we are older, through singing, instrumental, listening, drumming …

Some of these ways of playing with music also involve face-to-face behaviour too, for example in drumming circles. A double dose of regulatory support! Drumming provides rhythmic deep tone which can also be relaxing as well as animating and releasing. We can also use musical instruments and singing to change the way we breath. Wind instruments are obvious contenders for this. Listening to different types of sounds/music can also really support our regulation needs (*see* The Listening Project, p. 122).

SINGING

Singing changes how we breathe! Many of our traumatised pupils have learnt to breathe in an unhealthy way when their nervous system went into overdrive to protect them when they got into stuck states of alarm, fear and terror. How we breathe is one thing we all have a capacity to change, even if we can't change anything else. So look for (or create) opportunities for children and young people to sing. At TouchBase we have set up a choir called Belong. It's not your usual kind of choir: we don't just sit down or stand up, we experiment with a range of different regulatory tools and strategies because everyone attending has experienced relational trauma and loss, and needs over-compensatory support with their regulation. If you walked by, you'd see lots of movement, as well as children, young people and adults singing together. It's a wonderful creative and relational space. What might be available in your area? Could you team up with existing projects, or start something yourself? (*see* Additional Interventions p. 263).

DRUMMING

Where at all possible, drumming is something that is easily facilitated in the school context, whether alongside singing or standalone. Drumming can bring about the kind of endorphine rush which is only stimulated by playing music, not simply listening to it, and also increases pain thresholds. It's also been found to increase positive emotions and leads people to work in a more co-operative fashion - what's not to like?

Calm boxes (Bombèr 2007), Calm bags and SOS bags ... and hoodies!

A Calm Box or bag is a container for several 2-3 minute sensory bits and pieces which can shift the pupil's state in the direction of calm and alert. We tend to use boxes with younger pupils and purses/pencil type cases or toiletry bags for older pupils. We encourage staff to carry their own to explicitly model regulation for everyone. Obviously sensory bits and pieces are helpful for all pupils, but it's very important to stay attuned to an individual's precise needs at any given time: we can sometimes dysregulate a pupil further by not realising that a particular item is actually inadvertently activating their fight/flight or freeze systems. Please pay careful consideration to how they are before you use an object, how they are during and how they are after.

At times of crisis/challenging behaviour, for example when a pupil has run off we use SOS bags! These can be grabbed for crisis times and include a microtowel to sit on, some chewy sweets, mindful colouring book/postcards and pens, other sensory bits and pieces. Rather than chasing the pupil or merely following them, you set up a base nearby, or within their gaze. Then you engage with the contents of the bag, and occasionally smile and wave at the pupil to come join you. You give intermittent eye contact. Most of the time, pupils will come and join you, as they can sense this is a safe interaction and that whatever you have will soothe their dysregulation. A no-brainier!

In Nicky Murray's former school (he is the progressive Headteacher in Scotland mentioned on p. 77) staff wear hoodies, not shirts and ties. This can support not only the regulation needs of staff but those who come into contact with them, both pupils and parents. They can help everyone feel more at ease, more comfortable in the school context. And in Murray's school everyone is offered breakfast and everyone has calm boxes. You can watch video clips of Burnside Primary in Carnoustie, Scotland online - do take a look!

Movement (sensory breaks)

- **Power posing**: stretch as big, wide and tall as you can, for two to three minutes, either in real time or in your mind. Check out the work of Amy Cuddy (2012)

- **TRE**: this is short for tension and trauma releasing exercises. It involves a series of movements that encourage your muscles to shake, with the idea that this helps release tension in your body caused by the build-up of stress. TRE is a safe and natural process to reboot overprotective reflexes. Check out courses on bodycollege.net

- **Walking**: simply going for a walk together can be very helpful. It's rhythmic and repetitive, and thus soothing for those lower parts of the brain

- **Running**: simply going for a run together, not in a competitive way but collaboratively, as if with a fellow coach, can also be helpful. Like walking, it's rhythmic and repetitive, and soothing for lower parts of the brain

- **Cycling**: cycle together side by side, either on a usual bike or standing bikes

- **Sensory breaks**: spend 10-15 minutes doing resistance exercises together, where you need to use your body weight in order to move

- **Gonoodle.com**: there are lots of fun activities to do that involve movement on this free website!

Safe touch

We have found in our work that many children and young people who have experienced relational trauma and loss have touch deficit. Many really appreciate respectful, comforting touch, as long as they have control over when, what and the type of pressure involved.

Of course we need to be mindful of attuning to the state of the child or young person *and* our roles, responsibilities and policies. There are many studies which promote the use of safe touch for brain development, relationships, mental health and wellbeing. So it's important that all schools incorporate the use of safe touch within their policies and practices. Safe touch needs to be used in a context of both transparency and accountability. Do check out that your school has a safe touch policy. If not, write one using the ideas mapped out here!

I will outline three uses of safe touch that I recommend are used in schools by the small familiar Team Pupil. We must learn the specific pupil, know their developmental age, know their story, know what their stressors and calmers are, know what their zone of intimacy tolerance is and what their different states look like in order to use touch appropriately and well. It's important that we only engage in touch once a relationship is well established, once we've earned the right to become close over time, as we develop mutual trust. We must use attuned practice and be sensitive with our timings!

- **Casual/informal/incidental touch**

  This might be used to give reassurance, comfort or to communicate gratitude or success. For example, taking a pupil by the hand, patting on their back, putting an arm around their shoulders, doing a high five ...

- **General reparative touch**

  This might be used to support a pupil who is distressed or dysregulated. For example a hand massage, stroking a back or an arm, rocking gently ... (lap cushion may be used)

- **Massage**

  We tend to focus on heads and hands in schools as these seem more appropriate in that context. However in other contexts do consider feet and backs too. Remember that some children and young people can apply touch themselves, or there can be indirect touch from, say, rolling a Pilates ball over them. Some children and young people prefer light touch, others much firmer. You will remember that we explored the art of attunement earlier. It's so important that we keep watching what kind of state the pupil is in, as we may need to stop or to switch to another way of working at any point. And if you don't want to go in for any kind of massage for whatever reason, that's fine: find a different way they can experience the effects, there are inexpensive gadgets out there to give themselves a massage!

Interactive play

This might be used to deepen the bonds of attachment, to strengthen the relationship in school. This sort of play releases:

a) Opiodes - which calm and soothe the mind and body and brings reward

b) Dopamine - which supports focus and an alert state of mind

c) Brain Derived Neurotropic Factor - which supports brain growth

For example, thumb war, twister, passing balloons to each other, popping bubbles with different body parts, building towers with hands, moving the pupil like a wheelbarrow, the adult chasing and catching a pupil.

Safe spaces

Create different types of spaces somewhere in school. Ensure they are smaller, cosy and more comfortable than the other spaces the building provides. We can learn from special school contexts who already use sensory rooms for pupils, which can also be appropriate for traumatised pupils. And please note that these spaces don't need to be expensively kitted out. Just a lamp, some simple throws, cushions, a beanbag, a splash of paint and some aromatherapy oil on the radiator can easily provide the right kind of ambience.

The outdoors

It's well documented that being close to the land and working the land can support regulation needs, along with promoting relaxation, mental and physical health and wellbeing. Too many of our traumatised pupils have never been supported to feel at home in the natural world. Try and get outside as often as possible: even if it's only a small area of green, or from where the natural world can be seen, and enter that space of DMN (*see* **Reclaiming Discipline**) and what's known as 'soft fascination' where we're more oriented towards being present and in our senses than concentrating on particular tasks: creativity and new thinking can emerge.

If you have the access and the means, allotments and other open spaces of natural beauty offer marvellous options. At TouchBase we partner up with Plot 22 (*see* **Useful Organisations**), renting a space on Tuesdays for our families and for members of Team Pupil. After a pilot project we will also be working with a group of refugees and asylum seekers and a group of care leavers, offering the explicit therapeutic value inherent in being outdoors and working on the land. We have witnessed first hand the power of nature on those with faulty alarm systems and other developmental vulnerabilities (*see* **Additional Interventions** for more on this). What might be available in your area? Could you team up with existing projects, or start something yourself?

More complex dysregulation

Because of their dissociative tendencies, some will need everyone in Team Pupil to help bring them back to the here and now, the present, especially if there are unusual or challenging behaviours or a serious incident of some kind. I believe all of us can do this. Have a look at the following for more ideas …

Orient-Move-Ground

If I'm dissociative please use this with me...

ORIENT

Tell me where I am
Tell me who I'm with
Engage me in the game 5,4,3,2,1
Gently sing over me if you can
Remind me to identify someone with warm, smiley eyes and a warm face, who looks safe.

MOVE

Support me to make myself as big and tall as possible using my body - power posing!
Get me to wriggle my toes
Get me to stretch
Encourage me to splash my face with cold water
Encourage me to come with you to go and get a hot water bottle or an ice pack or some menthol rub to use against my skin
Support me to rub my hands together or even give me a hand massage with cream if I like it!

GROUND

Help me to think of why I am ok and safe right now by supporting me to use my senses...
'I'm ok because...'

Finally there will be some children and young people who will need you to go one step further. A pupil may need to be referred out to specialist Occupational Therapists trained in SAI (sensory attachment interventions) and others may need to be referred to different therapists specialised in EMDR, a highly effective NICE-approved therapy for working with trauma. There are a couple of organisations who work in both these areas, *please see* **Useful Organisations**.

The Safe Anchor

In the process of exploring and experimenting with all of these things, we can support the child or young person to start developing their own, unique, safe 'anchor', as I mentioned in **Respecting Biology,** made up of the kinds of things I've mentioned above once the pupil has been supported to explore and experiment with what works for them. We are all so different.

> For example I like warm bubble baths, cold water swimming, back massages, floral scents, gardening, the texture of velvet, photography, playing with Maisie my dog, watching open fires and the sea; and hanging out together with my closest buddies of course!

This may not be your idea of a safe anchor! Or, what's available within education, so we have to be practical.

> As a member of education staff in the school context, I carry around a calm purse. In this I have my lip balm, hand cream, an aromatherapy oil to sniff, a yogi tea bag, a couple of boiled sweets and a mint. I also use my Calm App or my LivingFromRest app for 5-10 minutes in the middle of the day, whilst going for a walk off the school premises.

All these things top up my regulatory needs, not only to benefit my own mental health and wellbeing, but also the pupils in my care. I'm aware we can influence each other for better or worse. If I am grounded and calm, I'm in a far better position to download calm into those around me. Why not consider carrying around your own mini mobile kit? Ensure you use it at regular intervals!

HOW TO USE THE ANCHOR

Complete an anchor by thinking about the resources you have in your life. When you feel wobbly, you can turn to these people and things and feel anchored!

When using it with our pupils, we don't necessarily give them the template at the beginning of the work. This is because quite a lot of the pupils I work with who have experienced relational trauma and loss have limited resourcing. Instead I would use the template for my own guidance, supporting me to give the pupils in my care the right kinds of opportunities to experiment with bits and pieces so that they could complete it at some point.

Safe people you can connect with

Pets or animals that make you smile

Activities that leave you feeling warm inside

Visualisations of safe, relaxing places

Special memories that leave you feeling happy

Exercise you enjoy

Meditation

Music that leaves you feeling calm or inspired

Art or scenery that you love to look at

Sounds that you love to listen to

Breathing exercises that bring you
back to your body

Textures that you enjoy the feeling of

Sensations you enjoy on your skin

Favourite smells

Favourite tastes

Complete an anchor for yourself

When you feel wobbly use your anchor!

Enable your pupil to make choices that work for their own Anchor

MY ANCHOR

TouchBase

Reproduced with kind permission from
TouchBase Centre CiC (2018)

These pupils need access to many different types of experiences now and lots of time to test them out and experiment both at home and school! To discover what works best for them individually.

For example,

Shaun (10) might experiment with different collaborative games that are both regulatory and relational. He might experiment with different textures to determine which are his favourite to feel.

Kelly (15) might experiment with different scents from a selection of aromatherapy oils. Which one alerts her, helping her focus? Which one helps her to feel relaxed and happy? Which one helps her to go to sleep as she has difficulty sleeping through the night?

REGULATE - using sensory interventions to quieten the alarm first

We must be open, honour and respect difference and leave our own preferences aside. Let's take every opportunity to facilitate our traumatised pupils' growing capacity for self-regulation. Now is the time! I hope this chapter has given you many ideas on how to do this, and you'll find more alternative interventions in Chapter 10.

Let's look at four short case studies integrating sensory, Theraplay® and DDP informed practice in action. You'll meet these children and young people and the staff working with them in the next three chapters as well.

REGULATE: Mini case studies

ARTHUR IN PRIMARY	Ms Lees notices that Arthur is looking agitated. She knows something happened at break but isn't sure what it was. He swings back and forth on his chair, with a scowl on his face. Ms Lees sidles up to Arthur. *"I can see that something is really bothering you right now. Let's go get some space together, you and me"*. She takes him outside to dig a big hole with her in the school's allotment space. *(downregulating)*
ADELE IN PRIMARY	Adele is sitting at the back of the classroom, looking listless. The rest of the class are getting stuck in to their numeracy problem solving, but she looks like a lost child. Ms Arbour walks over and smiles, suggesting they go for a walk as she has something to show her. Once outside she shows her the trim trail and with a wink in her eye says, *"C'mon - you and me let's try it out!"*. Before too long, Ms Arbour and Adele are laughing. Adele returns to class with a new energy and starts her work. *(upregulating)*

TYRONE IN SECONDARY	Tyrone has his hoodie up and is lying across his desk. His Key Adult Craig passes by: *"Hey Tyrone, Maisie needs a walk! C'mon. You and me. Let's take her for a walk on the school field. She might do a wee if we don't take her out in a minute!"*. (upregulating)
ASCHA IN SECONDARY	Ascha bursts into the Head of Year's room complaining loudly about the fact that Ms Wheeler has marked her down in her maths test. *"She is a bitch. I hate her. I'm not going back to that class ever again. I knew she didn't like me!"*. Ms Webb stands up and comes round the desk: *"Hey, hey hang on a minute ... let's breathe Ascha, breathe ... that's great, well done, keep breathing. I can see you're really upset right now. Ms Wheeler has marked you down and you are letting me know you are really, really angry with her, so much so that you don't want to ever go back to her lesson. And you feel she doesn't like you. No wonder you're so upset. Whoa ... Before we talk this through, let's get you a hot water bottle and a hot chocolate. Do you want to get snug in that blanket over there while I make it?"* (downregulating)

Chapter 7

A Way of Connecting **Relate**

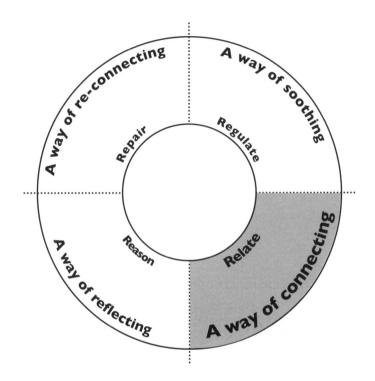

Because humans are inescapably social beings, the worst catastrophes that can befall us inevitably involve relational loss. As a result, recovery from trauma and neglect is also about relationships - rebuilding trust, regaining confidence, returning to a sense of security and reconnecting to love.   Perry & Szlavitz 2006, p. 232

Relationships matter: the currency for systemic change is trust, and trust comes through forming healthy, working relationships. People, not programs, change people.   Perry & Szlavitz 2017, p. 85

The limbic brain - the emotional, relational brain is our next port of call. According to Perry (2019) and our experience out in schools, the way we address this part of the brain is through human connection. We need to find ways to communicate with children and young people so that they feel seen, heard and understood, especially at times when their behaviour is creating disturbance and communicating their underlying state of dysregulation and distress. If we have a relationship with the child or young person, we'll be in a better position to support and influence them.

However: in the context of relational trauma and loss, one of the next biggest asks of our traumatised pupils, after felt safety, is being in relationship. If you've been wounded in the context of relationship, of course vulnerability, dependency and trust are going to be hard! There may be inner monologues going on inside our traumatised pupils, such as,

I don't want to ever feel vulnerable, small or weak ever again ...

If I let myself be still and open myself up to others I'll get hurt again

In fact the very thing our traumatised pupils need in order to heal and recover is likely to also be a significant trigger of anxiety and alarm, fear, even terror states for them. So we're not going to be able to 'just relate' in the way we usually might. Even with pupils who seem OK with adults: don't be fooled! All too often they've learned adaptive strategies to keep us at a safe-ish distance. Many traumatised pupils have learned not to allow themselves to be small, weak, vulnerable, dependent or powerless, ever again: their childhood wounds came about when they were very young with no control whatsoever over what happened to them and what they witnessed, and their every instinct is to stop this happening again. Powerlessness is at the very essence of trauma.

Navigating their way through life has meant the need to use defences. These defences *solidify into walls*, the blocked trust referred to by Baylin & Hughes (2016). Obviously when life is risky and there is unbearable pain, it's a very helpful and *adaptive* strategy. However, when later you're in a healthy context where there is safety, security and stability, for example in foster care or adoption or school, relating from behind solid defences becomes a *maladaptive* response. The way these walls are built and how they present themselves to us are determined by attachment styles. You can find out more about the different insecure attachment styles by reading Geddes (2006) and Golding et al (2013 & 2016).

Blocked trust is 'helpful' in that it keeps out the possibility of pain, just like a wall forms a barrier if you need security around something significant. However, walls don't differentiate: these walls also compromises the capacity to be sad, to receive comfort and to experience joy (p. 49). There's also limited access to oxytocin, the feel-good hormone involved in the formation of social bonds, and in play and laughter, making immobilisation without fear possible, blocking defensive freezing behaviour. Oxytocin suppresses the impact of stress. But these particular children and young people are oxytocin-deprived, joyless, comfortless. So blocked trust comes at such a great cost (*see* Bomber & Hughes 2013, p. 321).

In addition, the child's needs for nurture become so hidden away that the adults around them can easily wrongly assume they don't need any help, when actually, they do. It's easy to make such an assumption, not just because the child is hiding but because they are also mis-cuing us based on their expectations of adults. This mis-cuing and hiding can mean they elude, confuse or irritate education staff in everyday practice, as also happens with their parents and carers. As discussed previously in **Reframing Discipline** chapter, blocked care (*ibid*, p. 324) then becomes a real possibility, as none of us are immune to the powerful impact of relational trauma and loss on the dynamics that transpire within relationships. When the child's trust in us is blocked, it has an impact on *our* capacity to sustain relationship with them, so we have to work that much harder to stay open and engaged, accepting, empathic and curious. We need to resist any urge to respond to the transference and projection of challenging feelings that come our way, so that our pupils won't feel cornered.

Let's move along what Treisman (2019) calls the 'trauma river', and through what Education Scotland identifies as these stages of experience:

- TRAUMA-SENSITIVE   understanding that trauma refigures everything
- TRAUMA-AWARE   recognising the signs
- TRAUMA-INFORMED   attuning their way of relating
- TRAUMA-RESPONSIVE   using state dependent interventions

We need staff robust enough to withstand the inevitable rage and rejection which will come as our traumatised pupils introduce us to their inner worlds, where life is so different to how we might perceive things, through our relatively secure attachment lens, within our school systems.

> *Martin raised his eyes, sighed and flung his bag on the table, 'Oh great, just what I need today. I'm not in the mood for this stupid lesson. They are always SO boring. What's the point of all this ****? I don't care about stupid earthquakes!'.*
>
> *In a warm, playful manner, with a smile and a knowing look, Ms Tomlinson said, 'Hi there Martin. I'm glad you are here even if you are not. I miss you when you are not around! And actually I think earthquakes are quite interesting myself. You never know, it might be amazing. Give me a chance!'*

So that we don't get discouraged, let's remind ourselves that even when trust does start to grow, it's rarely a straightforward, linear process! There are so often a whole host of insecurities, which means there can also be many false starts along the way. Many of the children and young people I support believe that we only support them because we only partially know them. There's often a deep fear that once we know more, we'll reject them. Just let's pause a moment and recognise that probably all of us have some kind of sense of this: *'If that person really knew me - would they really love me?'* However, for children and young people (and adults) who've too often been on the receiving end of relational trauma and loss, this sense is so much more heightened, with a strong dose of toxic shame thrown in the mix, perhaps nowhere more so than when things start unravelling and their distressed behaviour begins to challenge us. Might they be provoking our rejection, because they can't bear waiting for it to happen anyway? Do we want to confirm or challenge their belief that life will always be about exclusion, rejection, abandonment, isolation and pain, exactly as they've experienced before? Is that how we want them to see life? Or, do we want them to know that they can also be met with empathy, acceptance and clear, containing boundaries, with adults alongside who genuinely enjoy getting to know them and helping them learn to like themselves as well? As the adults, that's our choice. 'Every relationship has the power to confirm or challenge all that's gone on before ...' Bombèr 2007).

Our traumatised pupils' presented needs are so often very different to their hidden relational needs. We need to discover their hidden needs, and this understanding will come gradually for us if we pay attention to increasing their felt safety. If we simply focus on the relational needs they present overtly we can all too easily get the wrong end of the stick about a pupil's motives and intentions. For example, a pupil can be seen as lazy when they are frozen, or we might view a pupil as controlling when they are actually feeling very fragile inside. In both instances, teachers may reprimand the pupil - but what might they actually need? What would we need, in those moments, to enable us to feel safely met and supported in relationship?

We're going to need to find ways to facilitate both novelty and play opportunities. Novelty that surprises the brain! Novelty will not only capture their attention but will gently challenge everything that's happened before, allowing them to build new neural pathways or to re-organise and update ones they had. Play (another of Panksepp's emotional systems, *see* **Reframing Discipline**) and playfulness will gently weaken their relational defences and buffer them to manage the everyday, ordinary stressors.

Yes, we can be involved almost literally in neuro-sculpting in our classroom and in our homes, schools and out in their communities!

Healthy attachment is very much like a dance of a balance of togetherness and separateness. We all need togetherness:

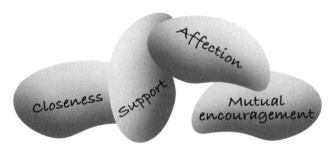

And we all need separateness:

When we are seeking to develop our relationships with traumatised children and young people, it's important that we don't do this in isolation - we need relationships too, in many ways. I've witnessed lone staff members becoming marginalised within big school systems, like some of our focussed pupils in this book. For example, a pupil gets sent to the Inclusion Department to go and work with their Key Adult after having been disruptive. I've seen for myself how *both* the pupil *and* the Key Adult can then be on the receiving end of tutting, raised eyebrows and unhelpful comments, isolating both the pupil and the Key Adult. Let's remember that school is a community of fellow travellers, a relational community of which we're all part and in which we all have value and to which we all belong. Every single pupil. Every single adult. Whatever our roles or responsibilities. Whatever our strengths and weaknesses. We are in this together as a community, our shared responsibility.

Relating to these pupils is just as important as teaching: in fact it is a *critical part* of teaching. As Headteacher Nicky Murray comments, learning and wellbeing should be our first priority in schools, not attainment (Conference, Adoption UK, Dec 2019). So whenever possible, work together with others to build relationships with your pupil, for example your colleagues in Team Pupil (*see* **Regulate**, p. 163). It's a 'community of care' that will enable a child or young person to start to realise their value, and for dignity to be restored. To support hurting children and young people into connection and to encourage 'togetherness', let's look at two different ways of being which greatly complement one another - the use of Theraplay® and DDP informed practice. I'd really like to signpost you towards these two really helpful ways of being and relating which time and time again have been effective in reaching and working with our traumatised pupils. (I'm not a trainer in these practices, but I've found that being informed by and integrating them into all of my relationships now, with children, young people, parents, carers and professionals, is so, so helpful, and I very much want to recommend them to you). I'm so glad I discovered them along my own professional journey and hope others will also recognise the huge contribution they can make within our UK education system. More information and the specialist training in these two fields can be found on the TIE website: traumainformededucation.org.uk (*and see* **Useful Organisations**).

Ogden (2015) explains how we need to cultivate an *attitude of generosity* in order to increase felt safety. She encourages us to find *something heroic*, something that we can connect with that symbolises both the gift and burden of the human condition. We can all offer these children and young people opportunities to experience different, safer relationships: over time, these will help to reduce their blocked trust. We need to support them to find a way to 'be safe in the arms of another', even when the 'arms' are not literal but experienced through our care and approach. Let's facilitate opportunities for these children and young people to be around others in shared, relational, collaborative situations as well. For example drum circles, orchestras, choirs, team activities/games … where they can and need to learn to rely on each other. And if this is too hard to begin with, we could consider using pets as stepping stones into relating to humans.

How does a focus on building relationships relate to discipline? Well, increasing a pupil's sense of felt safety and consequently trust will bring easier relationships between both staff and pupils. This will lead to more peaceful environments so that we won't have as many relational ruptures. And when there *are* ruptures, which is inevitable on this long and winding path, we'll be in a better position to know how to enable the pupil to return increasingly swiftly to a calm state of regulation: because we'll know the pupil well, and they'll trust us to have influence with them to help them move back towards social engagement again (*and see* **Reason**, *and* **Repair**). Sadly, without understanding and without relationship, there is increased risk of conflict and a resulting increased risk of further punitive disciplinary measures. Let's not go down that road. Let's provide relational buffering instead.

The difference this makes | **EVIDENCE FROM PRACTICE**

In reflecting on this work, it really has to be a whole school approach. Staff have to buy into the theory and accept that time is needed for these interventions. We have been lucky to be able to re-deploy staff to build Key Relationships with and Teams around pupils - Team Pupil. This has had such a positive impact, rather than plodding along with academic interventions, that weren't having the impact we hoped for.

Sitting back and reflecting as part of our different teams - Team Pupil has been really vital. It's helped us to recognise changes and improvements e.g. in number of incidents and shorter recovery times, things that can be hard to notice when you are embroiled in the work.

Alison West, Assistant Headteacher & Attachment Lead, Enfield

Without any shadow of a doubt the most powerful tool we as educators can use is the power of relationship!! The success observed in these young people who often come to us after experiencing much rejection, and have an ingrained sense of alienation, those who learn to trust and form better working bonds with their KAs have much improved outcomes and go on to FE with positive engagement.

After 20 years of teaching I have found that the students who seek out the ears and presence of those they feel they can trust fare much better overall. I have now seen many of these pairings. It's clear that the young person feels safe - not judged. We see them grow beyond previous expectations.

Lisa Fabian - Head of Art & Design & Attachment Lead, Croydon

The singularly most important provision we provide for our most distressed young children is a consistent adult to play and find joy with, understand and calm. The safety this relationship provides alone, reduces fear and stress levels and allows for emotional and physical regulation.

Daniel Thrower, CEO & Attachment Lead,
Anne Oakley, SEND & Attachment Lead, Norfolk

Dyadic Developmental Practice (DDP)

Traumatic events strike against our minds and hearts and create a story that is fragmented, with gaps, and is distorted by strong emotions from which the child shrinks and hides. Those stories are rigid with meanings given to the child by the one abusing her. From these jagged stories and the shame and terror that arose from relational trauma, DDP is creating stories, connection, strength and resilience.

Hughes, Golding & Hudson 2019

The acronym DDP stands for three different types of support - *dyadic developmental psychotherapy*, *dyadic developmental practice* and *dyadic developmental parenting*. DDP was created by Dr Dan Hughes, a clinical psychologist in the US who recognised very quickly that behavioural approaches were not supportive to the cohort of children and young people he was seeing, who had all experienced significant relational traumas and losses in their early years. He came to realise it wasn't so much behaviour that was getting in the way of their basic functioning in themselves, their families, their peer groups and in education, but a *lack of trust*.

It became clear to Hughes that until their basic need for felt safety was met, there was no point attempting to adapt or modify their behaviour through usual behaviourist strategies. As we know from the work of Dr Stephen Porges described in the earlier chapters of this book, this lack of trust goes deep and becomes wired into the nervous system. So what Hughes originally discovered in his practice has been further backed up by neuroscience.

As I mentioned on p. 173, DDP was originally a form of psychotherapy used with children and young people, those in care or adopted. However, once Dan Hughes had started training people in the UK, there was soon the realisation that this approach, or rather a way of being in relationship, could actually become a practice model in the UK that could be supportive for many different people with varied roles and responsibilities, including education staff as well as parents/carers who were attempting to get alongside those children and young people who had been wounded relationally. So here I'll be discussing DDP as *dyadic developmental practice* in education. This is described more fully in Golding, Philips & Bombèr (2020). DDP is based on attachment theory, intersubjectivity theory and object relations theory as well as extensive clinical practice, and is underpinned with an understanding about how developmental trauma impacts upon the child and their development.

DDP practice is fundamentally rooted in facilitating connection and security. My own dyadic developmental practice involves the following:

- Setting up a supportive environment for the grown-ups, which encourages and allows reflection.

- Encouraging *humility* in the grown-ups - an attitude of us 'not knowing', but *wanting to know* and understand what is happening in the inner, emotional world of the child or young person, so that we can support them with this experience. Being curious.

- Supporting *vulnerability and awareness* in the grown-ups - knowing our own triggers (or 'shark music' - Circle of Security, *see* **References** and **Useful Organisations**) which might have been activated by the behaviour of the child or young person (shark music is when we are reminded of something negative from our past, in the present). We can either be unconsciously driven to react defensively, or, we can work to become aware of our triggers and choose to recognise and override our reflex response: in other words, not let it influence us in the present and to remain open and engaged.

- Enabling opportunities for delighting in the child or young person.

- Expressing playfulness and humour, rather than rigidity and defensiveness.

- Reflecting on what is going on in the moment for the child in their feelings, thinking and beliefs, whenever they become defensive.

- Communicating our curiosity and understanding through wondering aloud.

- Filling up and then drawing on our compassion tanks so that we can open and keep open our door of empathy towards the child or young person.

All this changes our …

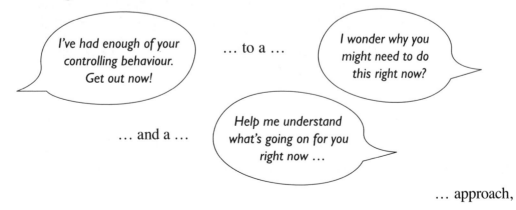

I've had enough of your controlling behaviour. Get out now!

… to a …

I wonder why you might need to do this right now?

… and a …

Help me understand what's going on for you right now …

… approach,

communicated with a gentle and kind curiosity, focussing on the pupil's needs at that moment, however maladaptively they are being expressed.

Of course we'd need to stop behaviour which is damaging, to someone else or to property; this approach doesn't suggest otherwise. However the approach is a *way of being* that conveys genuine acceptance (of the pupil), curiosity and empathy, conveyed with appropriate playfulness (*in other words* PACE, created by Dr Dan Hughes), setting the stage for the child or young person to experience felt safety with us *because they feel we are interested in them, in their core self.* Not merely preoccupied with their behaviour, and controlling it and them. This leads to feeling understood. When any of us feel understood, our state, feelings and behaviour naturally start to relax, to change …

I advocate that we integrate PACE, a key element of DDP, into all our work in school, so let's now explore it in more detail, and its relevance to the school context in the interests of reclaiming the use of discipline.

Dr Dan Hughes' PACE

We need to *embody* PACE in everything we do, whatever our role or responsibility, as we make and develop our relationships with our traumatised pupils: skilfully weaving in and integrating playfulness, acceptance, curiosity and empathy as we go.

Playfulness

Let's find a way to embody playfulness, by seeking joy in the relationship, together with the child or young person. We can only be genuinely, lightly playful when we ourselves are comfortable in our own social engagement system (p. 26), and so it serves us well to be mindful of our own states. Then we can determine when we are in the right place to get involved, or whether we need to let someone else (ideally from Team Pupil) step in to support the pupil. When we're open and engaged ourselves, we will come across naturally as warm and accessible. However, if we are intentional about this we can also go further: using chat, humour, being a little cheeky ... taking them by surprise! Communicate your delight in just being with them.

POSSIBLE BODY LANGUAGE:

♥ Sparkle ♥ Cheeky grin! ♥ Wide open mouth! ♥ Sitting back in shock ♥
♥ Sitting forward in surprise ♥ Big gestures ♥ Big animation ♥

POSSIBLE LANGUAGE:

Hey! Gotcha! No way! What?!

☺ Giggling ☺ Laughing ☺ Varying tone of voice ☺

I think we're far too serious in our schools at the moment. I actually heard a pupil in secondary say, *'Why can't the staff lighten up a bit and make learning fun?'* Wise words from a 15 year old! Playfulness can pave the way to more curiosity, to more exploration. Basically the exploration system comes online - isn't that what we're aiming for? Using playfulness will also reduce the sense of threat that these pupils experience frequently because of everything they've experienced (*remember faulty neuroception in the* **Reframing Discipline** *chapter?*). Less threat will mean fewer challenging incidents, less confrontation. So let's connect and chat first!

> *'You thought you were getting a boring lesson of science today but oh no, you will not believe what Miss has rustled up! We're definitely having some fun today! Yes - we are learning about how our bodies work. I don't want any of you getting mixed up! Who knows what might happen then!'*
>
> *'Oh Miss,' Sian moans, putting her head promptly on the desk. 'I don't wanna know about all that … I don't care'.*
>
> *'Oh my word Sian, you will once I get going! You won't be able to stop me. It's my favourite topic!' said with a wink. Sian looks up and shakes her head in disbelief. 'Oh Miss!!' says Sian, now smiling.*

> *Mr Lee (grinning and with much enthusiasm): 'Adam … look at those fab trainers. Are they new? They are SO, SO white. I bet they won't be after you have been out on the field at lunchtime. I know how much you love your football!'*
>
> *Adam's grinning, looking at his trainers. 'Yeah I got them last night. My birthday money! I'm pleased with them. Will see if they prove me lucky today with Toby's crew.'*
>
> *Mr Lee: 'Ah … are you playing Toby's team later? I want to know how you get on. Now you have those fab new trainers on, I'll come and find you!'*

Acceptance

At any given time, communicate acceptance of what the child or young person is experiencing in their feelings, thoughts or beliefs. Be aware that what's happening for them may well not match up with your own interpretation or meaning. We're not going to contradict them, or convince them they're wrong - instead, we're aiming to communicate understanding of the child or young person's perspective, validate it and empathise with how they must be feeling, given what they have just told us about their experience (*'Wow, if you heard what she said that way, I can imagine how hard that must be for you, how difficult'*). I think this is the hardest part of PACE for teachers and schools to enter into and communicate - their acknowledgement that traumatised pupils may *experience a different reality to the one we do or think they should do.*

In fact we all experience slightly different realities, affected by all kinds of things - experience, unconscious bias, transference, and so on: the difference is just starker, when we're in a position of power, and we have things we want or think we need to do, and the pupil's experience is so different and, apparently, getting in the way … as the adults, we have to take responsibility, a deep breath, and recognise that validating someone else's viewpoint is not only the right way, but often the quickest way (however hard sometimes) to show respect and bring them back into relationship with us. We have this cultural belief that children need to be told what to think and feel, when in fact they are more likely to make healthier choices if we first give them opportunity to feel deeply understood and heard, *as they are, in this moment, right now.* Phrases such as *'Help me to understand? (… what's happening for you, what that's like for you, what you were thinking/feeling/hoping for/scared about?' and so on)* are so helpful here. Another thing I have as an inner mantra in my own practice is to remember to stay with the uncomfortable feelings, for longer than I feel comfortable. It's really hard sometimes not to jump in and reassure, problem-solve, fix or rescue the children in our care, or simply tell them what to do. It can be so emotionally painful and so mentally frustrating at times - or is that just me?!

POSSIBLE BODY LANGUAGE:

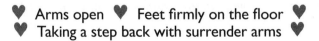

♥ Arms open ♥ Feet firmly on the floor ♥
♥ Taking a step back with surrender arms ♥

POSSIBLE LANGUAGE:

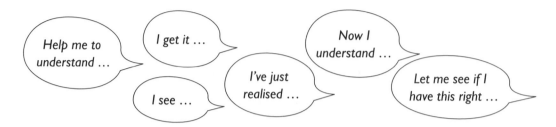

Acceptance will pave the way for a shared understanding of each other and for truly hearing each other. Pupils experience this as respect, and so have increased respect for us and for learning from us, the education staff, when they first feel 'heard', and obviously this has a knock-on positive impact on behaviour in class.

> *'That's it! I'm not ever going to that stupid Maths lesson ever again. I've had enough, I really have!'*
> *'Sanjay, what's happened?'*
> *'Mr Bell walked in and just shouted the whole lesson. He's always in a bad mood.'*
> *'So you were in class and there was shouting and you didn't like it?'*
> *'No, I didn't. It freaks me out when teachers shout.'*
> *'It freaks you out?'*
> *'Yeah …no-one should shout …'*
> *'No-one?'*
> *'Yeah, my parents shout all the time.'*
> *'Sanjay, it sounds as if all this shouting really stirs you up and make you feel overwhelmed. Have I got that right?'*
> *'Yep'.*
> *'I get it. Such a lot of shouting, so hard for you. How about you and me have a think together about what might help, when that happens?'*

Curiosity

If we're curious, it will support our pupil to develop curiosity about themselves, other people and the world we share. Curiosity leads to self-awareness: self-awareness leads to self-control. In our schools we focus too quickly on self-control, when in fact we need to spend a lot more time on *being curious*. Rather than making assumptions about the children in our care, let's instead try and remain in that uncomfortable place of '*not knowing'*, of seeing ourselves as fellow travellers setting off together with the child on a journey of discovery, together. Wondering aloud (Bombèr 2007). Making tentative connections. *'I'm wondering if you may be feeling …' 'I can see that …', 'You don't think it could be … ?' Do you think it might be because … ?'* Our wonderings are simply *offers*: we're not imposing our truth on the child or young person. They may reject what we say, and that's OK; it's our willingness to have a go that will mean the most to them. And what you've offered may help you both get closer to what's actually happening for your pupil, working it out together.

POSSIBLE BODY LANGUAGE:

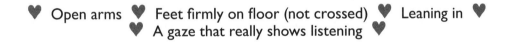

♥ Open arms ♥ Feet firmly on floor (not crossed) ♥ Leaning in ♥
♥ A gaze that really shows listening ♥

POSSIBLE LANGUAGE:

I'm wondering … *What if …* *You don't think …*

I wonder if … *I can see that …*

And curiosity breeds curiosity! We want to facilitate this for learning! We want our pupils to be more curious, not just about themselves but about everything that's going on around them, their world. A curious pupil is like gold dust in a teacher's hands! (p. 169 in **Regulation)** Curiosity will also communicate loud and clear to this pupil that you are genuinely interested in them. This is especially important with blocked trust in the mix. If they view us as *genuinely* wanting to learn who they are and why they do what they do, then of course behaviour will in turn become more appropriate and healthy as their confidence builds.

> *Craig starts rocking back and forth on his chair, eyes darting all over the place.*
> *'Craig, you seem really unsettled by something. I wonder what it is? ... mmm, I wonder if you felt wobbly when the teacher marked your work? Maybe you were worried? You don't think you were worried that she might be cross with you, do you, because of the marks she gave you?'*
> *'I dunno.'*
> *'You get worried about what people think of you don't you? I'm just wondering if your alarm started going off just then?'*
> *'Yeah maybe ...' Craig starts to calm as his Key Adult speaks in a gentle, warm, enquiring manner. It's the fact of her enquiry, indicating that his feelings are important to her, and her caring approach, that both matter as much as what she actually says.*

Empathy

How do we go about deepening our empathy? Our traumatised pupils are not stupid: they can tell if we really care, and when we don't. It's hard to care when we don't always know all the facts and figures, as to why a child does what they do, especially if you are on the receiving end of distressed behaviours such as spitting, swearing, screaming, kicking or biting. However, as we gradually come to understand more about what's going on underneath the behaviour, how the child or young person is feeling or what he is thinking, it can become easier to experience empathy for them. So at times of calm we need to do all we can to top up our compassion tanks with some reflection with an adult who has empathy for us! So then, at times of relationship rupture with the young person, when we don't feel empathic at all, we can still draw on our compassion until our empathy catches up with us.

Behaviour is communication, and often what the child or young person is communicating to us is deep anguish and grief. What will help is being a detective and knowing the story so far. Each child has their own unique journey of relational traumas and losses. So let's gather everything known to date, whilst also being mindful that this will only ever be part of the story. The child's body and mind will 'hold the score' (Van der Kolk, 2015) and will, over time, introduce us to the rest of the story, insofar as they trust us, know it themselves and are willing to. At TouchBase we write up a Factfile for these children with a summary of all the relational traumas and losses they've experienced, written from the child's perspective, not the adult's. This may include having lost their beloved rabbit at their foster home or not being with their brother anymore, despite him having been their carer through their early years of neglect.

We need to communicate with our body and mind that we 'feel' all this. I sometimes get the children I work with to take a peek, if they can, at what is happening with my eyes and my body language when we're talking about something, so they can sense my sadness for them, whilst they may not feel safe enough to feel or express their own sadness - yet.

POSSIBLE BODY LANGUAGE:

♥ Interested and alert posture ♥ Tears in eyes, if authentic ♥
♥ Face expressive of emotion that may mirror the child's experience ♥

POSSIBLE LANGUAGE:

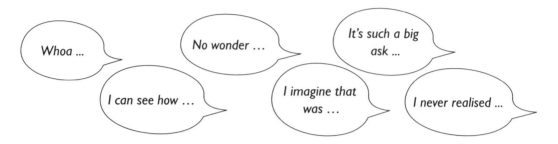

Empathy will give your pupil a strong sense of you being alongside them. Over time, that togetherness will soothe and reassure your pupil that they're not alone. This alleviates fear, meaning they'll be in a better position to learn, to take the risks required in learning. Having an explicit secure base will in turn also mean that their threat responses are diminished. If you feel you have someone watching your back, it is harder to move into defensive actions, and less important to do so.

Vikki burst into form. 'That's it. We are over. I can't believe it,' under her breath.

'Vikki, I can see something has happened. What's up?'

'Lily isn't responding. I contacted her and she can't be bothered to respond. I always respond when she texts me.'

'You have sent a message to Lily and she isn't responding. What does that mean?'

'She can't care less anymore about me, that's it.'

'Whoa … no wonder you are upset. You send a message to Lily, she didn't respond and you think she can't care about you because of that. No wonder you're upset! If her lack of response means that, that is tragic. You've been friends for ages and that would really hurt you, if that's what's happening … '

After using empathy I pause. Then I wonder out loud about all the possible alternative meanings behind Lily's behaviour (see 'The Hand of Options', Bombèr 2011, p. 186), in order to open up other possibilities for Vikki to consider: but only once she's felt heard and begins to calm and settle. Then her thinking brain and her social engagement system has a chance to come online (see **Reason***). Until then, she's unlikely to even hear me very well, but will gradually be influenced and settled when I maintain my calm and empathic tone and words.*

Entering the dance

What we are really after is supporting the child or young person into an 'affective-reflective connection' or dialogue (*see* DDP, p. 197), with us: in other words, a joined up heart-mind response, rather than merely saying what they think we want them to say - we'll know it when we see some vulnerability, some unguarded communication, a huge mark of their growing trust in us. This in turn supports their recovery, strengthens their attachment systems and opens up their exploratory systems, supporting their learning. Practising attunement, which we already explored earlier in this book, we need to use sensitive timings (Hughes & Bomber, 2013), and a balance between empathy (affective) and curiosity (reflective) in our interactions with these children and young people. If you spot that a child or young person is struggling with empathy, you need to switch to curiosity (*'I wonder what might be happening for you right now?'*). And back the other way - if you spot that a child or young person is struggling with curiosity, you need to switch to empathy (*'I can imagine how hard it is for you to let me be with you right now, and I can see that you've decided it's just about OK'*).

This way of being can feel clumsy to begin with, but with practice, you'll integrate it (into your everyday relating): it can have a profound impact on everyone you're attempting to relate with. And with respect to discipline, it will be such an investment, because your pupil will start to realise that you're actually on their side, celebrating them, gently challenging them on into security. This communicated value speaks volumes to those wounded by others. Meaningful relationships disarm those who feel the need to defend. And just to be clear. When I say 'on their side', I mean as an ally and advocate, not 'siding' against or blaming anyone else. Just in their corner, supporting them. Being there. Empathic, attuned, and responsive.

Theraplay® informed practice

We know that attachments are often compromised for those impacted by relational trauma and loss. *Learned secure attachment* is necessary for learning to take place, because, as we've seen, our attachment systems are directly correlated to our exploratory systems. As we know, traumatised children and young people have likely learned to distance themselves from genuine intimacy and the adults around them, through having experienced relational deprivation or disruption, and in some cases, intimacy betrayal. No wonder their learning is also compromised! So we know that relating to them will be tough for us and a big ask for them. No wonder so many distressed behaviours show up in our classrooms, when so many pupils are having to manage their states by themselves, without anyone having given them the tools to do so. However, as trauma experts in this field affirm, including Dan Hughes and DDP with PACE, *playfulness* can safely and gently weaken the defences that were adaptive at the time of crisis, but are now maladaptive in the healthy contexts our pupils now find themselves in, around us. Playfulness melts defences. Playfulness enables connection. Playfulness enables learning.

Theraplay® informed practice is an attachment enhancing, playful intervention that can be used in a number of contexts, including primary and secondary, mainstream and special schools. Jo Williams was the first to get this going with schools in the UK in 2004, starting where she was based at the Corby Supporting Schools Project in Northamptonshire. It's a way of being together, with the children and young people whom we get alongside. It can be used by people who have attended some form of Theraplay® theoretical training, but it's worth having a look at here so we can understand its relevance to our work.

As educational professionals, we can use it to enhance our core professional practice, to enable pupils to settle to learn, through the joint investment of adult and child into our relationships (Peacock, personal communication). Theraplay® informed practice involves facilitating playful encounters, skilfully attuned to the needs of the child, in order to build and deepen the bonds of attachment needed within our relationships with one another, so that we can function well in our homes, schools and out in our communities. The activities include increasing physical proximity, eye contact, touch and shared fun. Theraplay® training helps us know how to spot the signs of when a child or young person is being pushed outside their window of intimacy tolerance and we need to slow down, switch activity or stop.

Positive outcomes

When we invest in our relationships with our traumatised pupils in this way, we see significant, positive shifts in schools, just as Francis, Bennion & Humrich (2017) & Salisbury (2018) document in their UK school based research papers, backed up by what was predicted by the Theraplay® Institute (2015). There are a number of correlations between both these studies of Theraplay® projects with children in care, which add to the robustness of outcomes, (allowing for the small scale of both projects). Salisbury (2018) found that if a Key Adult in school engaged in 10 minutes of attachment-enhancing play daily over two weeks, the children's overall stress scores were found to have reduced over that period by an average of 29%, which is quite phenomenal. She also found that the children were more able to 'accept constraints' and 'accommodate and respond constructively to others': that there was an improvement in closeness and even better reduction in conflict in the relationships. There is ongoing research in this area, but the early evidence looks clear. If we invest in getting playfulness embedded within school culture, it's very likely to have a significant impact upon these particular children and young people. They'll be more free to settle to learn. This is key, if we want to see more appropriate, calmer, peaceful interactions and classrooms, as Salisbury (2018) found.

Theraplay® informed practice can be helpful in so many different contexts. I'd really recommend signing up for a training if you have the opportunity to do so. In Salisbury's work (2018) it was used within the dyadic relationship between a Key Adult and child or young person. It can also be used:

✔   between any member of Team Pupil and a child or young person
✔   in a small group of identified children or young people
✔   within a whole class (Sunshine Circles in **Useful Organisations**)
✔   within a whole school

You only need yourself and some cheap bits and pieces like newspaper, cotton wool balls, bubbles … in this time of austerity, what is there not to like?!   Through the trainings you will discover that the suggested activities are divided up into four dimensions, and through a specialist assessment you will recognise that the best Theraplay® 'diet' for the child or young person involves:

All our Attachment Leads at Touchbase go onto train in Level 1 Theraplay® as part of TIE; after a taster of it during their training, they are hooked! This is a fantastic way to get play back into schools, at any age or stage.

Coming out of hiding

Do be aware that even though these children fear intimacy, they will take small risks every now and then, coming out of hiding. When they do, ensure you are available physically and emotionally so that you can be responsive. Gently responsive - imagine how you'd greet a shy deer!

'I don't really understand what we have to do,' Sian muttered, under her breath, looking down: adding, 'Can you help me?' said in an even quieter, very hesitant voice.

Secondly, remember to give an empathic response. For example,

'Thanks so much for letting me know you'd like help, Sian. That was really brave to let me know. I'm sorry that I didn't explain it in a clear way.
Of course I will help you.'

RELATE - using quality moments to remind our pupils how important relationships are

Let's engage in quality moments (p. 132), let's 'show up' (Siegel 2020), so that the child in front of us feels seen and is heard. To do so, we need to be physically and emotionally present, attentive, attuned and responsive. In our schools we can sometimes be on auto-pilot because of the pace everything moves at. However, it's so important we engage in mindful teaching so that we can be present and available at appropriate times, as in the example above. Sadly we can overlook these 'cries for help' in the busy-ness of the school day. What's needed is sensitive attuned practice, and relationships.

The act of relating is needed to build trust during everyday school living. Relating is critical at times of distressed behaviour. This can be challenging for staff, but I'm hoping you can see how beneficial it is to invest as much as we can in this area, in a preventative way, so that we have the vehicle of shared relationships to draw on, for if and when the road gets rocky. In all my experience to date, it's been clear that even if you feel you have 'lost' a child or young person, they will remember your kindness, they will remember your connection to them and they may well return. This kind of relating will also set the scene for the learning that will go on next, at the **Reason** stage.

RELATE: Mini case studies

ARTHUR IN PRIMARY	Let's return to Arthur from Chapter 6. Ms Lees takes Arthur back inside to the safe space. She suggests they both have a drink and a snack together from the sensory snack tin. She connects with him and they chat, talking about the fun they had outside: Ms Lees communicates explicitly that she enjoys spending time with him, commenting on his strong arms! Great for digging!
ADELE IN PRIMARY	When they go back into school, Ms Arbour notices Adele's bright pink fluffy pencil case in her school bag. She connects and chats. "*Whoa!! Look at that. Can I hold that pencil case? That fluffy texture looks too good to miss!!!*" She strokes it and asks Adele where she got it, and asks whether she has any other fluffy things.
TYRONE IN SECONDARY	Craig says to Tyrone: "*We need a sit-down now and a cuppa I reckon! Let's go and get one. One sugar?*" With big mugs of tea in their hands, Craig checks in with Tyrone with some chat. "*So what's with the great hair cut? When did you get that done? And where do you go?*" Tyrone joins in, smiling now.
ASCHA IN SECONDARY	Ms Webb and Ascha are seated in the inclusion room, both with hot chocolates, Ascha cuddled up with her hot water bottle and blanket around her. Ms Webb connects with Ascha and chats. "*I was thinking of you the other day. I saw England play and I know how much you love football! What did you think of that final goal?*" Ascha grins, "*Oh my days miss, it was the best! I've never seen such a good win. It was awesome!*"

VOICE OF THE CHILD

WHAT'S IT LIKE TO HAVE A KEY ADULT IN SCHOOL?

It's good to have a Key Adult because they are the ones that you trust the most. Also because they will be the ones that can help you through anything

It's good because instead of just having yourself you have somebody to talk to. They support you

Good, as I have someone to support me and listen to me

It's cool: as I have adults I can go and talk to and support me. They have me in mind

Having a Key Adult is important to me because it gives me a chance to have my voice heard and someone to listen to. I can talk to my Key Adult when I am upset and this means I don't worry about things as much

It makes me calmer as my Key Adult talks things through with me and helps me to solve my problems

Cool because Miss B is fun!

Nice to talk when I'm a bit worried

Nice because I can talk to someone when I'm lonely

Really helpful and I can go to a safe space to calm down

VOICE OF THE CHILD (cont ...)

WHAT'S IT LIKE TO HAVE A KEY ADULT IN SCHOOL?

They are always there for me

Miss understands

It's amazing to have someone to help me in and out of class. She makes me feel safe

Mr X is always pleased to see me

If I feel cross Miss is there to help

Mrs A ... is my best friend. She helps me when my 'fizzy part' is too big

Good - helps me with my work in all subjects

Great - I like having my own person in school

School is too scary without her

It's amazing to have someone to help me in and out of class. She makes me feel safe

My Key Adult can be my voice when I don't feel confident

Sometimes good, sometimes not. Sometimes when I walk out of class I want to be on my own but they have to follow me. I like that they can help me if I need it, like if I am finding my work hard and if I walk out they don't give me a detention as they know that doesn't help

Nice. If I need help I go to my Key Adult. It makes me feel wanted and it's calm

I can trust them to help me

VOICE OF THE CHILD

WHAT'S IT LIKE TO HAVE A SMALL TEAM IN SCHOOL AROUND YOU?

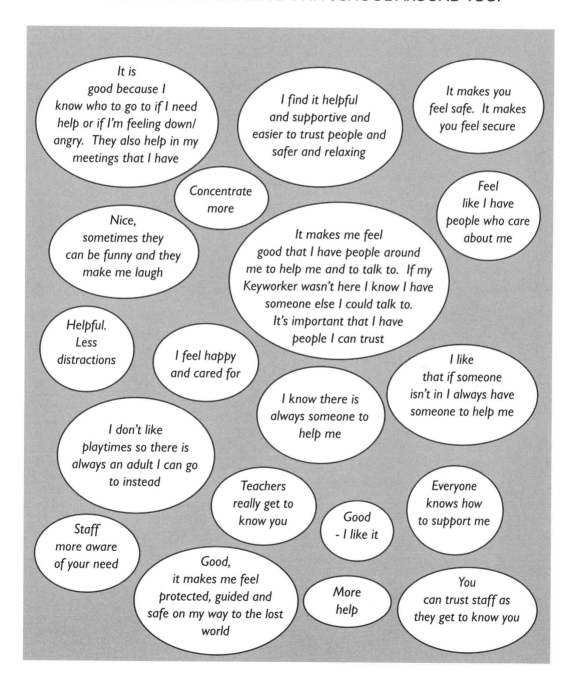

Chapter 8

A Way of Reflecting **Reason**

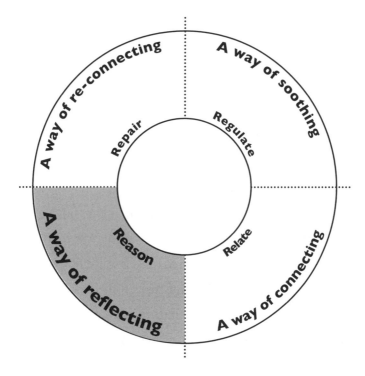

We must be guardians of spaces that allow students to breathe, be curious, and to explore.   Brene Brown 2019

As we've discovered in previous chapters we can't always move immediately into teaching, despite traditional advice: we must first support the regulation and relational (connection) needs of the pupil in front of us. I recognise from my own experience that it can be very hard to delay our actions when something has just kicked off in front of us: but if we *really* want our pupils to learn from our teaching, including learning about behaviour, then we must, in order to ensure these pupils can fully engage with the learning process, from a biological perspective. As Van der Kolk (2015) states:

'Children who defy the rules are unlikely to be brought to reason by verbal reprimands or even suspension … teachers' perspectives begin to change when they realise that these kids' disturbing behaviours started out as frustrated attempts to communicate distress, and as misguided attempts to survive' (p. 352).

This is why it's so important to not only soothe and quieten their nervous systems, so quickly activated as learnt survival responses, with our sensory interventions, but also to quickly reduce perceived threat by increasing our safety cues. We do this by communicating loud and clear that we are *'with'* them, rather than against them, through our way of being, verbally and non-verbally. Communicating that we hear them. Meeting our pupils in this way reassures them, thus freeing their exploratory system, crucial for being open and learning.

Essentially we are attempting to free up both bodies and minds within a rich context of safety, security and stability in school. When we really facilitate this well we're setting the stage for our pupils to begin to have a sense of mastery over themselves and their world. That way, when we suggest that calm is needed, they'll know what it means and have a fair chance of moving into that state. If we don't work this way, abandonment and rejection is repeated, and everybody loses. Again.

> The challenge of recovery is to re-establish ownership of your body and mind - of your self. This means feeling free to know what you know and to feel what you feel without becoming overwhelmed, enraged, ashamed, or collapsed.
>
> Van der Kolk 2014, p. 203

So once we are convinced that the pupil in front of us is in a state of either calm or alert, then we can engage their cortical brain, the top part of the brain, the thinking brain. It's at this stage that we can 'get cognitive'. When a child or young person is in this part of their brain, they are able to be fully engaged in learning. It is in this part of the brain where the following tasks can be engaged with and strengthened:

Reflective function ✔ Logic ✔ Cause and effect ✔ Predicting ✔ Organising ✔ Inhibitory control ✔ Mental flexibility ✔ Working memory ✔

I wonder what our school systems would look like if pupils were surrounded by an increased number of responsive adults? Where regulation and relationship were prioritised rather than solely focussing on attainment? Maybe then pupils would follow their natural curiosity and desire to excel rather than being shut down by hopelessness, fear and hyperarousal (Van der Kolk, 2014). This is indeed what the Educational Psychology Service in the local authority in Clackmannanshire, Scotland have discovered: they prioritise regulation and relationships as necessary precursors to attainment. They follow the neurosequential model of education (NME©) (**Useful Organisations**) - developed by Dr Bruce Perry (*see* p. 144). They have developed a programme called *Readiness for Learning* (R4L) which they are now in the process of rolling out to all their schools. Their work is respected by Dr Perry and the Child Trauma Academy in the US (*check out* Clackmananshire 2017-18, *and* Taylor & Barrett, 2018).

There is also a team of educational psychologists in East Ayrshire, Scotland, who are determined to integrate DDP, NME® and Nurture principles amongst other relational ways of being into schools, as they can see the benefit of doing so not only for this particular population but for all. In their practice they are especially focussing on ensuring safety for pupils. They already have data that shows a reduction in exclusions, although they are mindful that the success is determined by the leadership skills within each school system (Miller, R., private correspondence, 15/1/2020).

Nicky Murray, the Headteacher in Scotland, has also discovered the significant difference that focussing on the wellbeing of both individual pupils and the whole school community, can have upon learning. In his school of 500 children, located in a deprived area, there is no talk of attainment, only wellbeing and learning. The results? If you want to know whether school can really be done differently, have a look at this school and find out! (preview.tinyurl.com/ujotygn) (p. 178). Alongside the fact that Nicky is now being asked to speak all over the UK and share what he is doing, this speaks for itself! How wonderful to see such fantastic responses from children, parents, teachers - and Scottish inspectors!

So in this chapter we'll be looking at how our understanding of neuroscience can similarly help us use **Reason** wisely. And then in the next chapter, we'll focus on **Repair**, which I suggests needs to follow instances of supporting a pupil to think through their actions and choices, to bring resolution and closure; then the pupil can continue on with their learning.

This **Reason** stage is the one that many educators and parents/carers look forward to the most! The stage where they can actually have the opportunity to 'teach', whether that's an aspect of the curriculum or a behaviour matter. Yes, you will be able to teach! And your traumatised pupils will be actually ready and more able to hear you. Once we've fully attended to regulation and relationship, this will be our moment! So let's go through some important considerations here by exploring the importance of seizing the moment, our need to keep watching, and the need to build in the capacity to reflect by regularly pressing the pause button. We will then think about how best to teach, and what to teach.

Seize the moment!

For some of these children and young people we may only get a very limited window at this stage to communicate what we need to, because of how their nervous systems have developed *and* what they might be living through right now. Once they are in that open and engaged state, I'd urge you to prepare your very best lesson delivery and to get to the point of what you are teaching quickly - because it may not last long. Determine what your golden nugget is and go for it!

Keep watching!

I'd also recommend that you remain as present - physically and emotionally - as you can, so that you can be observant and attune to the possible state changes in the pupil you're teaching. It's helpful to have some kind of code that you can both use together to indicate that a pupil has shifted states. Children and young people love codes! Some schools use numerical scales, for example *'Where are you on the scale?'* (*one being when they are ready, settled to learn and five when their nervous system is firing up!*) and pupils may volunteer a number, which will help you too. Some schools use programmes like the *Just Right State* (SAI Centre) and pupils might volunteer a colour. One of our TouchBase associates Clare Langhorne speaks of some of her pupils showing her a clenched hand (in the shape of a brain!) if they are calm and alert, and an open hand to show when they are 'flipping their lids' (that is, when the pupil is in a state of feeling overwhelmed). This is based on Daniel Siegel's hand brain which she teaches them (*do check this out on YouTube - see* **References**). Once she has a sense of how they are doing, she can then naturally use the most appropriate sensory break or snack, depending on the pupil and whether they are exhibiting a hyper or hypo presentation.

I need to point out however that many of those I work with would have no idea where they were on the states continuum, as they haven't spent much time in a sufficiently grounded state to be able to 'read' themselves - yet! I'm sure you'll also have pupils in your classes who won't be at this stage yet and so will need your help in this. So with these pupils we have to reflect on their behalf, and commentate on what we can see: *'I can see you are getting a bit wobbly right now...'* or something similar. If they switch states at any point, you'll need to shift your way of being in response, your choice of intervention as well as what you're doing or offering, and move back through the cycle of regulation and relationship again.

It's true that we will spend a lot longer in those other two earlier stages than in **Reason** with some of our pupils. It can sometimes feel like an eternity! - but believe me, if those two stages are thoroughly worked with time and time again, then, over time, you'll be able to see your pupil remaining at **Reason** for much longer. It's so worth the investment. Bear with it. And yes, you will need relentless care for yourself, from your supporters, and a *lot* of patience is needed! Please make sure you get replenishing, restorative breaks; your longterm wellbeing is critical to helping your traumatised pupils.

Pressing the pause button!

When a pupil has the opportunity to pause, so much can happen, including accessing their DMN (p. 77), which is linked to increased creativity. Firstly they have the opportunity to process what they've just learned. Secondly, they have opportunity to integrate this into what they already know about the world. Finally, they have opportunity to cultivate their curiosity, since reflecting in this way will open up more questions and take them deeper into the exploration of the learning journey they are on.

So we're not just reducing stress for the sake of it, so that our pupils don't get triggered - we're not feather-bedding or wrapping them in cottonwool or pussyfooting around their sensitivities, as some critics suggest. What we're doing is consciously creating *increasingly prolonged periods of calm, alert brain activity*, so that new connections and new neural pathways have a chance of being laid down, to support their developing resilience and capacity for reflection, memory, planning, and all those necessary higher brain skills. In a warzone you only learn about war. In a state of stressful conflict, you only learn how to fight better or how to shut down into vengeful compliance toward the adults controlling you. We want our traumatised pupils to develop their brains, minds and hearts in a calm, caring ambience. And thus to learn everything that will help them grow.

IN ORDER TO SUPPORT **PROCESSING**, ASK -

IN ORDER TO SUPPORT **INTEGRATING,** ASK -

IN ORDER TO SUPPORT **CURIOSITY,** ASK -

In Scotland Headteacher Nicky Murray gives space within the school day for all his pupils to pause, to chew over, to think, to reflect. Pupils are asked to reflect regularly throughout the school day on how they are doing and what they have just learned. This school received outstanding from HMI Inspectorate in 2018. Here is one of their comments in the report:

> Highly motivated and articulate children who demonstrate an absolute commitment to be and to do their best. They are confident, responsible and show very high levels of empathy towards each other and respect for the school community. They demonstrate a high degree of resilience and readily seek out and take on new challenges.
> Slide from presentation at the ACE-Aware Nation Conference in Scotland, 21/10/18

OK, so let's now move onto what to teach and how to teach it!

The golden nugget

After working out whether you need to teach curriculum or something to do with discipline, then ask yourself:

> What is your teaching point?
> How will you teach it?
> How will you keep this child/young person engaged?
> How will you ensure understanding?

The Big 'D'

So now let's think specifically about discipline together. Before we get into the nitty-gritty of the real challenges before us I would like us to first consider our assumptions, our understanding, our empathy levels, the possibility of evaluating, our use of boundaries and the way we could offer alternatives ...

Assumptions!

Let's remember that we all bring our own meanings to events. These are informed by our experiences to date, in our past and present relationships at home, at school and now out in the workplace and our wider community. How we view something might not necessarily be how our pupil with their own unique experience and insecure attachment lens sees it. We can't afford to make assumptions. In fact making assumptions could actually alienate or rupture our relationship with the pupil further and whilst we're going to hold boundaries clearly and kindly, to keep everyone safe, remember we're doing everything we can to preserve and develop our relationship with our traumatised pupil.

Understanding

Ensure you take time to understand the pupil's perspective. If you don't understand this fully do not move on until you do! Ask them to help you understand:

> What was going on for them?
> How did they feel about themselves?
> How did they feel about the other/s involved?
> How did they feel about the context they were in?

Empathy

Do ensure you communicate empathy as you go, through your face, your body, your tone of voice, the pace of your voice, the intensity of your voice. Look actively interested. This is so important. If for whatever reason you can't find your empathy right now (and we all have those moments!) then choose another time when you have had your own regulation/connection needs attended to or swap in with another person from the pupil's team (p. 114). Remember that it's human not to find empathy when your own social engagement system is offline, when your own fight/flight/alarm systems are activated, when your own powerful feelings are reducing your capacity for calm reflection. So let yourself off the hook, and be self-compassionate first and foremost. It will become easier in time, as you get to know the pupil more and also get to know your own triggers and how to work with them.

Evaluations

Be very careful not to evaluate. It's easier said than done, especially since education staff themselves are evaluated constantly! Evaluation disables. Acceptance enables. By this I mean that the pupil in front of us is more likely to be in a position to continue thinking if we communicate that we are respectfully taking their experience into account. We might disagree with their perspective, but that's not the point. We need to acknowledge that *they see things the way they do*, and that they have a feeling response to that perspective. Think about how you might feel if someone tells you *shouldn't* be thinking or feeling what you actually do think and feel, or even that you're actually *not* thinking or feeling what you say you are, or even that you're *bad* to be thinking and feeling that way. Blocked? Angry? Frustrated? Unseen? How about, in contrast, when someone really shows you they 'get' where you're coming from, acknowledges the impact that must be having on you. Freed? Open? Understood? Willing to stay engaged, and listen? That's what we're aiming for. That's the starting point. Mutual respect will grow in this context and that's what will bring about the change we so desire for our pupils.

Use of boundaries

It is important that we hold boundaries firmly and gently. Be gentle with your strength and strong with your gentleness. Kindness when boundary-making goes a long way. Be careful not to use too much language (in other words, reduce the number of words wherever possible). Say what you want to happen. Get to the point. For example,

Endless possibilities

Something that traumatised pupils find especially hard is to consider the world from another person's perspective (if we find it hard to imagine their perspective, imagine how much harder it must be for them!). They are also often very rigid in their thinking. So something you can really offer at these times is the possibility of other ways of giving meaning to something. On my training I refer to this as the Hand of Options (*see* Bombèr 2011, p.186). I ensure I first pay a lot of attention to the pupil's perspective, acknowledging their thoughts, feelings, viewpoint etc.   Then I pause. Then I articulate other possible motives/intentions of the other people involved in whatever has happened, using *'What if … ?'*

Vikki's best friend Lily (p. 208) *never replied to her text last night. Vikki is now infuriated, saying that's the end of their friendship. That she obviously doesn't care! I explore her perspective with her for a while, not evaluating at all, just staying with her, acknowledging, empathising and reflecting back. For longer than feels comfortable, I must add! (as a teacher I have a default position of wanting to swoop in and rescue! I always encourage my trainees to 'stay with the uncomfortable feelings for longer than feels comfortable', and it's something I'll always need to keep practising myself).*

Then I pause and model thinking. I look earnest. I might tap my head. And then - 'What if they didn't have their phone?', pause: 'What if they have run out of credit?', pause: 'What if their mum has confiscated their phone?', pause: 'What if it has been broken?', pause: 'What if something has happened which we don't know about yet?'

What I've set out before Vikki may not have even entered her mind! For a traumatised pupil with a continual sense of powerlessness, offering alternative ways of thinking can reduce the pressure. Vikki is free to choose whether she keeps her initial perspective or whether she wants to alter this thinking. I see myself as merely offering some possible alternatives to work all this out. And to offer the possibility that maybe this might not be the end of the world, though it feels like it is to Vikki.

Cautionary note and the shame reducing language of parts

One final important point, as we need to be very aware of what toxic shame can do! It's very destructive to the person it haunts and to those who are nearest and dearest, as I know from experience. Because of this we're going to have to work very hard at also becoming *shame regulators,* as part of our role. Let's explore what this involves.

Many children and young people who have experienced relational trauma and loss will have a fragile sense of self because of the impact of toxic shame. So I'd like to revisit the use of parts language that can keep shame at bay, all too easily triggered if we're having conversations around boundary breaking and unhelpful choices (*and please see* Bombèr 2007, pp. 178-80).

Rather than being all good or all bad, each of us is a combination of parts. Parts we like and are proud of or don't mind others meeting, and parts we don't like and don't really want others to meet. For example, I like my creative part but I really don't like my impatient part! Hopefully you won't get to see it, but some of those close enough to me will have done, especially when I've been over-tired, not feeling on top form or even hungry! We need to help these children and young people to be curious about themselves so that they start to slowly realise their own mixture of parts, over time: because as has been said elsewhere, '*We learn who we are through the hearts and minds of another'.* Having built your relationship through co-regulation and a lot of quality moments together, you've now 'earned the right' to use this kind of language with the traumatised pupil you are working with. They can see - and feel - that you are genuinely concerned for them, so you may be able to have some influence with them. Notice out loud parts that make them them. For example:

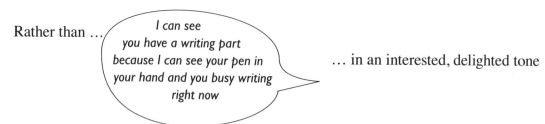

Rather than ...   *I can see you have a writing part because I can see your pen in your hand and you busy writing right now*   ... in an interested, delighted tone

Introduce the more difficult aspects of self by whispering them.

For example, for me you could say,

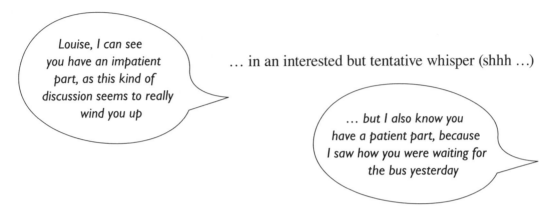

Louise, I can see you have an impatient part, as this kind of discussion seems to really wind you up

... in an interested but tentative whisper (shhh ...)

... but I also know you have a patient part, because I saw how you were waiting for the bus yesterday

This can lead to easier dialogues around discipline. For example, with a student whose behaviour has become verbally abusive,

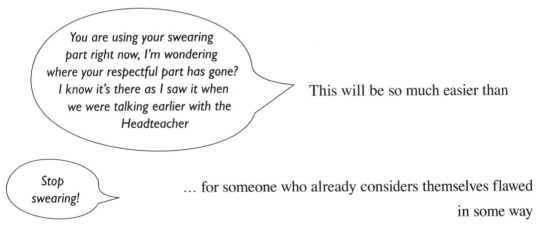

You are using your swearing part right now, I'm wondering where your respectful part has gone? I know it's there as I saw it when we were talking earlier with the Headteacher

This will be so much easier than

Stop swearing!

... for someone who already considers themselves flawed in some way

Please bear this in mind, especially at this particular stage, since the very nature of what we may be having to discuss is likely to evoke a shame response. Remember the aim is always to keep the traumatised pupil in a calm and alert, open and engaged state, so that they can actually learn from what we're saying, laying down new brain pathways. That won't happen if they're getting agitated and dysregulated.

Low-level disruption

Now we have the foundations for support in place let's think together about some of what might come our way and the educative opportunity possible! Hopefully you've read the other chapters before this one and so won't be moving into traditional discipline when your pupils haven't yet reached the point where they can actually manage it, because of their additional needs. We need to differentiate our discipline according to developmental needs and regulatory states, just as much as we differentiate our teaching in response to pupils' learning needs. So as a word of caution, please don't discipline for:

X Turning around
X Fidgeting
X Calling out
X Poor working memory
X Staring into space
X Not (appearing to) hear everything you are saying
X Poor organisation

X Magical thinking (when it doesn't cause harm to anyone else)
X Making odd sounds
X Being hyper-aroused
X Being hypo-aroused
X Not being able to follow an adult's instructions

For these areas, please consider increasing structure and supervision, as part of their individual development plan, so that these developmental vulnerabilities can be practised and strengthened. Also consider what else you could do to overcompensate meeting their regulation and relationship needs. There's always more we can do to support in these areas of developmental vulnerability.

The Big Four

So let's think about the most challenging four behaviours that could stem from their developmental vulnerabilities but will need special attention, because of the possibility of the serious impact on others. I have clustered them in a way that works for me, but I do realise that you might have different examples under different headings to me, so please consider your own as well. The basic principles however will be the same.

✗ Disrespect ✗ Damaging belongings ✗
✗ Injury ✗ Taking from others things not ours to take ✗

Let's first ask ourselves, what might be driving these behaviours? Are there any clues in the pupil's background and present circumstances? Remember that behaviour is communication. Often actions are used because these pupils don't have the words - yet. They are going to need us to help give them the words. Secondly, let's ask ourselves, what we can do to ensure the pupil continues to feel connected to us? How can we ensure this pupil knows we genuinely want to understand their struggles? Then and only then should we consider what is necessary to teach. As Forbes (2012) says, 'The way to change challenging students in the classroom is through influence, not control' (p. 77).

BEHAVIOUR	TEACHING POINT
Disrespect	In this school we respect one another
Damaging belongings	In this school we care for belongings of our own and each other's
Injury	In this school we value all living things
Taking from others things not ours to take	In this school we respect others' boundaries around their bodies and their belongings

How best to teach?

There are many different ways to communicate, not just through words. As a neurological consequence of getting stressed, traumatised children and young people tune out human voices when they are triggered; it's not a conscious choice, it's a deep-seated defence reaction. Some of the factors that might impact them in relationship with another person include: gender, posture, physical proximity, tone of voice, facial expression, mannerisms, the need for turn taking, perceived motives and intentions of the other, including feeling controlled by the other person. A recipe for a possible disaster! Remember how to increase felt safety cues (*see* **Regulate**) and over compensate these, especially at times when discipline is needed.

So with this in mind, it's worth spending time preparing *how* you will communicate in ways that safely and gently surprise the child or young person. Surprise creates novelty and novelty can build or strengthen undeveloped pathways in the brain. I strongly encourage you to consider a healthy, varied diet of forms of communication! Here are a few ideas to help you make your point in fresh and different ways:

Drawing	created by you or created together with the pupil
Comic strip conversations	create dialogues in relation to what you want to communicate
Everyday objects	placed, moved, used to demonstrate
A story or book	reading something together that already illustrates what you want to say
Pictures	communicate with images from magazines, photos, the art world, the internet
Poems/Songs	find one that communicates your point, or find them together
Clip	is there a section from an animation or film you could use?
Animals	the real thing (p. 259), or puppets or pictures can all help make the point
Music	find one that communicates your point or find some together

What to teach?

We will always be teaching either curriculum or behaviour. For both these areas it's important that we consider what our golden nugget might be, as referred to earlier. What is it that we actually want to communicate? For example using one of the big fours: *In this school we value all living things.* We could use any of the ideas above to communicate this teaching point. We could ask ourselves some further questions to unpack the teaching point - for example:

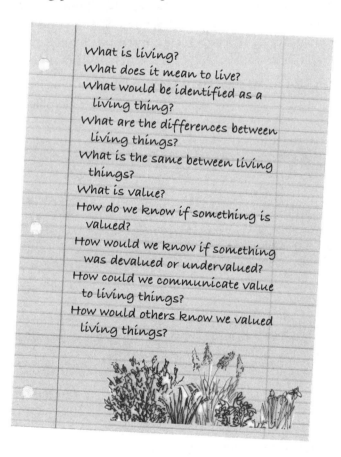

How much we explore and the depth we go to will be determined by the pupil's state as we keep watching and interacting. Remember to keep engaging the pupil in reflection as you go (*using the reflective questions on* p. 229).

> The difference this makes | EVIDENCE FROM PRACTICE

Here at Wyke Regis Primary Federation we understand how important it is to recognise and talk about our feelings and emotions. We understand that all members of the school community have life events that impact on their emotions and wellbeing. We understand that these emotions can show themselves in behaviours that do not meet the expectations of the school rules. We understand that these behaviours are a form of communication. We have a specific wellbeing section of the Federation development plan. We use the detailed scientific research linked to attachment theory and the impact of early childhood trauma to support all members of our school community through periods when their behaviour impacts upon learning and positive relationships.

Duncan Kirwin, Assistant Head Teacher, Dorset, from his promoting positive relationships policy, Sept 2019

Proactive checking in so that the pupil has opportunity to express their feelings as they go.

Attachment Lead, Brighton

Using props to explore feelings rather than direct talk.

Attachment Lead, Brighton

Sitting side by side can be better than face to face if a pupil has limited tolerance around intimacy.

Attachment Lead, Brighton

Consistency will be key when teaching your traumatised pupils. They will need to *consistently* experience our openness, our warmth, our care and our hearts and minds joining with theirs as we teach. Having a fellow traveller will mean that these pupils will be able to take the risks necessary for facing new challenges, in unchartered territories - learning. Emotional growth and wellbeing are directly connected to learning. And that's what we're there to support.

The need for psychoeducation

I imagine as you've been reading through this chapter you may have been asking yourself about whether our pupils need to understand about all this themselves? Yes! Why is it that we wait to talk about the brain, nervous systems and stress until the exam stage, from age 15 onwards? Just as we teach maths and science, surely we need to teach our pupils about how our bodies and our minds function best from an early age. It needs to be taught together with relational experience, since it's relational experience that will pave the way to deeper understanding and for making all this real and relevant to our traumatised pupils. What should they know?

- ✔ The functions of both bodies and minds
- ✔ How the nervous system works
- ✔ What happens when we experience toxic stress
- ✔ What we can do to maintain healthy bodies and minds
- ✔ What we can do to calm or quieten our nervous systems
- ✔ The use of stressometers (Bombèr 2011, p. 187) so they know their own personal stressors and calmers
- ✔ How to repair things when times get tough and things go wrong
- ✔ How to strengthen natural resilience

There are some great resources out there to support us with all this, such as:

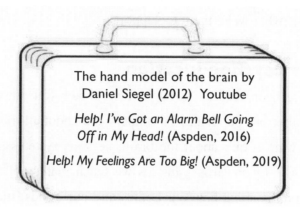

The hand model of the brain by Daniel Siegel (2012) Youtube

Help! I've Got an Alarm Bell Going Off in My Head! (Aspden, 2016)

Help! My Feelings Are Too Big! (Aspden, 2019)

An additional word

In Headteacher Nicky Murray's school, regular check-ins throughout the day with every child offer reflective opportunities, not to only to see how they are, but also to offer space to reflect on what they've learned.

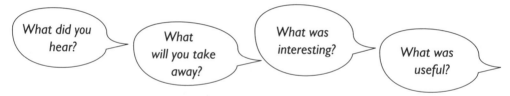

What did you hear?   *What will you take away?*   *What was interesting?*   *What was useful?*

Murray knows that there can be no learning without reflection. He's even created a 'book of whispers' for a class to have in turn to write their reflections about the stories shared in assembly! This book is then shared around the school. He describes 'cold and hot tasking', which is what children can do first and what they can do after teaching. He talks about progress through compassion. He's also created an acronym - GRIT - which all the children and parents know means Get Really Into Trying! He talks about the way that there is only so much we can control, but we CAN influence!!!

So let's influence! Whatever our pupils have lived through, which have created a series of specific needs for them, they also have the many ordinary needs we all have, because of our shared humanity. So in order to help them learn well, do ensure you include the following as you go!

Ordinary needs

Drawing on and expanded from Tobin (2018, p. 119).

Acknowledgement	*Do give traumatised pupils a task that makes them feel important, that they have something to contribute to the life of the school*
Nutrition	*Do ensure traumatised pupils have enough to eat of the right kinds of foods*
Communication	*Do ensure you find whatever means you can to communicate with each other*
Socialisation	*Do ensure you open up opportunities for all kinds of connection so they are not alone*
Touch	*Do ensure you facilitate opportunities for safe touch and sensory comfort, for example hugs*
Humour	*Do ensure that humour is welcomed in all your classes!*
Physical activity	*Do ensure there is space for movement in your classes in whatever way you can manage*
Structure	*Do ensure there are clear expectations and boundaries - be consistent, but not rigid*
Relaxation	*Do ensure you honour and model the need to rest*
Encouragement	*Do find any opportunity you can to be generous with your gratitude for who they are*
Reflection	*Do press pause from time to time so that the DMN can strengthen (p. 77).*

REASON - enabling our pupils to learn that they and their choices matter

We need to teach our pupils that they can impact their world, in increasingly positive ways. That they matter: that their choices matter. With us alongside them, we can open up all kinds of possibilities and opportunities together. An alternative way of living. Knowledge is gold! Life must be seen as a worthwhile adventure before recovery can really take place. Learning will be their resilience, so we must do everything we can to ensure they get to this stage.

Earlier Reina had lost it (as she put it). Another pupil had dissed her mum. Reina didn't live with her mum so this was especially painful for her: she was still in the process of grieving for everything that could have been. She had lived through a lot of neglect and witnessed domestic violence, as well as there being suspicions that she had possibly experienced sexual abuse too. Reina was in long-term foster care.

Reina, like many other pupils who have experienced toxic stress, moves up the stress continuum within milliseconds because of her limited window of stress tolerance. She had screamed hysterically, attempted to fight the other pupil yelling obscenities at her, and in the process had smashed a vase in the reception area and knocked off all the paperwork which had all been filed in alphabetical order for distribution to classes that afternoon. Mr Williams (Head of Year 9, part of Team Reina) had separated the two girls, using brief, assertive commands: 'Stop', 'No'. 'Now'.

Ms Taylor (Reina's Key Adult) had been called to support Reina. Ms Taylor had already spent time speed-walking around the field, actively listening, matching the intensity of Reina's agitated state and communicating empathy, big empathy for Reina's experience of what had happened. They had also had hot chocolate together at the school base and had engaged in a mindfulness exercise together using CALM. It was clear from connecting with Reina that she was actually deeply, deeply sad, despite the presentation of anger (we know that anger is the 'bodyguard' to fear and sadness). She was missing her mum. She was grieving her mum.

Ms Taylor felt Reina was now in an alert state, in her social engagement system and ready to move into Reasoning. This was her moment to teach Reina a couple of very important things:

- *That it's important to **respect** others around us even if we don't experience respect from them.*
- *That it's important to stay as **calm** as possible especially when we can feel our alarm kicking off.*

Ms Taylor decided to encourage Reina first.

'Reina I just have to say that I have noticed that when your alarm gets activated inside, when you flip your lid, you are getting quicker at recovering. In the past it would have taken you hours, or at the beginning, even days to recover! You must be getting stronger at managing all this.' Ms Taylor pauses and smiles.

Reina: 'Yeah Miss! I'm not as bad as I used to be eh?', grinning.

Ms Taylor: 'Now we both know you have an over active alarm system that you are trying to tame AND that you can get triggered very easily, especially at the moment as you are missing your mum and hurting a lot.' Reina nods, looking more at peace now, probably because she can sense Ms Taylor just seems to get it.

Ms Taylor: 'However, it's not OK to be disrespectful to others through what we say or what we do or to damage property. We don't do that here. In this school we choose to respect everyone and to value each other's property'.

Reina: 'I know Miss. Lisa really wound me up but I know what you are going to say ...'

Ms Taylor (smiling): 'Yes you do! However much someone else winds us up we don't lower ourselves to do the same and we definitely don't hurt others or damage property because we are frustrated or angry. That must stop'.

Reina: 'I know.' She holds her head low. She is sad to have disappointed Ms Taylor as she really likes her and values her. She's beginning to feel agitated.

Ms Taylor, noticing the return of Reina's agitation: 'Shall we walk again? How about we shake our arms a bit, shake out some tension?' Ms Taylor sees Reina is calming again, and they carry on walking: 'Reina, I know you have a respectful part in there (pointing to her head) as I've seen it! The way you speak to the year 7's when you do student duties and the way you care for our therapy dog and the way you now speak to your subject teachers. Your respect part has grown big and strong since I've known you! I think we have just got to now work on you quickly switching to using one of your de-stressors, as soon as you feel your blood starting to boil! We need to try and shrink your frustrated part don't we? Maybe you could decide in advance which one to use?'

Reina: 'Yeah.'

Ms Taylor: 'Let's spend this session thinking about what happens to our nervous systems when a stressor occurs and consider some quick wins, what you can do when this happens ... '

They go indoors and watch a clip online and problem solve together. Reina completes the lesson by drawing up a picture of her own nervous system and what to do to de-stress.

REASON: Mini case studies

ARTHUR IN PRIMARY	Ms Lees: *"Arthur, help me to understand what happened back there. Something happened at playtime to really upset you."* Arthur: *"Bill grabbed it. He grabbed the ball. It was my turn and I grabbed the ball back. He shouldn't have grabbed the ball."* Ms Lees: *"So let me get this right. You were playing ball and it was your turn to take the ball but Bill grabbed it. You were cross as you thought he shouldn't have it so you grabbed it back?"* Arthur: *"Yes, he can't have it. I want it."* Ms Lees: *"Remind me. Whose ball is it?"* Arthur: *"The school's I think."* Ms Lees: *"So let me check. You are playing with the school ball. You felt it was your turn. You saw Bill grab it and then you grabbed the ball?"* Arthur: *"Yeah ... that's right. He got all upset and yelled at me saying I shouldn't have grabbed the ball."* Ms Lees: *"Ah, so he yelled at you? I get it. So you were upset because he took the school ball and you felt it was yours to have? Ah ... that makes sense as to why you were upset."* PAUSE Ms Lees: *"Wait a minute! It was the school ball? It wasn't your ball? Oh ... I'm just wondering something ..."* Arthur: *"What?"* Ms Lees: *"What if Bill thought it was the school ball which belongs to everyone, so it was OK for him to have it? In this school we don't take what isn't ours to take. But this ball was everyone's to take ... Ah, everyone could play with the ball. So everyone needed to share! I get it!! What does sharing look like? Can you draw it?"* She passed the paper to Arthur, and together they worked out what sharing looked like. She then used a social story to communicate sharing at playtime. Arthur: *"Oh I didn't think of that ... "*

ADELE IN PRIMARY	Ms Arbour: *"Adele I noticed you sitting at the back of the classroom looking so alone. Did you feel like that?"* Adele nods and puts her head down. Ms Arbour: *"Oh my word. You were sitting in our classroom feeling alone? What could be going on to make you feel so alone I wonder?"* Adele: *"My dad never showed for contact yesterday. I don't have real family."* Ms Arbour: *"Oh my. Adele. You feel so alone because your dad didn't turn up for contact and you feel you don't have real family. Have I got that right?"* Adele: *"Yes he never turns up anymore. He's forgotten me."* Ms Arbour: *"Adele as you are telling me about your dad, I can hear real sadness in your voice and I saw that sadness when I saw you looking so alone in the classroom. It is really sad."* Miss Arbour puts her hand on her heart and says quietly *"So, so sad."* Adele wipes a tear from her eye and quickly tries to compose herself. Ms Arbour, very gently: *"It's ok to cry as you are sad"*, passing Adele a tissue. *"I'm so glad you showed me you were sad about this as now I know and we can be sad together, so that you're not alone with all your sad feelings."*
TYRONE IN SECONDARY	Craig: *"Help me to understand what was going on for you in class … ?"* Tyrone: *"What? I don't know what you mean?"* Craig: *"I saw you lying across your desk … I was wondering what this might mean?"* Tyrone looks away: *"Dunno …"* Craig: *"I wonder if you are feeling tired, or maybe something has upset you or disappointed you … Just wondering …"*, with an empathic look. Tyrone: *"I dunno … yeah tired, … tired of everything."* Craig: *"Everything?"* Tyrone: *"Yeah everything … It's just too much. What am I supposed to do? They're always fighting … always going on and on and on …"* Craig: *"You're letting me know everything just feels too much right now. It sounds like you're really down about this."* Tyrone: *"It's not just now, it's been going on for ages. I hate it. What can I do? Nothing. They got themselves into this mess and now we are all paying…"* contd…/

TYRONE IN SECONDARY	As they continue in this vein, it transpires that Tyrone's parents have been taking drugs and have got themselves into debt, unable to pay the bills and now in constant daily altercations as they can't manage the stress. Tyrone is bearing the brunt of it. Craig: *"No wonder you are not able to focus in class Tyrone. That's a lot for a 15 year old to try and get his head around. I get that. Sounds like you are feeling overwhelmed."* PAUSE. Craig: *"I'm so glad you let me in, as now it's not just you thinking about all this, it's me too. Two heads together has to be better than you on your todd. We're not going to sort this all out straightaway, but I reckon together you and I can think up some ways to cope, to make life a little easier right now. Shall we give it a go?"* As this was also a disclosure, Craig explains he needs to pass it on to a senior manager, as it may be that together they will have even more ideas.
ASCHA IN SECONDARY	Ms Webb: *"Now then. Help me to understand why you think Ms Wheeler doesn't like you, it sounds like you think this is why she gave you a bad mark?"* Ascha: *"It so is. I just know."* Ms Webb: *"How do you know? Help me to understand."* Ascha: *"She's got this look!"* Ms Webb: *"Tell me more."* Ascha: *"She never smiles and looks straight through me. It's spooky. I feel I have to watch her constantly as I've no idea what she's going to do next."* Ms Webb: *"Right. So she has a still face? A face that never moves?"* Ascha: *"Yeah, its freaky. It only moves when she shouts."* Ms Webb: *"So let me get this right, you're in class, you see her face and it makes you feel uneasy like she doesn't like you ..."* Ascha: *"Yeah."* Ms Webb looks intent. *"Oh no ..."* contd.../

ASCHA IN SECONDARY	PAUSE. *"I've just realised something. There's a science to all this. Let me show you something …"* Ms Webb proceeds to explain to Ascha how our neurobiology works, how we are impacted more positively by smiles, openness and warmth but also how rightly or wrongly our neuroception can sense danger if we are met with a still face. Ms Webb uses a video clip and some drawings to help her understand.
	Ascha: *"That's SO interesting Miss."*
	Ms Webb: *"If this is the science, what if this was nothing to do with whether she liked you or not, but more to do with just what happens in our physiology? And if that's the case, what if you just didn't do well in your test, but this has all been made so much worse for you because of this science?"*
	Ascha: *"Yeah maybe."*
	Ms Webb: *"So if we could have got Ms Wheeler to smile or to look supportive in some way, you may have found this news so much easier to take? You never know!"*
	Ascha : *"I think you are right."*

These pointers opposite for working with crises are based on and adapted from Sally Donovan's helpful therapeutic parenting work with teenagers (2019); but are applicable with children of all ages, not only adolescents.

In the next chapter, we'll think about what to do when there is a *relationship rupture*. We need to know what we can do to facilitate an opportunity for *relational repair*. This is both an important and fragile transitionary phase, since what happens between relational rupture and relational repair can either break us or make us. It holds yet another educative opportunity with such a powerful message for all of us in this life.

That we can start over. That it's possible to put things right.

WHEN CRISES ARISE

Based on Sally Donovan's therapeutic parenting work with teenagers (2019):

Hold your own boundaries:
• Ensure you pull in all your support so you can remain boundaried. Don't get entangled in the mess.

Connection:
• Maintain a connection with the pupil in whatever way you can.
• Be glad to see him/her: *'Hey, really good to see you!'*
• When something difficult has happened stay open, *'Tell me about it.'*
• However disturbing it is, *'Let's sort it out.'*
• Express how you think the pupil. might have felt in the situation, *'that must have been so hard.'*
• Use different means to communicate - text messages, post it notes, postcards, hand on the shoulder.
• Quick in and out - do and say what you need to in brief. Don't go around the houses to get your point across.

Micro nurture:
• Consider if there is anything small you can do to communicate you still care. For example give pupil a snack, a drink, a small object to keep, a random act of kindness. Don't go too overboard.

Maintain your boundaries:
• Consider taking time out and swapping in with someone else from time to time.

• Only focus on dealing with what's really important, rather than all the finer details.
• Remember this is only for a season.

Safety:
• If the pupil is likely to get aggressive make a safety plan together with them when all is calm. Explain what you are going to do and what they need to do if their upstairs brain goes offline due to alarm.

Sensitive timings:
• Don't tell pupil some difficult news immediately they ask you a question, e.g. *'can I go and ...'* Bide your time. *'I just need to have a think about that'.* Choose when it might be appropriate to share possibly triggering news, for example when there are others around, when the pupil is regulated ...
• Loosing is good.
• Don't try and win battles!
• Don't join the fight!
• You will inevitably be tempted to be drawn in to fight too. Don't.

Recovery time
• Allow things time to diffuse.
• Repair
• Prioritise facilitating any reparative opportunities. Don't let anything compromise your relationship.

The difference this makes | EVIDENCE FROM PRACTICE

With thresholds for EHCPs ever increasing and placements for specialised schools ever decreasing, mainstream schools are finding themselves in the new terrain of having to integrate attachment aware and trauma informed provision at school. Such 'hard to teach' pupils are just that: hard to teach, because they remain in such an aroused state that they are too unsettled to learn. Becoming stress regulators, as opposed to the more traditional behaviour managers, has transformed the terrifying world of school for our pupils. It has allowed them to integrate successfully into a world where they once thought they did not belong. It has allowed them to recognise, just like every other human being, they are 'the same but different', like two award-winning actors of two opposing genres, rather than the 'unworthy comparison' to another student. Bouncing chairs, balance boards, sensory breaks of walks and adaptive games of 'squash', 'time in', longer transitions between lesson times away from crowded corridors, snack time, fiddle toys, group games of a 'matching and sorting' theme, to integrate the two sides of the brain, are just the frosting of the piñata cake we're making. But what's going on inside this cake is ever so colourful.

One parent notes, '*The work you have done is making a noticeable positive difference. I have noticed [a particular pupil] linking his difficult behaviour to feelings of increased anxiety, being able to identify and express when feeling anxious and the reason behind why. [The pupil] also recovers more quickly from outbursts of volatile behaviour. After incidents [the pupil] is able to reflect that, apart from said incidence, the day had been good. This is an amazing development. I want to thank you for the work you have done.*'

Staff colleagues have said, '*Thank you for the time and effort you have put in to reflecting for us using your training and experience which is invaluable in supporting us. The impact of being a stress regulator for these pupils is so apparent that it cannot be questioned. Instead, what is questioned is 'how and why?'.* Curiosity and empathy are reborn. Not only within the pupil, but amongst all those who surround them ... and this is just the very beginning of an incredible journey of recovery.

> '*[You] ... have made incredible progress with our most traumatised students and the impact of your work is evident. Your work has transformed [child] responses to school.*'

An extract from Nicola Yeandle, Attachment Lead, Eastbourne

Chapter 9

A Way of Reconnecting **Repair**

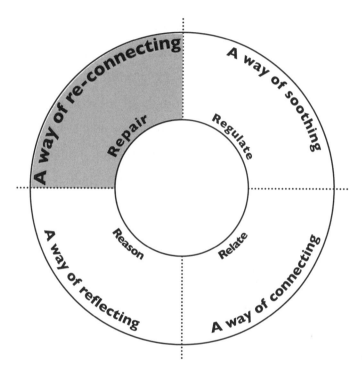

Troubled kids are distinguished by their regrettable ability to elicit from others exactly the opposite of what they really need.   Tobin 1991, p. 20

The difference this makes	EVIDENCE FROM PRACTICE

Repairing relationships was not an area we had focussed on previously. This has now become a real area of importance to ensure children don't carry guilt, shame or fear from a previous day when they return to school. Saying sorry together with a child is a really empowering feeling and holding them through these difficult moments is very rewarding.

Alison West, Assistant Head Teacher & Attachment Lead, Enfield

So as we start this stage, you may well be thinking what a lot we had to do before getting here. You'd be right in thinking this! However each of the previous stages have been essential, because our traumatised children and young people don't have the necessary foundations we all need to view ourselves from a secure perspective. Instead, they have a fragile sense of themselves and poor internal controls, until our over-compensatory support is provided for a considerable time. As I described earlier, we can get away with not going through all these stages for those who *have* experienced 'good enough' care, as generally they'll be able to manage navigating their way through the ups and downs of life, including school, thanks to their robust sense of self and their internal controls. But we *must* honour biology with our traumatised pupils when their biology has been impacted and compromised through being exposed to toxic stress whilst living, as they have, through a range of ACEs.

> What happens between rupture and repair builds resilience. Reparation makes relationships stronger   Schore 2014, youtu.be/cbfuBex-3jE

Surrender

It's important that we first acknowledge that we may well need to apologise ourselves, and apologise many, many times! Let's lead by example. If we've not been on best form, if we've messed up or overlooked something, let's take responsibility. If you have gone too quickly, or the child or young person has experienced you as overstepping what they feel comfortable with, step back with arms up in surrender and say: *'I'm so sorry for … May I have another go …?'* I've had to do this countless times within my own practice.

Let's be respectful of those in our care. Mutual respect will deepen respect in the other person. I can't stress how important humility is, especially around these children and young people who may have previously experienced attachment failures and inadequacies in their early years, with no-one owning up or taking responsibility, leaving them feeling they are probably to blame exactly as they may have been told they are.

Stress regulation and shame regulation

We need to give ourselves new roles, in order to navigate this stage well, together with a child or young person. As I've mentioned in earlier chapters, we need to be stress regulators and shame regulators, rather than behaviour managers (pp. 84, 124 and 251). Reframing the language we use to describe ourselves will be very significant for how we and others view our roles and responsibilities.

This particular stage - **Repair** - has the capacity to be a life-changing opportunity but also the capacity to hamper new growth. Relationship ruptures are inevitable. We all mess up from time to time. We break things, we say or do things we later regret: we don't think carefully enough, we stand by when we should have acted, we are selfish ... I could go on! (or is this just me?!) Unlike us, if our traumatised pupils think they've made a mistake or messed up, they can quickly feel like their back is against the wall with no exit strategy available. They can get themselves very stuck. That's where we come in!

As I've said before (p. 223), when the need arises, be prepared to switch back to the previous stages of **Regulate**, **Relate** and, when they're ready, **Reason**, at any point, and go around the cycle again. Whatever you do, don't, please don't, give up!

Reparative opportunities

So I'm sure you'll remember the days when children and young people had to write lines or to write long confessionals! Though that was a while back now, we continue to ask pupils to complete reflection forms on what they did, what was wrong, why they did it, what they'd do next time and how they are going to make amends. And worse - have a look back at the list gathered from both pupils and education staff on p. 42 in the **Reframing Discipline** chapter. Please note these are all going on right now in the UK, as the evidence was gathered over the last couple of years.

When relational withdrawal is routinely employed as a discipline technique, attachment security may be compromised, which could then activate further behavioural problems. Even if such problems are not created, routine withdrawal is likely to create a distance in the relationship that will undermine its strengths and influence on the child's life in the years ahead.   Hughes 2009, p. 82-3

For repair to actually mean something and to make a difference going forward, there are some principles we must adhere to.

Six principles for repair

This work must happen with an adult the pupil trusts, ideally their Key Adult.

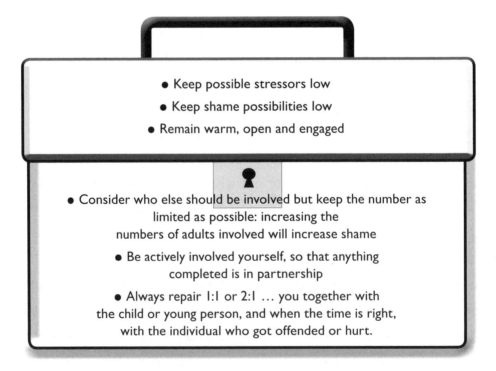

• Keep possible stressors low

• Keep shame possibilities low

• Remain warm, open and engaged

• Consider who else should be involved but keep the number as limited as possible: increasing the numbers of adults involved will increase shame

• Be actively involved yourself, so that anything completed is in partnership

• Always repair 1:1 or 2:1 ... you together with the child or young person, and when the time is right, with the individual who got offended or hurt.

Felt safety

The most important principle here is the first point; as we've seen throughout this book, it's attachment security that brings about felt safety for the child at these times of tension. Their compromised state with respect to lacking trust because of what they've previously experienced is the very reason why we must pay special attention to this at these fragile times of rupture and repair. Over-compensatory relational input would be ideal. We must always engage in relational proximity, not relational withdrawal, for these pupils (p. 65). What happens within this fragile window between a relational rupture and a repair can either strengthen or weaken this pupil's attachment security: 'Safety should never be a reward that we have to earn ...' (Hughes 2009, p. 170).

How to repair

There are many creative ways to do this but here are three particular options that are especially helpful with these children and young people: using visuals, the use of random acts of kindness, and paying back time. Within these examples there are many creative possibilities, to get you thinking! They can all be done together with someone from Team Pupil (*Attachment Aware School Series*, Bombèr, 2016-2017). It's important to clarify that the person who has been offended or hurt wouldn't be the appropriate person to have alongside, creating the reparative opportunity. It needs to be someone else from Team Pupil pro-actively supporting the child or young person to form a bridge into re-connection with that person hurt or offended. So, in effect, this further staff member would be swapping in, on behalf of the offended/hurt member of Team Pupil, who had been working alongside the pupil but was attacked or insulted (for example) in some way.

Using visuals

At TouchBase we have created *Sorry* cards for our young clients to use as and when they need to, designed by previous young clients. We also offer a selection of postcards, notelets and plain paper so that they can be creative with us, in terms of how they say sorry. Some pupils may want to just draw a picture of something the other adult or child likes. Some may want to write something but we don't push this. We avoid long confessions! We join in and get alongside, using picture (pictures speak a thousand words). For example I would appreciate a dog lying down or with its head tilted, in a picture, if someone had offended me. What sort of visuals might you appreciate?

Random acts of kindness

Knowing a little about the person the child or young person has offended or hurt helps. Together you can then consider doing something that the child or adult might really appreciate. For example I would appreciate someone watering my plants, giving me a bunch of flowers, washing my car, making me a cup of tea, taking my dog out for a walk, making me dinner, baking me a cake or painting me a picture … (those closest to me might remember this list ☺ !). What might you appreciate?

Payback time

Sometimes it can be important to pay back time instead. An example of this might be if someone smashed a window or trashed a room when in a state of alarm, within their fight/flight nervous system, because they were feeling threatened in that moment for whatever reason. In both these instances, we could time how long it might take for an adult to sort this out, for example, if the caretaker or the teacher were to sort out the breakage or clear up the messy room. Then, together with the child or young person, we would determine what we could do, using that same time frame, to pay back time. In the example of the caretaker, it may be that we go sweep up with or for them, collect the bins and tidy their space over a few days to pay them back for the time they lost sweeping up the broken glass, ordering a new pane of glass and fitting the new pane of glass. Notice that I say 'we'. Let's not stand back and watch the child or young person but get stuck in alongside them as well, to model repair. Co-modelling is so powerful when an additional attachment figure is involved: and that means, us!

Increasing structure and supervision

Once we have repaired whatever has gone wrong, as the grown-up we will then need to decide whether there is a need to increase structure and supervision for a time, in the context of whatever has gone wrong. For example, structuring play times, rather than allowing spontaneous play for a while: or being in charge of their money for a while, if they have misspent it. If this were the case, you would explain to the child or young person that you are being supportive, providing some protective boundaries for a time, until they had had enough opportunity to practise and get stronger in this specific area.

Using words such as *'practising'* and *'getting stronger'* keep shame levels low (remember we are taking up the role as stress and shame regulators). Ensure you keep your body language and tone of voice warm, open, calm and engaged, when talking about something like this, as it mustn't come across as a punishment or in any way evaluative of the pupil in and of themselves. You are simply affirming and honouring where they are right now, what their needs are and what will help: and also communicating hope for all that could be. Remember as human beings none of us are static: we're constantly growing and changing.

Remember Reina in the previous chapter? Her random acts of kindness included getting a vase, using découpage and flowers from the allotment to make a display for reception, offering to pay back time for messing up papers by running errands for the staff. And a mediation session with the other girl, with practice beforehand to help her state what she could have said:

"Don't ever put my mum down. My mum is very important to me and you have no right to disrespect me or my mum. Respect is taken seriously in this school."

Educative opportunities

Some educational staff may feel discouraged having to go through these cycles time and time again. However, I want to encourage you to re-frame what you are doing, as you're actually quite remarkably creating an educative opportunity at each stage of the journey. Let's consider together what the child or young person will learn as a result of navigating each stage.

Regulate

Every time we regulate together with a child or young person, we teach our pupil that it's possible to shift states, sensations and feelings by engaging with something on a sensory level. That all important life-changing message that it's possible to learn how to soothe, quieten and calm the alarm system in each one of us, so that we can then use our social engagement system.

Relate

Every time we relate through quality moments together with a child or young person we teach them that connection is paramount, that relationships are necessary in order to live well. That relationships can be safe and positive, and can bring safety and comfort, love and joy. The message of health and wellbeing.

Reason

Every time we reason together with a child or young person, we teach them to pause, reflect and consider something in the higher part of their brain, their thinking and cognitive brain. The message that it's possible to override the emotional limbic brain from time to time, to extend ourselves outside what's known and familiar, to tap into our exploratory system, be curious, interested, excited: to settle to learn.

Repair

Every time we repair a relationship together with a child or young person we teach them that there is usually an exit strategy. That it's usually possible to put things right and that we are often made stronger as a result of difficulties. So there is no reason to panic or be afraid of ourselves or of each other. The message of hope.

Resilience building practices can happen any time ...

Yet another great idea from Headteacher Nicky Murray (p. 77): he encourages the practice of gratitude in his school, which can be so supportive for strengthening resilience in our children and young people. Research has clearly shown that regularly bringing to mind, listing and sharing what we're grateful for can actively promote an optimistic state of mind. Can you think of other ways you could encourage this in your everyday practice?

REPAIR: Mini case studies

ARTHUR IN PRIMARY	Ms Lees: "*I wonder whether we could help put a smile back on Bill's face, I heard that he was also unhappy after play? At this school we're generous and kind. What could we do, I wonder?*" Arthur: "*I don't know … *" Ms Lees: "*Hey! He likes football! How about we set up a football practice circuit and let him try it out? What do you reckon?*" Arthur: "*Ah he'd love that! I will too! Let's do it Miss!*" They go off and create a circuit and send Bill an invite to come and use it with them for 20 minutes.
ADELE IN PRIMARY	Ms Arbour: "*I wonder whether we need to let dad know that you missed him? How about us making him a card and giving it to your social worker? What do you reckon?*" Adele: "*Yes please! I could draw me waiting and looking sad.*" Ms Arbour: "*A 'Missing you' card.*"

TYRONE IN SECONDARY	Craig: *"I've had an idea! How about we create a first aid kit together?"* Tyrone: *"What do you mean Sir? I'm not hurt!"* Craig: *"You may not be hurt physically, but I can tell you are emotionally? So we need to come up with a kind of self-care plan, so that you can feel better inside to help you get through this. For example, I know you love hiphop. We could put 30 minutes of listening to hiphop on there! What do you think? We could think of all the things you love and put them on a piece of paper so that whenever you're feeling low, you could do one of them … "* PAUSE. *"How about we experiment and just see if it helps?"*
ASCHA IN SECONDARY	Ms Webb: *"How about we go and see Ms Wheeler together and we ask if there is any way that she could smile at you every now and then in class … might that help you?"* Ms Webb had prepared Ms Wheeler for this meet-up and asked if she could do all the talking, on behalf of Ascha to keep her stress low. She remembered one of the DDP informed practice principles of speaking about pupils to reduce the intensity of the interaction (see Golding, Philips, Bombèr, 2020) *"Is that maybe a plan?"* Ascha: *"It's a plan."* Ms Webb and Ascha do a high five.

The difference this makes	EVIDENCE FROM PRACTICE

One more difficult part of this work was letting staff know that this was a process that needed to be seen through before the adult could talk to the child about their behaviour. Often, at first, staff were more interested in consequences. Now, through training, talking and watching the work I think staff can see that the children are unable to talk things though straight away. Training adults enough so they can thank children for saying sorry, without talking though the incident has taken lots of work. Some still need reminding or need the Key Adult to cut short their response for them!!

Alison West, Assistant Head Teacher & Attachment Lead, Enfield

Chapter 10

Additional interventions

In addition to everything I have already included as good practice, I thought it might be helpful to share some alternative practices for schools, that can support and strengthen the first two **R's** - **Regulation** and **Relationship**. Let's continue to think outside the box to extend our thinking for supporting traumatised children and young people.

Because of the fragmenting effects of trauma on minds and bodies, it's always better to integrate these sorts of activities into everyday home, school and community life, together with other people who are familiar, rather than setting up a discrete provision in a time-limited way, with strangers. Remember many of our pupils have already experienced multiple transitions and had lots of people involved with them. So it's important to keep the group of people directly and closely involved with the child or young person to a minimum. A small number of adults (4-5), preferably just those already identified as Team Pupil.

Using pets therapeutically

We have a small, apricot cockapoo called Maisie, who works with us here at TouchBase. She is now four years of age but we have had her around the base and children since she was 18 months. She loves children. In fact, she lights up around any human who comes anywhere near her, but especially children! She is one of the best investments I could ever have made in both a personal and professional sense.

For those who have experienced intimacy betrayal at the hands of human beings, pets provide a gateway to connection. There are some for whom therapeutic work is a necessity but because trust, vulnerability and dependency are such big asks, there is no way they would have willingly come to our base. However, an introduction to 'someone' like Maisie can make all the difference!

Maisie doesn't judge, shame, hurt or make any demands inadvertently. She simply wants to connect. Originally, I had thought she would just be around in the therapy rooms, but on discovering her playful personality I started working with her in schools too, as part of our Theraplay® informed practice. She encourages a sense of felt safety with her smile, sparkly eyes, comforting curls, wagging tail and physical proximity. She seems to know how important sensitive attunement is and tunes in beautifully to a child's regulating needs, responding by getting them grounded or energised as appropriate She even engages in huggles on demand (what the children call her attempts to hug them!). Maisie is a valuable part of our team and has her own bio page on our TouchBase website.

How about considering a pet for your school? It doesn't have to be a dog, but any animal who enjoys the attention of being handled by children and young people.

Five points to consider:

- 👍 Do consider possible allergies and ideally choose a pet or breed that is hypoallergenic.
- 👍 Do ensure you have received as much training as possible, and recognise the needs of the animal as of paramount importance. For example, Maisie has a few extended breaks throughout the day when she is off in the countryside enjoying being a dog, with The Dogs Club.
- 👍 Do ensure that you have set up a pet policy for insurance purposes.
- 👍 Do include opportunities for psychoeducation on being around pets. For example how children need to behave around animals, for example being gentle in their voices, body language and movement and respecting the animal's need from time to time for time out. There are some great dog posters available (doggiedrawings.net, for example: 'How not to greet a dog')
- 👍 Consider the health and safety needs of the children/young people, for example including hand washing after spending time with pets.

VOICE OF THE CHILD
ON BEING WITH ANIMALS

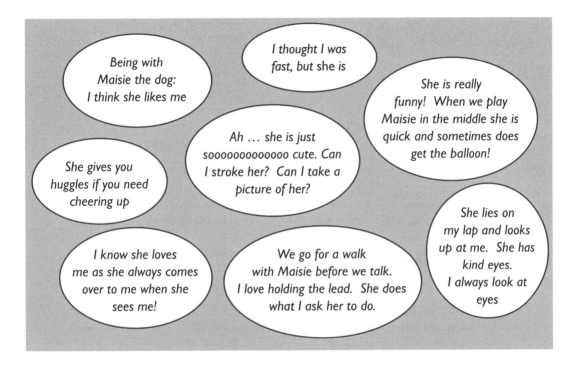

Being with Maisie the dog: I think she likes me

I thought I was fast, but she is

She is really funny! When we play Maisie in the middle she is quick and sometimes does get the balloon!

Ah ... she is just soooooooooooooo cute. Can I stroke her? Can I take a picture of her?

She gives you huggles if you need cheering up

She lies on my lap and looks up at me. She has kind eyes. I always look at eyes

I know she loves me as she always comes over to me when she sees me!

We go for a walk with Maisie before we talk. I love holding the lead. She does what I ask her to do.

Using the arts therapeutically

We have found that many of our children who have experienced deep internal pain are often the most creative. Open up different opportunities and model how to use different types of media, and it seems that their imaginations are captured and another means of communication is created. Over the years we have facilitated groups using the arts, through therapy, arts workshops, exhibitions and competitions. We've been deeply moved by the work our children and young people produce. Often their artwork tells their story, which in turn deepens our empathy and compassion.

Most importantly it becomes a vehicle for communication with both themselves and those around them who don't always get what's going on. It offers a window into some of the more vulnerable, unseen places that have often been hidden, through the need to defend themselves against psychic pain. Unfortunately, defence walls don't differentiate; they can keep out everything, not just the pain. So often, our traumatised pupils are described as 'hard to reach'. The arts provide the means to connect. You don't necessarily need words to communicate. And some have experienced such powerlessness as a result of their own or others' words, that they've given up using them.

How about considering whether you could facilitate access to a wide range of media so that your pupils have this opportunity if they so wish? Partner up with those who are skilled in this area, who know how to optimise the use of different materials and tools so that the children and young people have more options.

Five points to consider:

- 👍 Be aware of your own arts' bias and ensure you allow the child/young person plenty of opportunity to experiment and explore the use of different media.
- 👍 Don't translate their work. Let them explain their work if they want to. Otherwise be respectful and just be alongside, open and engaged.
- 👍 Encourage visits out to art galleries, exhibitions and museums.
- 👍 Encourage the creation and use of a diary which includes photos and other visual bits and pieces.
- 👍 Give them opportunities to exhibit their work if they'd like to. It can be very valuing to express yourself in this way, though never obligatory.

VOICE OF THE CHILD
ON WORKING WITH THE ARTS

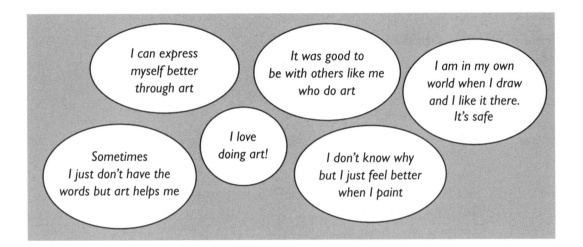

I can express myself better through art

It was good to be with others like me who do art

I am in my own world when I draw and I like it there. It's safe

I love doing art!

Sometimes I just don't have the words but art helps me

I don't know why but I just feel better when I paint

♪ Singing together

The Virtual School in Torbay have been running a choir for years now. All different ages, all different backgrounds but they come together around a song. They don't all sing in pitch but they all sing. Together they sound amazing. The facilitator, Tracey Powell, describes them as being like the dawn chorus! Together the music is brought alive. They have inspired me to create *Belong* - a choir in Brighton & Hove for those aged between 10 and 16 under the direction of a vocalist. Singing together not only supports the individual with their own regulation needs but supports the wellbeing of the whole community too, through both co-regulation and relationship. Check out the popular BBC programme, *The Choir*, to see very visual evidence of the power of groups singing together in diverse settings - including in a school near Grenfell Tower and one in prison, explored and facilitated by choirmaster Gareth Malone (tiny.cc/13lyiz)

How about considering setting up a choir? How about joining in yourself? Partner up with those who are skilled in this area who can support you to meet the regulation and relationship needs of these children.

Creative therapies … enable a therapeutic attunement, through an embodied awareness of rhythmic flow, and the mutual connection that occurs where there is an intense process of deep listening, kinaesthetic awareness, and deep attention to what is happening in the moment.   Kossak 2008

Five points to consider:

- There are many different ways to warm up! Have a go at using your body like percussion!
- Ensure you keep any practice upbeat and fun, using actions and movement wherever possible.
- Be aware of your own music bias and ensure you give the child/young person opportunity to experiment with different styles of music they are interested in.
- Don't be an observer, do join in!
- Create opportunities to perform so you have something to work towards.

VOICES OF PARENTS/CARERS
ON SINGING TOGETHER

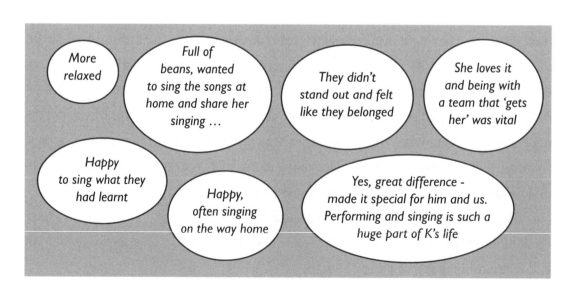

More relaxed

Full of beans, wanted to sing the songs at home and share her singing …

They didn't stand out and felt like they belonged

She loves it and being with a team that 'gets her' was vital

Happy to sing what they had learnt

Happy, often singing on the way home

Yes, great difference - made it special for him and us. Performing and singing is such a huge part of K's life

Working with the land therapeutically

We partner with a fantastic charity called PLOT 22, in Hove. They provide us with their community allotment space weekly for therapeutic work. We facilitate dyadic work with children and young people who have been wounded relationally. This work is carried out either together with their adoptive parent/carer or together with their Key Adult from school, wherever the bond needs to be repaired, or strengthened further, or both.

The interventions during the day are pitched at the child's stage of development and their varying states throughout the day so that our interventions are both developmentally appropriate and state dependent (p. 139). There is always a specialist therapist and teacher on site. We adhere to the health and safety procedures on site written by PLOT 22. On a day when we have observed how mutual trust seems higher than usual, we sometimes get involved with the more risky tasks, for example fire making and sawing of wood, factoring in a risk-benefit analysis.

Through sensitive, responsive care, the children/young people are freed up to enjoy the space together with their key person. As you can imagine, the land provides us with a rich array of sensory comfort - smells, textures and colours, together with many possible regulatory activities such as weeding, planting, foraging, cooking and eating together. This seems an ideal space in which the DMN is likely to come online, strengthening incredible new neuroconnections for our children and young people (p. 77).

Rich, relational interventions over the course of the day, informed by both Theraplay® and DDP informed practice, enables the connection between the child/young person and their key adult to grow and deepen. The day is photojournalled so that a special memory between the adult and child is created and then anchored. To support this memory creation, transitional objects are created and swapped between the child and their adult, for example friendship bracelets and small treasure boxes containing little bits and pieces from the garden that the other person might appreciate, for example a petal, a small pine cone, some rosemary and a pebble in the shape of a heart! We encourage the adults to follow up the day with reference to these pictures

VOICE OF THE CHILD

ON WORKING AT PLOT 22 WITH TOUCHBASE

We loved the day it was so much fun! It was very special to pick our own lunch and eat together. It was very special to spend time with my mum. I hope we can come here again

What a wonderful day to be able to pick and eat our lunch and enjoy all the fresh smells and tastes from a garden directly into our cooking pot

I really enjoyed the sound of the popcorn and the wind in the trees

We had a lovely day! Great to concentrate on the important things and work together

A perfect opportunity to escape real life for a day and focus on accomplishing so much together while getting close to nature

Thank you for such a super day. All together it has been a very special experience for us both which I shall treasure and reflect on a lot

You help everyone calm down. Thank you

We've had the most wonderful day in this peaceful, calm, relaxed environment. This really is an amazing place

I really liked it and it helped me to get closer to my mum and dad. THANKS!

Thank you for a lovely bonding day

A wonderful day full of joy and laughter

Thank you for a lovely, peaceful, foodie day. This really is a little piece of heaven

and transitional objects as they so beautifully provide the visual evidence of the joy of connection to oneself, each other and nature.

The feedback we have had from both the children, young people and the adults experiencing Plot 22 has been so positive. Witnessing what goes on has been fascinating. Step onto the land and you actually see defences melting away. The difference from entering the space to leaving the space at the end of the day is considerable!

How about considering using some land, whether it is a small patch of land just outside the school, an allotment or a woodland area … ? There is also real value in finding a piece of wasteland and enabling it to become a place of natural beauty together with a child or young person who has experienced trauma and loss. There is something deeply transformative about this process on a personal level. There are many, many possibilities … Partner up with others who know how best to work and connect with the land. Together we can be so creative. It's our experience (alongside others up and down the country) that something mysterious, healing and special happens when hurting children and young people are surrounded by such a rich context of sensory experiences and immersed in beauty.

Five points to consider:

- How can you create a sense of privacy in the outdoor space you are using?
- How can you ensure there is shelter if there is wind, rain or very strong heat?
- How will you ensure all are comfortable temperature wise?
- What provision is there for toileting?
- Are you able to provide different types of seating and areas for sensory comfort?

Using baking therapeutically

We partner up with another amazing organisation, Stoneham Bakehouse in Hove. Preparing, kneading, waiting, baking and then eating together provide important regulatory and relational experiences for recovery. Simon Cobb works with young and old, and together they have realised the mental health benefits and transformative impact of baking.

The new economics foundation (neweconomics.org) analysed a huge number of studies into health and wellbeing and came up with five 'Ways to Wellbeing' that are consistently evidenced as making a positive contribution:

	Connect	talk, listen, be there and be connected in relationship with other people
keep	**L**earning	embrace new experiences, see opportunities and surprises yourself
be	**A**ctive	do what you can physically, enjoy what you do, move your mood
take	**N**otice	note and remember the simple things that give you joy
	Give	your time, your words and your presence

Three additional elements have been added more recently: **E**at well, **R**est well and **S**leep (all of which follow easily after a good session with the Bakehouse!). The key letters form the easy-to remember acronym **CLANGERS**.

Baking is a great way to do all these things in the interests of supporting mental health. It's social, it can be done together. Kneading is a physical activity. You need to take notice of how the dough changes as you work it. There is lots to learn! And you can share what you create. In our new project ConnectIN, we have trialled work with care leavers, refugees and any other young people who experience isolation in many different forms. Baking offers the opportunity for connection, with oneself and together with others. It also supports social skills and life skills.

Through the experience of baking rolls, cakes, bread and pizza, the young people are offered a body-mind intervention. For someone who has experienced the fragmentation of trauma this is healing, integrative work. The kneading of dough and proving especially allows the protection of time and time to rest, time to be, time to become … perhaps the DMN comes on line here too (p. 77). Important lessons for all of us but particularly for those with disrupted early attachments who don't know how to rest, to be, to become …

The children and young people are usually proud of what they produce, so baking can facilitate a sense of efficacy. They are also quite keen to share what they have made with others which encourages interdependency, which is often so hard for traumatised children and young people.

How about creating space to bake at school or home? Or considering joining up with a local bakehouse or bakery and enabling children to have access to this experience?

Five points to consider:

> 👍 Be mindful that some children and young people don't feel at all comfortable with sticky textures. You may need to take over at that stage of the process.
>
> 👍 As there are five different stages to bread making you can easily use baking as a sensory break between other interventions
> (i) Knead it, (ii) Wait to prove, (iii) Shape it, (iv) Wait to prove, (v) Bake it. And of course a sixth vi) - Eat it! 😊
>
> 👍 Be aware that the transitions involved in baking - for example waiting to prove the bread - may prove hard for some children and young people, so be prepared to be patient and to offer support.
>
> 👍 Some think you can only bake in schools with pizza ovens or big commercial ovens but the domestic oven is absolutely fine! It offers many possibilities.
>
> 👍 It is recommended that you work either 1:1 or in groups of 4-6 over a period of two hours.

VOICE OF THE CHILD
ON BAKING TOGETHER

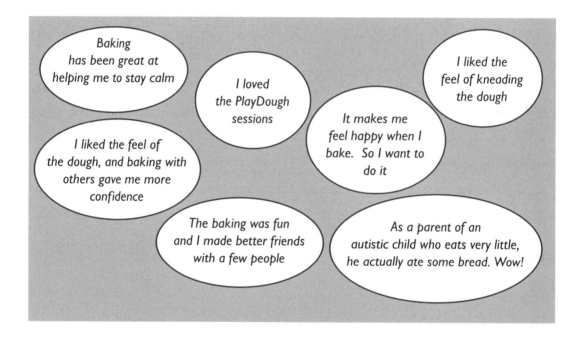

Baking has been great at helping me to stay calm

I loved the PlayDough sessions

I liked the feel of kneading the dough

I liked the feel of the dough, and baking with others gave me more confidence

It makes me feel happy when I bake. So I want to do it

The baking was fun and I made better friends with a few people

As a parent of an autistic child who eats very little, he actually ate some bread. Wow!

Using sport therapeutically

In Brighton & Hove there is an amazing table tennis club set up by Tim Holtam, Harry McCarney & Wen Wei Xu called Brighton Table Tennis Club (BTTC). It's widespread knowledge locally that this club is one of the most inclusive clubs you will probably ever come across! If you ever get opportunity to visit please do - you will be blown away! Some of our most vulnerable children go there, but so do many others of all different ages, who may well have been marginalised in many other contexts.

The table provides that extended physical proximity that is needed as the intimacy zone of tolerance of traumatised children and young people is often so limited. The bats and ball facilitate the rhythm, repetition and physical regulation needed by those with faulty nervous systems caused by toxic stress. The game itself requires at least two players, and so connection is facilitated. There is no expectation to engage verbally but before you know it, the social engagement system is activated through smiles, laughter and chat. Some of their players have gone on to win matches and to play locally, regionally, nationally and internationally. Within the game children learn about practice and about becoming stronger. They learn through the relational experience involved that connection is rewarding. All of this builds resilience - natural resilience.

How about purchasing a net, a couple of bats and a ping pong ball and considering setting up an area at school whereby you could facilitate sport therapeutically? If not table tennis, how about investing in a couple of rowing machines? A couple of upright bikes? Gorilla gym? We don't have to continue 'doing school' the way we always have. These children don't need more of the same, they need something different, novel experiences that support them to update their templates of how they see themselves, others and the contexts they find themselves in. Let's surprise both their minds and their bodies!

Five points to consider:

👍 Ensure you choose Key Adults in school who are up for getting physical as they need to join in! We can't have observers!

👍 Always start in a collaborative way, beating 'personal bests' before competition is introduced. Many of our children/young people have a fragile sense of self.

👍 Be wary not to create more discrete support provision but rather integrate sports into everyday home and school life as these children need support to generalise.

👍 Add variety in the mix

👍 Model practising and getting stronger as this is the best way to evidence what might be possible!

All these different examples meet both the regulation and relationship needs of traumatised children and young people, moving them back into their social engagement system. In effect, for these pupils who so easily get stuck in alarm, we're getting their 'seesaw' moving again (p. 113-4). And often having a lot of fun together whilst we do so.

> *T had feedback from the Head Teacher on one of their players, H, who said: "In my opinion, the table tennis club has nurtured and guided H through challenging times. You have tapped into his sporting talents and given him a sense of belonging and self-belief. As a team you go above and beyond for our diverse community - I cannot praise your inclusive ethos highly enough." H told us about how he feels being part of the table tennis club:*

> *"It makes me feel good, I can get all the frustration out of my head. I feel relaxed there because the adults are like teachers, but not as strict. I have learnt to spin on my forehand and backhand and when I'm 13 I reckon I'll be able to beat T and W in a proper table tennis match. It's a good experience to be with different types of people. I feel special there. Today some of the team came to support me - I'm going to put the photo on the front of my bedroom door. I'm doing a week residential trip with them this summer. Everyone will be older than me but that's OK."*

> *A's mum says he was bullied at school and after trying lots of activities unsuccessfully, he has now become really enthusiastic about table tennis. He says it "keeps his legs going ... and I feel fit afterwards." He likes striving for the medals, and says it 'pumps me up' when he does. He says his coaches are very encouraging, but also "... in control. If stuff crops up with other kids in the sessions then things get sorted".*

VOICE OF THE CHILD

ON PLAYING SPORT TOGETHER

> Playing table tennis as well as I can has made me think that I am not just a normal talent ... and I didn't think I could have friends, but I have made them through playing table tennis

> [the sessions] ... have had a massive impact ... coming here helps me back at school

> ... very sad because I'm not able to see my dad until I'm 15: table tennis helps me have some fun

> ... the people are kind and I've made some friends

Chapter II

A relationship policy for schools

In this book I felt I really wanted to write a policy that schools could adapt as their own - see what you think. Do you want your school to be *truly* attachment aware and trauma responsive, not just one that takes a training and then moves on? If so, have a go at implementing these recommendations in practice, and integrating the key elements into your policy documents in your own language.

WHAT WE BELIEVE:

- In this school we integrate Attachment Aware and Trauma Responsive interventions into our everyday practice.
- From research we are aware that any disruption within the early years from pregnancy onwards can impact minds and bodies in three key areas: affect regulation, attachment and executive function.
- From research we understand that the toxic stress involved in ACEs impacts the nervous system of human beings.
- From research we know that over-compensatory, rich, relational interventions can bring about recovery so that children and young people can function well at home, school and out in their communities.
- We view ourselves as an important part of any pupil's recovery journey. We believe in recovery in community.
- We will not discriminate how we relate to the pupils in our care as we believe each pupil is worthy of our time, energy and patience. However we will differentiate, according to need.
- We will have compassion for those who have muddles, are hurting and/or grieving for whatever reason.

WHO WE ARE:

- We see it as our responsibility to be stress and shame regulators for the pupils in our care.
- We see it as our responsibility to learn all about our assigned pupil: what they have lived through to date, their resilience factors, their stressors and their calmers.
- We do all we can to ensure that our assigned pupils do not lose their thinking capacity (*see* **Respecting Biology**)
- We will be wise with our words, ensuring we do not label any of the pupils in our care.
- We will be gentle with our strength and strong with our gentleness, remembering that some pupils in our care have a very fragile sense of self.
- We see it as more important to always prioritise maintaining connection with our assigned pupil than aiming to prove a point or to get our point of view across (*see* **Relate**).
- We utilise all and any opportunity to communicate delight to the pupils in our care, rather than relying on conditional acceptance.
- We communicate with both our minds and our bodies that these pupils are not alone, that they have fellow travellers supporting them along their life course whilst at our school.
- We see it as our responsibility to remain regulated throughout the school day, taking regular, quality breaks and pressing the pause button occasionally to re-resource ourselves (*see* **My Anchor** p. 184)
- We see it as our responsibility outside of school to attend to our own regulation and relationship needs, to keep healthy and well in both our bodies and minds.
- We remember that everyone is doing the best they can, with what they have lived through to date.
- We try really hard to remember not to take personal insults and rejection personally, or get triggered, as we know that some pupils have experienced intimacy betrayal and do not trust adults in the moment.
- We will engage in relentless care.
- We will let others know if we are struggling, so that we can engage in safe, quality practice.
- We will do all we can to ensure we stay connected to our family, friends and colleagues so that we can experience the relational buffering we need to do our work well.
- We will be aware of the boundaries of our skills set and refer on to trauma recovery experts, as and when appropriate, for specialist advice and support.
- We will identify someone we trust in our work capacity to be our own professional Key Adult, to give permission to them to check in on us on a regular basis, to support our self care.

HOW WE WILL WORK WITH OUR PUPILS WHO HAVE EXPERIENCED RELATIONAL TRAUMA AND LOSS

- We will know their story.
- We will trace back to what a child or young person has lived through, from pregnancy onwards, taking special note of any relational disruptions, ACEs and toxic stress.
- We will try and find out whether there were any others around the child at the time of difficulties, who were physically and emotionally present, attentive, attuned and responsive, for example an auntie, or a neighbour or a youth leader.
- We will provide relational buffering
- We will allocate a Key Adult to all those who have experienced disruption in their early relationships, and a formalised team of 4 or 5 significant adults will be created around them in school (see *Attachment Aware Schools Series* (Bombèr 2016/17) *for more details on the roles and responsibilities of each of these team members*).
- We will prioritise spending quality time with our assigned pupils, being physically and emotionally present, attentive, attuned and responsive.
- We will always prioritise maintaining positive relationships with our pupils whatever other demands are going on, engaging in quality moments.
- We will intentionally use warm and open faces and body language, a varied tone of voice, humour and playfulness, in order to support felt safety.
- We will engage our playful parts wherever possible, not taking ourselves too seriously.
- We will be curious about why pupils do what they do, wondering aloud so that our pupils have opportunity to be curious too and start to make links between states, sensations and feelings.
- We will not problem-solve or reassure our assigned pupils before first really communicating that we have heard what they are trying to tell us about their internal feelings and thoughts.
- Drawing on Perry's NME® model, we will use the **4 Rs** and ensure we are mindful of the order needed: **Regulate**, **Relate**, **Reason**, **Repair**, as well as acknowledging the need to circle back through the stages if our pupil's stress levels and state indicate they are not yet or are no longer ready for a particular stage.
- If we have received the appropriate theoretical and practical training around Theraplay® and DDP informed practice we will use this within our work.

TRANSITIONS

- If an adult needs to change their regular commitments with their assigned pupil, we will take all necessary efforts to communicate this change to the pupil directly and with compassion. The adult will also give the pupil something to support them to manage the separation or change of plan; for example a note or a card, or will swap something like a pen or a pencil case.

- If an adult needs to leave the school for whatever reason, we will make all efforts to ensure the assigned pupil has a carefully thought through and staggered goodbye (see Bombèr, 2011 *for details on how to handle longer term transitions well*).

- If the pupil needs to leave suddenly, for whatever reason, the KA and Team Pupil will make all necessary efforts to say goodbye by visiting, by using Skype, letters or cards. Genuine care will be communicated and a sense of them 'not being forgotten'.

PROVIDE RELATIONAL REPAIR

- We will never leave a pupil on their own after a difficulty or a relationship rupture. This is the time they need us the most (*see* **Repair**).

- If there is a difficulty between ourselves and our assigned pupil or another member of staff, we will do all we can to resolve it so that we can be at peace with one another.

- If an interaction with a pupil becomes difficult for the adult, the adult will take time out to get themselves regulated before re-engaging at a later stage: another familiar adult from Team Pupil will swap in, to be with the pupil.

- As adults we will always apologise directly to the pupil if we mis-attune to them, and their state becomes aggravated.

- When a pupil is aggravated we will match the intensity of the pupil's affect so that the pupil feels heard and validated.

- If something needs to be repaired we will join in too, even if we don't consider the difficulty to be our own personal responsibility.

- If we notice a pupil becoming stressed by any of our interventions we will switch what we are doing, recognising that relationships can be stress-inducing for pupils who have experienced relational trauma or loss (*see* **Regulate**).

- If there is a tension build-up in a classroom we will ensure we check in with our assigned pupil with a smile, and a *'It's going to be OK'*.

- If something goes wrong we will seek understanding from the pupil themselves, rather than making our own assumptions. We will communicate curiosity: *'Help me to understand …'* or *'I wonder what was happening for you …'*

OUR AIMS INCLUDE SUPPORTING ALL PUPILS TO:

✔ Function well at home, school and out and about, in their communities.

✔ Experience safety, security and stability with us.

✔ Reduce their blocked trust.

✔ Increase their tolerance of intimacy.

✔ Increase their comfort zone.

✔ Increase their stress tolerance.

✔ Increase their self-awareness.

✔ Strengthen their sense of self.

✔ Increase their internal controls.

✔ Strengthen their resilience.

✔ Feel confident and secure enough to explore, experiment, be curious and open to learning (enable their exploratory system to come fully online).

✔ Develop a personalised tool kit that will support them to move from alarm to social engagement.

✔ Integrate their body and mind.

✔ Integrate their past experiences into a coherent narrative.

✔ Move towards interdependency with others.

WE WILL MEASURE EFFECTIVENESS BY:

- Checking our attendance data.
- Asking the children and young people themselves to complete a 'Relationships' Circle' (see over).
- Seeking the pupil's own views about their mental health and wellbeing.
- Timing how long it takes our children and young people to recover from everyday, low-level stressors in school.
- Logging how many times senior managers have to deal with serious incidents.
- Measuring their learning progress, in comparison with themselves, not their peers.
- Logging any transitions made between classes or schools mid-year.

Signed: ....

Dated: ....

One final thought on evaluation

On our Attachment Lead course, Key Adults work together with their focussed pupil to find out a little more about how they see their support network and the contexts they find themselves in. We ask children and young people to complete a relationships' circle, indicating who they think is around them. We also give them a blank piece of paper and ask them to 'Draw you and your home' and another blank piece of paper, 'Please draw you and your school'. We also give them a template of a person holding a rope on the side of a mountain and ask them to draw who would hold the rope (the mountain climb exercise). We're not seeking to interpret every detail in their pictures but simply to see who they include in their pictures: people or animals or objects? Children or adults? Those present in their lives now or not? Real or imagined? We carry this out near the beginning of our year together and then again at the end.

It's quite striking how, initially at least, many who have experienced significant relational traumas and losses choose themselves, animals, objects, imaginary others, those not around and peers, as opposed to grown-ups, especially those who are now caring for them. This is a pattern we've noted over many years now. The saddest pictures are those where the child or young person is alone or when they draw something like a lone rock or an animal, stating clearly, 'I don't trust anyone'. Tragically we always have quite a few of those represented in our work out in schools.

Remember we are designed to function best in the context of relationships with others. It's important that we keep an eye on their relational health. To encourage you: after a period of over-compensatory care, we start to notice one or two adults start popping up.

This is recovery in progress!

The impact of working within a Relationship Policy which honours the 4 Rs

The difference this makes │ EVIDENCE FROM PRACTICE

Staff have been given training on the **4 Rs** and we have posters displayed in each classroom and in corridors to remind staff of this when supporting children in overwhelm. This has enabled staff to see difficulties differently and has changed the way that our children with the most significant attachment needs are supported. In turn, this has resulted in a complete transformation of these children.

Aimee Cave, Assistant Head & Attachment Lead, York

We have a Key Adult/mentor for all our learners, even if it is only someone they 'check in' with throughout or at the end of the day.

We find that offering a variety of responses, we can support individuals more effectively. When we limited ourselves to just one methodology, we quickly learnt it did not work for some. I have invested heavily in our own people. It has cost a huge amount of school funds but I am finding it so worthwhile on so many fronts. I get the commitment from staff because relationships are robust between staff and children. Learners respond more readily to the therapeutic intervention than with a stranger. This is an important point. Most of my learners will not access CAMHS even though they need to. They cannot manage the transition to another building with an individual they have failed to secure a relationship with, so they NFA for appointments and of course lose their booking. A negative cycle.

If I were to say anything to [other] schools about this, it would be, every time, understand the needs of your children then crisis will be averted.

Lyndsey Brown, Headteacher with two Attachment Leads in the school, Bradford

Our pupil has blossomed under her Key Adult and team, using AATI strategies (for the duration of 3 years). She was able to attend the residential school trip this year without any difficulties and has managed other children in care coming and going in her family, without any major difficulties in school.

I think the school now seems a calmer place with the **4 Rs** being used. Staff feel better prepared to manage difficult situations and know which Key Adult to call for different children. It has been amazing to see, after relationships have been built, how children can trust their Key Adult to come to them in times of distress and believe them when they say 'Let's go and ...' in order to help regulate. It's helped staff to see that these strategies work and can prevent situations from escalating.

Spending time building relationships with these children has been insightful and fascinating. This has helped adults to be able to offer the most effective strategies to children to help them regulate, after outbursts. Staff have been amazed at how quickly children can leave situations for co-regulation with adults, and has reminded staff that the children themselves don't want to be in that state either.

Watching the children instantly calm when adults relate to them and acknowledge how they must be feeling has been great, it's like watching a weight being lifted from their shoulders.

It's interesting to try to walk the tightrope of support, trying to make each step in the journey at the right time but also knowing it's OK to make mistakes and go back to the Regulate activities if you have moved on too quickly.

Alison West, Assistant Head Teacher & Attachment Lead, Enfield

The use of attachment aware practice in our school has had a significant and positive contribution to the very chaotic lives of our most vulnerable and traumatised young people, often those young people who are in foster care or state care - or who are transitioning into semi-independent living. The use of the **4 Rs** clearly brings about security for the young person and is also useful to remind staff to manage their own feelings and expectations when in the stressful times of supporting a student in crisis or meltdown.

Lisa Fabian, Head of Art & Attachment Lead, Croydon

All 11 schools across the three phases within the Trust have received training on how to be attachment aware and trauma informed and responsive. We are in the process of changing or implementing new Behaviour Regulation Plans, incorporating our policies on relational safety, language of parts (for the youngest children), PACE and regulation ideas specifically appropriate for the age of the pupils or the specific developmental needs of the child.

Daniel Thrower, CEO & Attachment Lead, Anne Oakley, SEND & Attachment Lead at The Wensum Trust Norfolk

All of our schools do not exclude any child with SEN or CIC and exclusions have reduced significantly in all. Many of our primaries (ours included) have a 0% exclusion rate, in favour of using the **4 Rs**. This is embedded in our policies.

Tracy Jones, Vice Principal, Trust SEND Lead & Attachment Lead, Bristol

Conclusion

When we each find the courage to look this problem in the face, we will have the power to transform not only our health, but our world.

Burke-Harris 2018, p. 222

Life began with connection, in relationships. Let's ensure life progresses with and ends with relationships. This is the way we were designed to function best as human beings. We can't 'do life' alone: no matter how independent we are, we can't survive or thrive completely on our own. We need one another. Healthy interdependence needs to be facilitated throughout the lifecourse, in homes, in schools and in life beyond school within our communities, for the sake of our health and wellbeing and for our population's sake. We need to build communities which connect well, which promote safety and wellbeing, and which value secure, sustaining relationships for everyone.

When we're in a caring relationship with a child, young person or adult, it's not just our emotional response which is important. Actions matter. It's not enough just to be moved emotionally by the kind of distress experienced by our traumatised pupils; that I've shared within this book: we must be moved to act as well. Let's find the courage to disable the societal imprinting and cultural expectations that have been around for far too long. Let's be the ones who facilitate recovery for those who have been wounded to their core by ACEs, whatever they look like now, however this is communicated, through actions or through words, or both. It's not at all helpful to collude with the relational withdrawal or relational distance that we sometimes facilitate consciously and unconsciously. As Porges (2019) states,

> When we become a polyvagal-informed society, we're functionally capable of listening to and witnessing other people's experiences, we don't evaluate them.   p. 3

Instead of withdrawing and distancing, we need to draw close and find ways to connect with our traumatised pupils, even if they are resistant.

The documentary *Resilience* has created a new beginning for the conversation that was long overdue within education in the UK. No longer can we expect our pupils to just come into school, sit down and engage in the learning we provide. We need to know their story: what have they lived through? How are they currently living? We can't have been thinking straight to ever imagine that a pupil who was experiencing domestic violence at home, could simply sit up and get on within our classrooms. That a pupil who lost their friend to knife crime could automatically put it out of their mind and focus on their GCSEs. Now is surely the time to ensure *all* our schools are *person centred*, not curriculum centred.

Rather than merely applying rigid, rule-based systems to our fellow human beings, surely our pupils need to be interacted with relationally. Many are desperate for connection, human connection. This must always be our first priority in school: everything else comes next. Nothing should ever happen in our schools that costs us our relationship with our pupils. We must do all we can to protect and honour our relationships with one another: they are the heartbeat of learning.

> At their best, schools can function as islands of safety in a chaotic world. They can teach children how their bodies and brains work and how they can understand and deal with their emotions. Schools can play a significant role in instilling the resilience necessary to deal with the traumas of neighbourhoods or families.
> Van der Kolk, 2015, p. 351

We must hold a much bigger vision for learning. Learning isn't just restricted to the school years but spans a lifetime; so facilitating learning opportunities must be the responsibility of everyone, not just classroom teachers. There needs to be a level playing field for all types of learning too. Why do we only value academic learning? Now is the time to reinstate the value of all learning - the arts, sports, vocational, social skills, resilience … And we shouldn't just look at what we teach, but crucially, *how* we teach … We have known for a long, long while that there isn't a one size that fits all, so let's embrace all the different teaching and learning styles possible, including more active participation from our pupils and more hands-on projects: rather than reducing our education system to essay writing, SATS and exams.

Now is the time to reclaim the word discipline with its original meaning - 'to teach'. To view *discipline* as merely another mode of learning, and not to ever again allow *punishment* to attach itself to its meaning. We must use *differentiated discipline* with our traumatised pupils within our classrooms, so as not to alienate or isolate them further.

Let's also redefine the meaning of success. Success could be *recovering from stressors quickly*. Success could involve *having the resilience to manage something*, despite the odds. Success could be interpreted in the *practising and the 'getting stronger at'* … not just in achieving an A* in English Literature. Success could be starting up as a car mechanic. As a musician. As a cleaner. As a youth club leader. As a rap artist. As a builder. As a dancer. As a gardener, a bookkeeper, an entrepreneur. Equality is valued in education and yet not always practised by those who lead.

We need to understand why we have a duty of care to tame those who are hurting inside. Let's use different ways of being in our schools so that those pupils who struggle with intimacy tolerance experience therapeutic communication, not communication that aggravates or isolates them further. These can include sensory attachment, Theraplay® and DDP informed practice.

And as a matter or urgency, we need to realise how important it is to change tack in terms of supporting staff in schools. Rather than *reducing* the number of adults in school, we need to *increase* the number of rich, relational interventions available and on offer from adults skilful enough to get alongside those amongst our pupils who find connection hard. When we know relationships are the heartbeat of every school, ensuring life at every level, we cannot afford to merely say there are *'not enough funds'*. Whatever it costs, we must increase the adult:pupil ratio. Even if, for now, this means tapping into the voluntary sector, and charities, or even our own communities - aunties, uncles, grandparents ... we recommend TLG, a national charity, which provides mentors and coaches for children in schools (*see* **Useful Organisations**). We know, from trauma experts to what the children themselves say (*see* **The Voice of the Child**), that relationships are the healing agent that we need.

I am a strong believer that all of us can play a significant part in this recovery, having both experienced and witnessed it happening repeatedly in both my personal and my professional life journeys. Recovery takes place within community, not just together with a therapist, in an isolated room. There isn't a 'cure' for the serious impact of relational trauma or loss, but rather a physiological, psychological and relational 'place' that someone can get to as they begin to integrate what has happened for them previously. Then, they will be able to get on with everyday life really well, within relationship with others. As Babette Rothschild comments, the most important thing we can work towards and wish for, for those around us, is to be able to function and to function well in our homes, schools and out and about in our communities.

For recovery, we need to support the child and young person to both *safely* remember their life history of relational trauma and loss and to come to the realisation that they can now become *active authors* of their own continuing biographies. Together, with us alongside them, they need to gradually become aware of their patterns of both their defensive positions - their protection - and of their relationship styles - their connection. Only then will they have the self-awareness they need to actually have a choice about the types of relationships they enter into and the types of lives they lead. Relationships that can bring joy. And a choice about how to engage with the opportunities that come their way at home, school and in their communities. A life that is both meaningful and purposeful.

On her website, Deb Dana (rhythmofregulation.com - *see* **Useful Organisations)** states that in order for full engagement in the therapy process, therapists need to attend to the 3 Ps - the **p**lace, the **p**erson and the **p**rocess. As educators, I believe this is really helpful for us to use as our focus too, in our schools, our homes and other contexts where these traumatised children and young people find themselves. I've summarised below the key points discussed in this book, using the helpful structure of these three Ps.

Place   Let's ensure we have increased sensory comfort (what they see, what they smell, what they touch, what they hear, what they taste) and also increase the availability of regulatory tools (rather than inadvertently overlooking the lack of warmth and security in the spaces in which these children and young people find themselves).

Person   Let's intentionally increase our own safety cues as we relate to these children and young people, rather than inadvertently using threat cues. We may send out threat cues through a lack of self-awareness around our own body language, together with our lack of awareness of the relational impact some of our policies and practices have on those who have experienced relational trauma and loss in their lives. So let's engage in intentional, warm and open body language. Let's smile - lots! And may our voices be engaging, with modulation, so that our pupils are curious about what we have to say.

Relationships are:

♥ The heartbeat to get learning going ♥
♥ The vehicle towards adaption and recovery from ACEs ♥
♥ What we all function best with ♥

Process Let's increase opportunities for flexibility rather than rigidity, within our policies and practices. With the knowledge we have now, we can no longer state: *There is one behaviour policy (and zero tolerance of deviation)*. It's so important we remember that our traumatised pupils have a rigidity themselves, because of the scar tissue from the relational wounds they have experienced. So to fully engage them, so they have a chance to genuinely optimise the educative opportunities we give them, we need to use a differentiated approach, rather than insist on one size fits all.

'Caring' should never encourage children and young people to lose their sense of control of their own future. Instead, caring should involve actions which empower them, actions that enable them to move forwards towards better relationships, better times, better solutions and better situations. This is a compassionate response.

We really need to know how to help human beings function best, to know the score. Neuroscience enables us to make connections on behalf of and for the children and young people in our care. It's an important backdrop and scaffolding to what we'll need when the going gets tough - and it does get really tough, from time to time. The recovery process includes many ups and downs.

It's critical that we take the time to truly *know* the individual child or young person we're working with, not just superficially, but knowing them through and through. Be curious. What's their story? What have they lived through? Have they experienced toxic stress? When was that? Was there anyone around to buffer that stress? What makes them tick? What are their triggers? What are their calmers? What has helped them make it thus far? What are their hidden dreams and desires? What gives them comfort, what gives them joy?

Let's all remember that the long term impact of ACEs is not all about suffering. For *some* children and young people, adversity may:

Adversity may ...	Why might that be
Enable them to develop **perseverance**	... since they've had to stick in there in order to survive overwhelming toxic stress
Deepen **empathy**	... since they know what it is to suffer and hurt deeply
Bring out **protective qualities**	... since they know what they could have done with, but didn't have
Spark mini **'super-powers'**	... for example, being hypervigilant, being able to multitask, having a fine eye for detail ... since these skills/powers were practised and developed in the midst of much turmoil and pain, in order to support survival

Adapted and expanded from Burke-Harris 2018, p. 218

And we must never overlook this. Though I'm sure we wouldn't ever wish suffering on any of our fellow human beings, we also must recognise that some treasures may have been collected along the way. These treasures could actually benefit themselves, ourselves and others, into the future. For example, I remember listening to an incredible woman - Sabrina Cohen-Hatton on Woman's Hour (BBC Radio 4, 11/4/19), who holds a strategic position in the fire service and is the youngest fire chief in the UK (as of 2020). She described how she had been enabled to make a significant life-saving decision on behalf of her fire crew, because of her heightened hypervigilance, which had developed as a response to her ACEs (do look her up and read her book, '*The Heat of The Moment*' (Society, The Guardian: 23/10/19).

But primarily, ACEs get 'under the skin' of children and young people impacting bodies, hearts and minds in a profoundly negative way. It becomes a significant part of who they are. So our goal is for us to be their supporters in the creation of integrated narratives, in which they can own their past, weave it into the colourful, broader tapestry of who they are, in the present, on the road to a better future.

It is only when we take time to know the child that we can even begin the journey of teaching them, including that aspect of teaching we call discipline. I hope by now you'll recognise that first and foremost, our traumatised pupils need rich, relational experience with us, relationships that communicate acceptance and understanding of everything that makes these children and young people feel, and think the ways they do. Together with us they'll learn about regulation and repair. Then we can teach them the facts and figures - the curriculum. Then we can teach them how to be and how to behave around others - discipline - so that they can relate well and fully function as the strong and valued member of our school community they really are.

In relating we must be sensitive with our timings: timing is everything! For a long time we've rushed on in there, attempting to get children and young people to understand important facts and figures when they weren't in anything like the right state to hear us. We've sent them off to isolation rooms and put images of sad faces on the board when things got out of hand because no-one had ever helped them experience co-regulation, and then learn how to contain themselves. Instead, paying attention to their body cues so that we know what's happening in their nervous system, is going to be pivotal. At any given moment, we need to know which of the three nervous systems they are in - their social engagement system (green), their fight/flight system (amber) or their freeze system (red) and which state they are in: calm, alert, alarm, fear or terror. Sensitive attunement to the specific nervous system and which of the five states the child or young person is in will pave the way to what is needed next: whether we speak or go sensory, whether we draw close or give space. All our interventions need to be state dependent: one size really doesn't fit all!

We need to follow the neuro-sequential order of the **4 Rs**, what Dr. Bruce Perry named as **Regulation, Relationship, Reasoning** (2014-2017), followed by what I'm calling **Repair**. Then we can invest in what matters most - safety, security and stability.

It's only when the regulation and relationship systems are well attended to that the exploratory system will have any opportunity to be fully activated. Shared learning will be possible, if we first learn how to respect and honour biology. When we know how to reach our traumatised pupils in each state, and support them back to or sustain them in a calm, alert, social engagement, settled to learn.

It's seriously tragic what some children and young people have had to endure in their early weeks and years, when they should have been held tightly, soothed, comforted, supported, enjoyed and taught. It's perhaps even more tragic that so many still go on to experience even more hardship, further relational trauma and loss, as a result of our collective naivety, a lack of knowledge being shared in our communities; and our systems don't respect or honour biology, haven't updated practice and policies - *yet* ...

Now is the time for us to lead the way: we must take up our rightful roles as fellow travellers. Our journey together with this tribe of children and young people will be influenced not only by thoughtful attention to what's being said, but also to what is being spoken beneath the words, through the body. We are going to need brave leaders who ensure all the latest information on child development, attachment and neuroscience is shared and fully integrated into everything we think and do. We owe it to our children. In the words of Nelson Mandela (former President of South Africa),

> Safety and security don't just happen, they are the result of collective consensus and public investment. We owe our children, the most vulnerable citizens in our society, a life free of violence and fear ... and there can be no keener revelation of a society's soul than the way in which it treats its children.
>
> 8th May, 1985 nelsonmandelachildrensfund.com

Most people come into education wanting to make a positive difference to the lives of children and young people. I hope this book will give you the courage, knowledge and ideas you need to be that difference, starting with one conversation, one child, one young person, one lesson, one school policy ... to play your part in revealing society's soul, for the better. It's up to us to be relational activists!

1000 TEAR BOTTLES

L M BOMBÈR (2019)

I stumbled across a room today

And didn't expect what I saw

1000 tear bottles positioned

Beautifully on the floor

Each one moulded

One lump of clay

The size - a human heart

Across the ages

They filled the room

Some hiding small and fragile

Whilst others stood tall and proud

I picked a small one up nearby

Considering you my child

Knowing the tears remain inside

Scaffolded behind your walls

But one day I pray they will come

That they will flow

And be released.

Until that day I will tell them

Of the tears that are inside

Why they can't be cried right now

Why you are so scared

Why you appear so tough, so still

The tears - trapped well inside

They don't know like I do

What broke you

They don't know like I do

That you feel so alone

They don't know like I do

That you're hurting - deeply.

I stumbled across a room today

And didn't expect what I saw

1000 tear bottles positioned

Beautifully on the floor

Acknowledgements to Deborah Tempsett, '1000 tear bottles', Ashburnham Installation 2019

There is a sacredness in tears. They are not a mark of weakness, but of power... They are the messengers of overwhelming grief, of deep contrition, and of unspeakable love.

Washington Irving

References and bibliography

APPG (2019) *All Party Parliamentary Group on Knife Crime. Back to School: Breaking the Link between exclusions and knife crime October 2019* preview.tinyurl.com/ukrrhx5

Aspden, K.L. (2016) *Help! I've Got an Alarm Bell Going Off in My Head!* Jessica Kingsley Publishers: London

Aspden, K.L. (2019) *Help! My feelings are too big!* Jessica Kingsley Publishers: London

Assets Publishing Service (2015) Use of reasonable force preview.tinyurl.com/vzm3x3h

Baylin, J. & Hughes, D. (2016) *The Neurobiology of Attachment-Focused Therapy* W. W. Norton: US

Bennett, T. (2017) Creating a Culture: How school leaders can optimise behaviour *Independent Review of Behaviour in Schools 00059* (DfE) March 2017

Bloom, S. L (1997) Creating Sanctuary: Toward the evolution of sane societies Routledge: New York

Bloom, S. L. & Farragher, B. (2013) *Restoring Sanctuary: A New Operating System for Trauma Informed Systems* OUP: USA

Bombèr, L.M. (2007) *Inside I'm Hurting: Practical strategies for supporting children with attachment difficulties in school* Worth Publishing: London

Bombèr, L.M. (2009) Survival of the Fittest in, *Teenagers & Attachment: Helping adolescents engage with life and learning* (Ed. Andrea Perry) Worth Publishing: London

Bombèr, L.M. (2011) *What About Me? Inclusive strategies to support pupils with attachment difficulties make it through the school day* Worth Publishing: London

Bombèr, L.M. & Hughes. D. (2013) *Settling to Learn: Why relationships matter in school* Worth Publishing: London

Bombèr, L.M. (2015) *Attachment Aware Schools Series: Bridging The Gap for Troubled Pupils* Box set (5 books) Worth Publishing: London

Bombèr, L.M (2015) in, *Capacity to Change* (Eds., Williams, B., Peart, E., Young, R. & Briggs, D. Family Law (a publishing imprint of Jordan Publishing Limited): Bristol

Boudreau, E. (2019) *School Discipline Linked to Later Consequences: Usable knowledge relevant research for today's educators online* Research story 53910 Refers to nber.org/papers/w26257.

Bhreathnach, E. (2006) *The Scared Gang* Northern Ireland: Alder Tree Press

Brooks, D. (2019) *The Wisdom your Body Knows New York Times.* nytimes.com

Brown, B. (2012) *Daring Greatly: How the courage to be vulnerable transforms the way we live, love, parent, and lead* New York: Gotham Books

Brown, B. (2019) BreneBrown.com Quote taken from p.1 of website, DaringClassrooms

Brunker, L. (2014) *The Kids' Guide to Staying Awesome and in Control* Jessica Kingsley Publishers: London

Burke-Harris, N. (2018) *The Deepest Well: Healing the long term effects of childhood adversity* Bluebird, Pan MacMillan: London

Busby, E. (2019) Number of pupil exclusions from schools rises to highest point in decade amid funding cuts *Independent* (online) *Education News*, 25/7/19

Cantor, P. (2002) Turnaround for Children turnaroundusa.org/

Children's Commissioner (2019) *Exclusions: Children excluded from mainstream school* childrenscommissioner.gov.uk

Circle of Security (2016) Shark Music youtube

Clackmannanshire Council Education Service (2017) *Boosting brains, boosting learning: A briefing to support educator understanding of the 'Readiness for Learning' (R4L) approach* Alloa: Author clacks.gov.uk

Clarke, J. I., & Dawson, C. (1998) *Growing Up Again* Hazelden: USA

Coan, J.A. (2010) *Adult Attachment and the Brain Journal of Social and Personal Relationships* (27): 210-18

Coan, J.A., Schaefer, H. S., & Davidson, R. J. (2006) Lending a Hand: Social regulation of the neural response to threat *Psychological Science, (17): 1032-39*

Cohen, D. (2020) *Saving Troubled Teenagers is a Tale of Two Cities* Evening Standard (8/1/20) Standard.co.uk

Cozolino, L. (2013) *The Social Neuroscience of Education* WW Norton: USA

Cuddy, A. (2012) *Your Body Language Shapes Who You Are* TEDGlobal. bit.ly/cuddy-ted-talk

Damasio, Antonio. R. (1999) *The Feeling of What Happens* Vintage (Random House): UK

Dana, D. (2018) *The Polyvagal Theory in Therapy: Engaging the rhythm of regulation* WW Norton: USA

Dana, D. (2019) *The Polyvagal Theory in the Classroom with Deb Dana* 5/4/19, accessed Oct 2019 YouTube

Desautels, L.L. & McKnight, M. (2019) *Eyes Are Never Quiet: Listening beneath the behaviours of our most troubled students* Wyatt-MacKenzie Publishing: Oregan, USA

DfE (2018) *Guidance for Designated Teachers* assets.publishing.service.gov.uk

Donovan, S. (2019) *The Lost Years: re-igniting compassion and ambition for our most vulnerable young people through an understanding of trauma and adolescence* Talk at the From Trauma to Trust Conference, 29/11/19 coaect.co.uk

Donovan, S. (2019) *The Essential Guide to Therapeutic Parenting the Teen Years* Jessica Kingsley: London

Eades, J. M.F. (2008) *Celebrating Strengths: Building strength-based schools* CAPP Press: Coventry, UK

Felitti, V.J., Anda, R.F., Nordenberg, D., Williamson, D.F., Spitz, A.M., Edwards, V., Koss, M.P., & Marks, J.S. (1998). *Relationship of childhood abuse and household dysfunction to many of the leading causes of death in adults: The Adverse Childhood Experiences (ACE) Study American Journal of Preventive Medicine 14(4), 245–258*

Forbes, H. (2012) *Help for Billy: A beyond consequences approach to helping challenging children in the classroom* Beyond Consequences Institute, LLC. beyondconsequences.com

Francis, Y.J., Bennion, K. & Humrich, S. (2017) Evaluating the outcomes of a school based Theraplay® project of looked after children *Educational Psychology in Practice: Issue 3* (2017) pp. 308-322

Geddes, H. (2012) *Attachment in the Classroom* Worth Publishing: London

Gillett, T. (2019) *Toddlers, Meltdowns And Brain Development: Why parents need to ditch traditional discipline* [Blog] Raised Good, Parenting by Nature raisedgood.com

Glenville, M. (2019) *The Role Nutrition Plays in Healing from Trauma*, presentation given at the Congress of Attachment and Trauma in London 15-17/11/19

Golding, K. S., Fain, J., Frost, A. & Templeton, S. (2013) *Observing Children with Attachment Difficulties in preschool settings* Jessica Kingsley Publishers: London

Golding, K.S., Fain, J., Frost, A., Mills, C., Worrall, H., Roberts, N., Durrant, E. & Templeton, S. (2013) *Observing Children with Attachment Difficulties in School* Jessica Kingsley Publishers: London

Golding, K., Turner, M. T., Worrall, H., Roberts, J. & Cadman, A. E. (2016) *Observing Adolescents with Attachment Difficulties in Educational Settings* Jessica Kingsley Publishers: London

Golding, K. (2014) *Using Stories to Build Bridges with Traumatized Children* Jessica Kingsley Publishers: London

Golding, K. (2017) *Everyday Parenting with Security and Love. Using PACE to provide the foundations for Attachment.* London: Jessica Kingsley Publishers

Golding, K.S., Phillips. S & Bombèr. L.M. (2020) *Working with Relational Trauma in Education Series: Guide to Working With Relational Trauma Using DDP* Series Editor Kim Golding: Jessica Kingsley. London.

Greenhalgh, P. (1994) *Emotional Growth and Learning* Routledge: USA & Canada

Haines, S. (2016) *Trauma Is Really Strange* Singing Dragon: London

Hambrick, E.R. & Brawner, T.W. (2017) *The Neurosequential Model: Introduction & research updates* static1.squarespace.com

Harrison, B. (2019) Too Fidgety to Meditate? Try TRE - the new tension-release technique *The Times* online thetimes.co.uk

Hobday, A. (2001), Timeholes: A useful metaphor when explaining unusual or bizarre behaviour in children who have moved families *Clinical Child Psychology and Psychiatry*, 6, 1, 41-47.

Home Office (2019) *An Analysis of Indicators of Serious Violence* (July 2019) gov.uk

Hughes, D.A. (2009) *Attachment Focussed Parenting* WW Norton: New York

Hughes, D.A. & Baylin, J. (2012) *Brain-Based Parenting* WW Norton: New York

Hughes, D., Golding, K. & Hudson (2019) *Healing Relational Trauma with Attachment Focused Intervention* WW Norton: New York

Ian, R. & Ross, F. (2011-2012) *Autogenic Dynamics : Physiological, Psychological & Research Matters: the Polyvagal Theory and a more sympathetic awareness of the ANS* (after Porges et al) atdynamics.co.uk

Johnson, S. (2008) *Hold Me Tight* Hachette Book Group: USA Published first in Great Britain in 2011 by Piatkus

Johnstone, M. (2012) *Quiet the Mind: An illustrated guide on how to meditate* Constable & Robinson Ltd: London

Kossack, M. from *Why Rhythm* on rhythm2recovery.com (accessed 16/12/19)

Knost, L.R. (2013) *Two Thousand Kisses a day: Gentle parenting through the ages and stages* Little Hearts Books: LLC, USA

Knost, L.R. (2013) *The Gentle Parent: Positive practical, effective discipline* Little Hearts Books: USA

Landor, M., Tod, L. & Kennedy, H. AVIGUK Home videointeractionguidance.net

Langton, E.G. & Boy, K. (2017) *Becoming an Adoption-Friendly School* Jessica Kingsley Publishers: London

Levine, P. (1997) *Waking the Tiger Healing* Trauma North Atlantic Books: Berkeley, CA, USA

Levine, P. (2010) *In An Unspoken Voice: How the body releases trauma and restores goodness* Berkeley, CA: North Atlantic Books

Lindaman. S. (2016) *How Polyvagal Theory Helps Us Understand the Effectiveness of Theraplay®* The Theraplay® Institute Newsletter, Winter 2016

Linley, A., Willars, J. & Biswas-Diener, R. (2010) *The Strengths Book* CAPP Press: Coventry, UK

Lucas, S., Insley, K. & Buckland, G. (2006) *Nurture Group Principles and Curriculum Guidelines: Helping Children to Achieve* The Nurture Group Network, UK

McAllister, J. (2016) *Reclaiming Discipline for Education: Knowledge, relationships & the birth of community* Routledge: Research in Education (Kindle Version)

McNight, M. (2016) *The Brain & Troubled Children & Youth in ACES & Education* Blog by Michael McNight 5 acesconnection.com 5/12/2016)

McTaggart, J. (2018) *Behaviour Model* Accessed online via social media July 2018 (Permission sought personally Oct 2019

Maté, G. (2019) *When the Body Says No: The Cost of Hidden Stress* Vermillion: USA

Maté, G. (2019) Dr Gabor Maté on *Childhood Trauma, The Real Cause of Anxiety and Our 'Insane' Culture* Human Window humanwindow.com

Miller, K. Connected Moments connectedmoments.co.uk

Mosley, J. & Grogan, R. (2009) *The Big Book of Calmers* Positive Press Ltd: UK

Murray, N. (2018) *One School's Story of Building Resilience* Presentation at the ACE-AWARE Nation Conference (2018) Nicky Murray, Headteacher. 21/10/18. youtube

Music, G. (2011) *Nurturing Natures* Psychology Press: Hove

Music, G. (2019) *Nurturing Children* Routledge: Oxfordshire

National Offender Management Service (2016) *NOMS Annual Report & Accounts* 2015-2016 gov.uk

new economics foundation (2008) *5 Ways to WellBeing* (pdf) issuu.com

New Zealand Education Department (2019) *Support for Schools to Manage Challenging Student Behaviour* education.govt.nz

New Zealand Education Department (2018) *Banning Seclusion and Creating a Legal Framework for Physical Restraint* education.govt.nz

New Zealand Legislation (2019) New Zealand Legislation - Education Act 1989. No 80 29/10/19 legislation.govt.nz

NHS Education for Scotland. (2017) *Transforming Psychological Trauma - A knowledge and skills framework for the Scottish workforce* Published May 2017 NHS Education for Scotland: Scotland, nes.scot.nhs.uk

Nouwen, H.J.M. (1997) *The Inner Voice of Love* Darton, Longman & Todd Ltd: Wandsworth, UK

Nouwen, H.J.M. (1982) *Compassion* Darton, Langman & Todd Ltd: Wandsworth, UK

Nouwen. H.J.M. (2017) *You are the Beloved* Hodder & Stoughton: Great Britain

Nouwen, H.J.M. (2018) *With Burning Hearts (2nd Edn)* Orbis Books: Maryknoll, USA

Ofsted (2018) *Positive Environments Where Children Can Flourish: A guide to inspectors about physical interventions and restrictions of liberty* No. 180006

Ogden, P. & Fisher, J. (2015) *Sensorimotor Psychotherapy: Interventions for trauma and attachment (Norton series on interpersonal neurobiology)* WW Norton: USA

Olson, K. (2014) *The Invisible Classroom* WW Norton: USA

Palmer, P.J. (2007) *The Courage to Teach: Exploring the inner landscape of a teacher's life* Jossey Bass: San Fransisco, USA

Panksepp, J. (2004) *Affective Neuroscience: The foundations of human and animal emotions* Oxford University Press: NY, USA

Panksepp, J. (2010) *Affective neuroscience of the emotional BrainMind: evolutionary perspectives and implications for understanding depression* Dialogues of Clinical Neurocience Volume 12, no.4

Perry, B. & The Child Trauma Academy (2004-2017) *What is NMT?* ChildTrauma.org

Perry, B. (2006) *Applying principles of neurodevelopment to clinical work with maltreated & traumatised children: the Neurosequential Model of Therapeutics, in, Working with Traumatised Youth in Child Welfare* The Guildford Press: New York

Perry, B. & Hambrick, E. (2008) The Neurosequential Model of Therapeutics *Reclaiming Children & Youth* 17 (3) p. 38-43

Perry, B. (2013) *Applying Principles of Neurodevelopment to Clinical Work with Maltreated & Traumatised Children. The Neurosequential Model of Therapeutics* Article can be found child trauma.org

Perry, B. (2014) Early Childhood Development 27/5/14 Youtube

Perry, B. (2017) *Early Brain Development: Reducing the effects of trauma* Youtube

Perry, B. & Szalavitz, M. (2017) *The Boy Who Was Raised As A Dog (3rd Edn)* Basic Books: USA

Perry, B. & Ablon, J.S. (2019) CPS as a neurodevelopmentally sensitive and trauma informed approach in Pollastri, A.R., Ablon, J.S. & Hone, M. J. G. *Collaborative Problem Solving in Clinical Psychiatry* Chapter 2, pp. 15-31 mgh.havard.edu

Perry, B. (2020) The Neurosequential Model: A developmentally sensitive, neuroscience-informed approach to clinical problem solving in Mitchell, J., Tucci, J. & Tronick, E. (2020) *The Handbook of Therapeutic Care for Children* Chapter 6, pp. 137-158. Jessica Kingsley Publishers: London

Porges, S. (2017) *The Polyvagal Theory: The New Science of Safety & Trauma.* Nerd Nite 4/11/17 Youtube

Porges, S. (2004) *Neuroception: A Subconscious System for Detecting Threats and Safety, Zero to Three* lifespanlearn.org

Porges, S. (2006) *How Your Nervous System Sabotages Your Ability to Relate*: An Interview with Stephen Porges about his polyvagal theory, by Ravi Dykema Nexus nexusalive.com

Porges, S. (2008) The Polyvagal Theory: New insights into adaptive reactions of the autonomic nervous systems *Cleveland Clinic Journal of Medicine* Volume 75, Supplement 2

Porges, S. (2011) Interview with Stephen Porges: Somatic perspectives on psychotherapy stephenporges.com

Porges, S. (2011) *The Polyvagal Theory: Neurophysiological foundations of emotions, attachment, communication,and self-regulation* WW Norton: USA

Porges, S. (2015) Making the World Safe for our Children: Downregulating defence and upregulating social engagement to optimise the human experience *Children Australia* 40, pp.114-123, doi:10.1017/cha.2015.12

Porges, S. (2015) Play as a Neural Exercise: Insights from the polyvagal theory in D Pearce-McCall (Ed.) *The Power of Play for Mind Brain Health* (pp. 3-7) Available from mindgains.org

Porges, S. (2017) *The Pocket Guide to The Polyvagal Theory* WW Norton: USA

Porges, S. & Dana, D. (2018) *Clinical Applications of the Polyvagal Theory* WW Norton: USA

Porges, S. (2019) Survivors are blamed because they don't fight *The Guardian* online: 02/6/19 theguardian.com

Porges, S. (2019) in *Stephen Porges on the link between feeling safe and making change* Youtube

Porges, S. (2019) *The Emergence of a Polyvagal-Informed therapy: How music and voice contribute to healing following trauma* Presentation at the Congress of Attachment and Trauma in London 15-17th Nov 2019

Post, B. (2018) *The Great Behaviour Breakdown* Post Institute: Palmyra VA, USA

Powell, B., Cooper, G., Hoffman, K. & Marvin, B. (2014) *The Circle of Security Intervention*, The Guilford Press: USA

Redford, A. (2016) *The Boy Who Built a Wall Around Himself* Jessica Kingsley Publishers: London

Redford, J. (2016) *Resilience: The biology of stress and the science of hope* (film) Dartmouth Films, USA

Rhodes, J. & Dearing, R. (2018) *Imagine Eating Lemons. A children's introduction to mindfulness* Happy Sappling Books: UK

RMPS Resources (2017) *Breaking The Cycle* (documentary) youth.be

Rosenberg, S. (2017) *Accessing the Healing Power of the Vagus Nerve* North Atlantic Books: Canada

Rothschild, B. (2000) *The Body Remembers: The psychophysiology of trauma and trauma treatment* WW Norton: USA and London

Rothschild, B. (2017) Autonomic Nervous System Table. (Laminated card) WW Norton: USA

Rothschild, B. (2010) *8 Keys to Safe Trauma Recovery* WW Norton: USA

Russell, R. (2016) *From Attachment Wound to Parallel Process: Embodiment, enactment, and complexity in body-mind relational psychotherapy* (unpublished article)

Salisbury, S. (2018) Using attachment enhancing activities based on the principles of Theraplay® to improve adult-child relationships and reduce a child's 'overall stress' as measured by the Strength and Difficulties Questionnaire (SDQ) *Journal of Emotional & Behavioural Difficulties* Vol 23, 2018, Issue 4

Sapolsky, R. M. (2004) *Why Zebras Don't Get Ulcers: The acclaimed guide to stress, stress-related diseases, and coping* St Martin's Press: NY, USA

Schore, A. (2011) The Effects of Early Relational Trauma on Right Brain Development; affect regulation, and infant mental health *The Infant Mental Health Journal* 22 (1-2) pp. 201-269

Schore, A (2014) *Dr Allan Schore on Resilience and the Balance of Rupture and Repair* Youtube 13/5/14

Sellgren, K. (2020) *Putting Pupils in Isolation Drives Poor Behaviour* bbc.co.uk 9/1/20

Shukman, D. (2019) *Football Pitch of Amazon Forest Lost Every Minute* bbc.co.uk

Siegel, D.J. (2012) *Hand Model of a Brain* Youtube

Siegel, D.J. (2011) *The Low Road* Dr Dan Siegel PsychAlive Youtube

Siegel, D.J. (2012) *The Developing Mind: How relationships and the brain interact to shape who we are (2nd Ed)* Guilford Press: NY, USA

Siegel, D.J. (2015) *No Drama Discipline: the whole-brain way to calm the chaos and nurture your child's developing mind* Scribe: London

Siegel, D.J. & Payne Bryson, T. (2016) *No - Drama Discipline Workbook* PESI Publishing & Media: Wisconsin, USA

Snunit, M. (1998) *The Soul Bird* Constable & Robinson Publishing: London

somaticperspectives.com (2011) *Somatic Perspectives on Psychotherapy*. November 2011: Stephen Porges. Podcast and transcript available through website

Stern, D.N. (1974) Mother & infant at play: the dyadic interaction including facial, vocal and gaze behaviours in, M. Lews & L.A. Rosenblum (Eds.) *The Effect of the Infant on its Caregiver* pp. 187-213 Wiley: New York, USA

Stern, D.N. (2000) *The Interpersonal World of The Infant: A view from psychoanalysis & developmental psychology* Originally published 1985: Paperback 2nd Edition, with new introduction Basic Books: New York

Street, K. (2014) *School as a Secure Base: How peaceful teachers can create peaceful schools* Worth Publishing: London

StrengthQuest (2000) Reference Card Gallup Press Retrieved from strengthsquest.com

Taylor, L. & Barrett, W. (2018) Developing a trauma informed approach to closing the poverty-related attainment gap. *Educational & Child Psychology*, Volume 35, no 3. p. 64-75

Taylor, S., Rizvi, F., Lingard, B. & Henry, M. (1997) *Education Policy & the politics of change* Routledge: London, New York

TES News (2018) Isolation rooms: should they be banned? 27/11/18 tes.com

Thierry, B.D. (2015) *Teaching the Child on The Trauma Continuum* Grosvenor House: Surrey, UK

Tobin, L. (1991) *What Do You Do with a Child like this? Inside the lives of troubled children* Whole Person Associates: USA

Treisman, K. (2018) *Neon The Ninja: Activity Book for those who struggle with sleep and nightmares, for children aged 5-10* Jessica Kingsley: London

Treisman, K. (2018) *Trauma, Adversity, & Culturally Informed, Infused and Responsive Organisational change* Winston Churchill Report.

Treisman, K. (2020) Trauma informed, culturally infused, trauma responsive services. Podcast 23/1/20, Season 2, Episode 3 of Lisa Cherry Trauma Resonance Resilience

Trevarthan, C. (2004) *Learning about Ourselves, from Children: Why a Growing Human Brain Needs Interesting Companions* Hokkaido University, Japan

Trevarthan, C. (2014) Child Flourishing Symposium 2014 youtube

Tronick, E. (2007) *The Neurobiological and Social: Emotional development of infants and children* WW Norton: New York

Tronick, E. & DiCorcia, A. (2015) *The Everyday Stress Resilience Hypothesis: A reparatory sensitivity and the development of coping and resilience.* Children Australia, 40,pp.124-138: 10.1017/cha.2015.11 quoting Leerkes et al, 2009; McElwain & Booth-Laforce, 2006: Thompson, 1994

Van Der Kolk, B. (1996) *Traumatic Stress* Guilford Press: USA

Van Der Kolk, B. (2015) *The Body Keeps the Score: Mind, Brain and Body in the Transformation of Trauma* Penguin Books: Great Britain

Wilson, C. (2018) *Grounded: Discovering the missing piece in the puzzle of children's behaviour* Chew Initiatives: UK

Wolfinger, L. & Holliday Lentz, M. (n.d.) *The Kids We Lose* mainepublic.org

Useful organisations

These are organisations that I know well and that I would recommend: some are local to me, many are national. Of course you might find similar organisations closer to where you are. It's good to surround ourselves with others who can support us in our roles. Remember, it takes a village to raise a child!

Attachment Lead Network
attachmentleadnetwork.net
A national network of those involved in education, who advocate for children who have gone through relational trauma and loss in their lives, using trauma responsive practice in their schools across the UK. There are strategic Attachment Leads (a leadership position that ensures attachment & trauma responsive principles are integrated into both education policy and practice) and Attachment Lead Key Adults (who provide more individualised, integrative support within education)

Beyond Consequences Institute
beyondconsequences.com
An organisation that provides resources and guidance on working with children who demonstrate challenging behaviour for parents, schools and professionals. They focus on teaching caregivers to be trauma aware and responsive; and to use alternative practices, rooted in love, rather than traditional fear-based discipline.

Body College
bodycollege.net
Steve Haines has been a body worker for over 20 years, as well as an award-winning author of books such as *Anxiety Is Really Strange* and *Trauma Is Really Strange* (Singing Dragon). Bodycollege provides information on training courses in Trauma Release Exercise (TRE); in which Steve is the leading certificated trainer in the UK, in addition to providing online courses and resources on anxiety, pain and trauma.

Brighton & Hove table tennis club
brightontabletennisclub.com
Table tennis can be used as a powerful tool in engaging people of all ages and backgrounds; and transforming lives. This club is well respected locally in Brighton & Hove as being a well-established community that brings all kinds of people together, regardless of gender, race, religion, disability, sexuality, background, experiences … successfully.

Centre for the Study of Emotion and the Law
csel.org.uk
A great multidisciplinary resource for research papers about the impact of trauma on executive functions, amongst others.

Childhood101
childhood101.com
Childhood 101 is dedicated to inspiring parents, teachers and other care givers to create playful learning opportunities in their homes and learning environments with children aged 2-12, for example, the free resource - *8 Fun Breathing Exercises for Kids*. These are eight simple breathing exercises that are perfect for use with kids at home or school. These exercises can be used as part of your calmdown plan, as a prior-to-sleep relaxation activity or as a brain break exercise to refocus and re-fresh.

Child Trauma Academy (CTA)
childtrauma.org
The Child Trauma Academy is a community of practitioners overseen by Dr Bruce Perry, working to improve the lives of high-risk children through direct service, research and education. By creating biologically informed child and family respectful practice, programs and policy, CTA seeks to help maltreated and traumatised children.

Children's Sensory Therapy Ltd
childrenssensorytherapy.co.uk
A team of experienced Occupational Therapists, with post-graduate training in Sensory Integration and Sensory Attachment Intervention. Specialist interest in how early life trauma affects the development of the nervous system, and how brain and body regulation helps children access their higher level skills. They work across the UK.

Circle of Life Rediscovery
circleofliferediscovery.com
This organisation facilitates exciting and highly beneficial nature-centred learning and therapeutic experiences for young people, adults, and families in the Sussex woodlands. The health and wellbeing of individuals, communities and the natural world are interdependent. Immersion in nature raises the impact of education, health and family support services and helps to sustain natural resources and woodlands.

Clackmannanshire Educational Psychology Service
clacks.gov.uk/learning/psychserevice/
Clackmannanshire Educational Psychology Service have a long history of embedding trauma informed approaches across education. Most recently, they have taken the work of Dr Bruce Perry to incorporate his Neurosequential Model in Education® into their Readiness for Learning Approach. This has resulted in significant improvements in learners' executive function skills, which is beginning to impact on attainment figures. Their work in this area has been identified as an area of good practice by Dr Perry's organisation, the Child Trauma Academy.

Connected Lives
connectedlives.org.uk
Connected Lives is a charity which provides early help for family relationships from an attachment perspective. They recognise the importance of healthy attachment relationships from cradle to grave for our mental, emotional, social and even physical well-being. At their hubs trained facilitators use evidence-based programmes such as Circle of Security Parenting©, Hold me Tight©, and Created for Connection©. Delivered in groups, these approaches give parents and partners a map for understanding relationships (attachment theory), insight into their strengths and their struggles and the opportunity to look at new ways of responding.

Connected Moments
connectedmoments.co.uk
An organisation that offers support to help communication between you and your child, helping you to understand each other better and to create calmer, happier relationships.

Daring Classrooms
brenebrown.com
Brene Brown has a free resource for teachers to support them to create Daring Classrooms. Based on her best selling book, *Dare to Lead.*

DDP UK
ddpnetwork.org/uk
Organise and provide training, therapy, education and parenting interventions in dyadic developmental psychotherapy, dyadic practice and dyadic parenting in the UK. Continuously developing their work and aiming to support those certified in DDP and those in training. Involved in cutting edge research as to the difference DDP can make in supporting traumatised children and young people. Part of Trauma Informed Education (TIE).

Do-BeMindful
do-bemindful.com
The vision through the Do-BeMindful Initiative is to provide communities with the opportunity to learn the life-enhancing tools of Mindfulness in practical, fun and enriching ways. The programmes aim to develop awareness, self-regulation and resilience in teachers, parents and children to encourage a calm, kind and compassionate culture. Online resources available so you can be mindful anywhere!

EMDR
emdr.com

EMDR (Eye Movement Desensitization and Reprocessing) is a non-intrusive NICE approved psychotherapy which enables people to heal from the symptoms and emotional distress resulting from disturbing and traumatic life experiences. Repeated studies show that by using EMDR therapy, people can experience the benefits of psychotherapy that once took years to make a difference. Eye movements (or other bilateral stimulation) are used during one part of the session. As this happens, for reasons believed by a Harvard researcher to be connected with the biological mechanisms involved in Rapid Eye Movement (REM) sleep, internal associations arise and the clients begin to process the memory and disturbing feelings.

Gonoodle
gonoodle.com

A free website that supports educators, parents & carers get children and young people moving, with short, interactive activities. This helps keep them engaged and motivated throughout the day, allowing children to perform better and keeps their body/mind healthy.

Home for Good
homeforgood.org.uk

A charity dedicated to finding a home for every child who needs one, by co-ordinating and resourcing a rapidly growing network of people, churches and local movements across the UK who are raising awareness of the needs of vulnerable children and young people, inspiring individuals to explore fostering and adoption, and equipping churches to better understand and support all those involved.

ISSTD International Society for the Study of Trauma & Dissociation
isst-d.org

The International Society for the Study of Trauma and Dissociation is an international, non-profit, professional association organized to develop and promote comprehensive, clinically effective and empirically based resources and responses to trauma and dissociation and to address its relevance to other theoretical constructs. Education is one of their primary goals, achieved partly through training programs, conferences and the *Journal of Trauma & Dissociation*.

Jigsaw
jigsaw-ot.co.uk

Occupational Therapy for children and young people across Sussex. They provide a number of different assessments and treatment packages individualised to a child's needs, including Sensory Attachment Intervention (SAI). They also provide training for schools, parents and other professionals.

Kind Kids club -
thekindnessconnection.org

Innovative, not-for-profit organisation that encourages children to volunteer and give their time/ resources. They provide special experiences for children.

National Association of Therapeutic Parents
naotp.com

A not-for-profit organisation providing support, education and resources for parents and supporting professionals relating to therapeutic parenting, effective interventions, compassion fatigue and the effects of early life trauma. Their aim is to promote better outcomes for children who have suffered early life trauma, by significantly improving the consistency and quality of support available to Therapeutic Parents in the UK and Worldwide, regardless of whether they are Foster Carers, Adopters, Kinship Carers, Special Guardians, Step Parents, or birth parents.

National Child Traumatic Stress Network
nctsn.org

The National Child Traumatic Stress Network is an American organisation whose mission is to raise the standards of care and improve access to services for traumatised children, their families and communities throughout the United States.

Neurosequential Model in Education® (NME®)
neurosequential.com

The NME® model is a neurosequential model in education that draws upon NMT® (a neurodevelopmentally-informed, biologically respectful perspective on human development and functioning) to help support educators to understand student behaviour and performance.

Neurosequential Model of Therapeutics® (NMT®)
neurosequential.com

The NMT® model is a developmentally informed, biologically respectful approach to working with at risk children. It is not a specific therapeutic technique or intervention; it is a way to organise, think about and work with a child's history or current functioning.

Pennies of time
penniesoftime.com

An organisation full of volunteers with the goal of creating compassionate, problem solvers. Its purpose is to be a 'go-to-place' for families to rely on, in the journey of raising children to also become compassionate problem solvers.

Plot 22
plot22.org

Plot 22 is a charity that facilitates communal gardening opportunities and cooking activities in a beautiful allotment space. They create opportunities for everyone to step into connecting with the land, working the land and taking up responsibility and leadership.

Random Acts of Kindness
randomactsofkindness.org

A small team that strive to make the world kinder; to make kindness effortless and to have selfless acts be a norm in society.

Relax Kids
relaxkids.com

This organisation offers child relaxation training, classes and resources to parents and professionals working with children. They use research-based mindful and relaxation techniques alongside values and positive psychology such as compassion, gratitude and strength-building. Their aim is for children to develop resilience and give them tools and techniques to manage their emotional and mental health.

Rhythm of Regulation
rhythmofregulation.com

An organisation headed up by Deb Dana that offers education around the use of the polyvagal theory in therapy. Includes many good free clips and a free guide for those wanting to understand more!

SAI (Sensory attachment interventions)
sensoryattachmentintervention.com

An SAI Centre run by Eadouin Bhreathnach, the author of *The Scared Gang* books (Alder Press) and the Just Right State programme for groups. The centre provides an integrative approach to the treatment of children and adults, who have suffered abuse or severe neglect. The work recommended seeks to regulate arousal states of fight/flight/freeze or dissociation, then modulates the senses through a combination of up and down regulating experiences. This in turn supports the child or adult to access high level sensory, emotional and cognitive functioning. The centre is currently involved in training, clinical supervision, research and designing regulatory spaces/gardens. There are free papers to download that support understanding.

Sunshine Circles®
theraplay.org/sunshine-circles

Sunshine Circles® are a registered service mark under the Theraplay® Institute. They can quickly and dramatically improve the quality of the classroom and provide a helpful focus on resources to maintain an emotionally positive and an enriched environment.

Stoneham Bakehouse
stonehambakehouse.org.uk

This is a community supported bakery based in Hove, Sussex. Community members bake bread for the community, for the benefit of the community's wellbeing.

The Listening Project
integratedlistening.com
Developed by Dr Stephen
Porges, the Safe and Sound
Protocol is a 5-day intervention
to decrease stress and auditory
sensitivity whilst enhancing social
engagement and resilience. Based
on Dr Porges' Polyvagal theory,
the door is opened for important
communication by calming the
physical and emotional states.

**The Natural Health Practice
(NHP)**
naturalhealthpractice.com
The Natural Health Practice
works closely with Dr Marilyn
Glenville PhD, one of the UK's
top nutritionists. She personally
recommends and, in some cases,
has even formulated the products
offered. Marilyn Glenville spoke
at an international trauma
conference in London in autumn
2019 presenting supplements for
mental health and wellbeing and
supplements for better sleep that
can be used with children, young
people and adults who have
suffered stress, toxic stress, trauma
and loss. The Natural Health
Practice provides 'expert advice' to
help you understand your health
problems, and discover what you
can do to alleviate them. You will
also find complete supplement
programmes.

Theraplay® UK
theraplay.org/uk
Theraplay® is way of being,
for building and enhancing
attachment, self-esteem, trust in
others and joyful engagement.
Focusses on four dimensions:
structure, engagement, nurture
and challenge. The sessions
help the child/young person and
parent/carer or member of Team
Pupil to have a changed view of
themselves and have a positive
impact on their relationship.
Theraplay®UK is part of Therapy
in Education (TIE).

TouchBase Centre CiC
touchbase.org.uk
A community interest organisation
(not for profit) under the
leadership of Louise M Bombèr,
which facilitates a range of
attachment aware and trauma
responsive interventions for
children and young people aged
5-25, families, schools and the
wider community. They aim to
support everyone to live well.
A team of specialist, strategic
Attachment Lead teachers,
therapists & psychologists who
have extensive experience and
expertise in relational trauma and
loss. Part of Trauma Informed
Education (TIE).

**Transforming Lives For Good
(TLG)**
tlg.org.uk
This is a national charity that helps
hundreds of struggling children and
young people every year, enabling
practical one-to-one coaching in
schools, hot meals during the school
holidays and alternative provision
for those at risk of exclusion from
mainstream school. Schools can
work in partnership with them.

Trauma Informed Education
traumainformededucation.org.uk
Three organisations (TouchBase,
Theraplay® and DDP Connects
UK) with a recommended,
developmental pathway for
supporting those impacted by
ACEs, within education. Provides
training, resources and support for
everyone advocating for inclusion,
so that children and young people
who have experienced trauma and
loss have access to the appropriate
kinds of practical interventions
they need.

Turnaround for Children
turnaroundusa.org
Dr Pamela Cantor is the director
of Turnaround for Children, an
organisation which uses science
to improve schooling for those
effected by Adverse Childhood
Experiences. The website
provides information on the ways
in which Turnaround for Children
are impacting schooling in America
as well as case studies, and tools
for educators.

**Video Interactive Guidance -
AVIG-UK**
videointeractionguidance.net
This is an organisation which
provides information and training
in the use of video interaction
guidance to support and
develop and strengthen attuned
relationships. The website holds
an overview of the practices
involved in VIG as well as a
directory of VIG practitioners and
information on training courses.

Index

Recovery badges

If you have been moved by anything you've read in this book and you'd like to join the inclusive revolution, I would like to offer you a badge, one that communicates to everyone that you're doing all you can to advocate for, and support, those who are currently at risk of being misunderstood and excluded.   The Recovery badge communicates that you understand how important it is that our communities take their place in supporting traumatised children and young people: that you recognise that it really does 'take a village to raise a child'.

I came up with the idea for the badges, which were taken to the design stage by Alice Harper, a member of our TouchBase Team, and to creation by John Timpson, the highly respected business man and entrepreneur behind high street shoe repair chain Timpsons. They were launched at St Peters Church, in Brighton, at the public screening of *Resilience* in May 2019. They are distributed at all our weekly training events run all around the UK.

To order your badge/s then please email info@touchbase.org.uk Voluntary £1 donation are welcome to cover production costs and to invest in community projects facilitated by TouchBase.